REDS IN THE HOOD

REDS IN THE HOOD

By Terry Christian

André Deutsch

First published in 1999
by André Deutsch Ltd
76 Dean Street
London W1V 5HA
www.vci.co.uk

ISBN 0 23399 427 0

Typeset by Derek Doyle & Associates
Mold, Flintshire
Printed and bound
by Werner Söderström Osakeyhtiö, Finland

1 3 5 7 9 10 8 6 4 2

Contents

Introduction

In the summer we played football in the park until our tongues hung down to our shorts and the sun was a Red globe bowing to the moon as it sank over the rooftops. Sweaty and thirsty we'd walk down Kings Road daring each other to knock on the front doors of the neat semis that we called posh people's houses to ask for a drink of water, in the hope they'd give us something better like lemonade. The ball would be dribbled all the way, playing one-twos off the walls. We didn't even think about having the latest replica kits – we had hand-me-down United and City shirts that had been washed so often you'd think the glorious Reds were the shocking pinks and wonder whether Manchester City ever played in shirts quite so sky blue. To say we loved football would be like saying mammals breathed air; in truth we had nothing else. Manchester United were the conquerors of Europe, Manchester City were the League Champions, Denis Law was king, George Best was godlike in his Old Trafford heaven and Manchester ruled the football world.

Footballers were our heroes, our role models. They weren't distant deities – we worshipped them from a few feet away. We knew where they lived, where they went drinking. We'd spot Nobby Stiles and Pat Crerand coming out of the Quadrant pub on the Gorse Hill roundabout and we all knew Matt

Busby lived off Seymour Grove. By and large United's players lived in Old Trafford, albeit the posh end known locally as Firswood. In the park we'd try and dribble the ball like George Best, score like Denis Law, tackle like Nobby Stiles, shoot like Bobby Charlton and accuse each other of diving like Francis Lee. We joked and looked forward to the day when we'd get our first pair of football boots and travel to exciting away matches in towns like Leicester, Sheffield, Liverpool, Newcastle and West Ham (which I always imagined to be by the seaside ...?). We wore any football shirts we could get, and though over the years they came in all shades, shapes, sizes and teams we were all, in the end, 100-per-cent Manchester United. Red to the core.

Football when we were kids was never mentioned in the same breath as fashion and we could never have imagined a day when it would become an unaffordable luxury, a subject for media networking or a form of corporate entertainment. In the eyes of the monied classes back then it was too downmarket for any of that, a sport for old men in flat caps and young hooligans. You see we took football for granted – it was all ours because no one else wanted or was interested in it and Manchester United was our salvation; it coloured our lives, gave us a place in the world and hope for the future. And after leaving school I was made to believe that my obsession with football was a childish eccentricity ... but they didn't understand.

Football meant Saturday and vice versa. Saturday was our day of pride, our couple of hours in the sun. Saturday afternoons we went to the match (or tried to), simple as that, because that's what everybody we knew did on Saturday afternoon. (You might say that Saturday was and is my favourite day.) For us second-generation Irish kids it was like going to church and going to school. To watch George Best drop his shoulder and run at the goal, leaving defenders on their back-sides dumbfounded by his supreme footballing poetry; to see the top corner of the net bulging after a twenty-five-yard screamer from Charlton; or Denis Law ghost in between a ruck of players in the area and foxily glance a well-aimed header past a hapless keeper ... that was something unique to Man. United and special to us, and there are no sophisticated inter-pretations as to why we felt that way, we just did

May 1995: I was slumped drunkenly in the Metropole Hotel bar in London. It was the night of the afternoon's defeat in the FA Cup – Everton 1, Manchester United 0. But what a differ-ence Eric Cantona would have made. I'd witnessed the black day, earlier that January, when Cantona had been sent off – and later banned for the rest of the season and the beginning of the following season – thanks to the actions of a foul-mouthed racist yobbo. And later I'd witness the profoundly blacker day when he announced he was leaving us for good. So I dallied and drank into the small hours, chatting to my United heroes – Paul Ince, Mark Hughes, Steve Bruce, Paul Parker and Lee Sharpe ... within a year they had all played their last games for Manchester United, spread their wings and brought over £15 million into the Old Trafford coffers.

Periodically I'd think, 'What if they all left United?! Giggs, Schmeichel, Beckham, Keane, Scholes ... even Alex Ferguson?' Then I'd remember. From Best to Brazil, Stepney to Bailey, Macari to Muhren, an endless river of talent had flowed through Old Trafford. Over almost 30 years of Saturday after-noons and cold Wednesday nights I'd watched the progress of hundreds of players, some from the Old Trafford ranks, others stars bought in to become legends, to say nothing of a variety of managers' tribulations. They all have special moments for me as a fan, but ...

Their association with Manchester United was transient, only a part of their lives, albeit a special one. No player could ever *be* Manchester United (even Best, even Cantona), no manager either (not even Busby). The supporters were Manchester United. We'd be there whatever division, whoever the manager and whoever the players were, from the cradle to the grave. It's supporters that make any football team. Old Trafford was my birthplace and not even Manchester United Football Club can claim that.

From our earliest days the golden centre of our universe had been Manchester United and Old Trafford Stadium. We were working-class kids of immigrant parents, with little self-belief, no wealthy relatives, no big plans for the future. Yet through all of it there was Manchester United FC, a pure, inspirational thing in an unfair and dirty world, and at that time we felt it was all ours.

This isn't so much a story about Manchester United, but about what they meant to us as youngsters in the Old Trafford where I was born and raised, in the days before everyone watched from seats, dressed in replica shirts like the participating audience at a *Rocky Horror Picture Show*. Before the suits invested in football like it was pork bellies and frozen orange juice. It's the story of the period from 1968 to 1977, when football at Manchester United was more downs than ups, more passionate last-minute semi-final failure than glorious victory. When despite this football belonged triumphantly to us Old Trafford boys ... the Reds in the hood.

1

Jam Butties and a Johnny Seven

Saturday night was sausages for tea, the football results, *Dr Who*, *Voyage to the Bottom of the Sea* and a bath before bed. Aged four and in the bath, subject as ever to my mother's patience and caring, I asked the burning question:

'Mam, are we rich or poor?'

'Poor.'

The answer was given in such a matter-of-fact fashion that I found it quite disturbing. My Saturday night feel-good factor was disappearing down the plughole with the six inches of lukewarm water I'd been splashing about in and I was not happy. Don't get me wrong, I didn't think we were rich, but as I've discovered more painfully since, it's often disheartening when your deepest suspicions are confirmed.

The house we lived in was on Duke Street, in the Brookes Bar area of Old Trafford. It was a largish terraced house with three rooms upstairs and three down. It was lucky for us that it was so large as, up to my fourth birthday, there had been two adults and four kids sharing the upstairs of the house with an old Welsh couple living downstairs (rent: 15 shilling a week). Like all houses in that area it had coal fires for heat and an outside loo. On winter days I'd scratch strange shapes and pictures into the thick ice that had formed on the inside of our bedroom window, scraping away until I could see through it to the entry that separated the backs of our row of houses from those on Clifton Street.

Nobody we knew had a fridge, car or telephone. Milk bottles perched leaning on the window ledge out in the back-yard in the autumn and winter and were placed in a bucket of cold water in the summer. The rooms at the back of the house, the kitchen and small middle room (a collecting point for laundry and clothes plus assorted children's junk), were always dark, permanently in the shadow of the backs of the looming terraces that hemmed us in. The Arctic coldness in these rooms clothed them in an austerity, misshapen and untidy, that signalled these were rooms for passing through and not sitting or playing in. There was damp everywhere downstairs that seeped into your nostrils and on cold nights, with our mam and dad's coats spread on top of our beds for extra warmth, the chill seemed to take a grip on our young bones. The houses along all those streets were due for demolition, but we weren't sure when, so everything from the furniture to the crumbling plaster on the walls had a temporary feel – we lived in a kind of limbo.

I was that not-uncommon wanton type of infant who never shut up. As the fourth of six kids I craved attention, and questions tumbled out relentlessly. Mam, why is the sky blue? Why is Christmas only once a year? Why haven't we got a dog? A car? A toilet in the house? Why is that woman sitting across from us on the bus so fat? Somehow things rarely made sense. Every toy other kids had I wanted, although this isn't surprising: though well looked after, us Christian kids didn't exactly have a cluttered playroom. I had a stuffed monkey, a broken fort, a six-shooter cap-gun and some toy soldiers, inherited mainly from older cousins and my older brother, that were so ancient they were drawing army pensions. When I'd enquire as to why a certain kid had a new Johnny Seven or some other toy completely out of our financial reach, like a Scalextric, my dad would say in his thick Dublin brogue, 'Dose kids only have jam butties for tea.'

I envied those kids and would gladly have sacrificed some of my mam's stews and the like for jam butties and a Johnny Seven. According to my dad, only having jam butties for tea was the explanation for every kid in the world having better and more toys and pocket money than us. 'But Prince Andrew's got a Scalextric, Dad.' 'Yeah but he only has jam butties for his tea.' I think it was that fixation the Irish have with food, a collective memory of the famines of the 1840s and '*an gorta* mor' ('the great hunger'), and nothing in the world it seemed was as horrific as not eating properly.

My father had been one of six kids, four of which made it to adulthood. His father had died when he was seven and the only association with him he knew was his name – he had been named Daniel after him. My dad was the only one of his family to move over to England; not that his upbringing in Dublin was one conducive to getting all dewy-eyed about the old country. He was brought up in one room of a tenement in Augustine Street in the famous Liberties area of Dublin, with his mother and two brothers and sister. His life had always been a struggle, with one bed for all of them, turf for the fire kept under the same bed, buckets of water from a pump in the yard to be carried up eight flights of stairs, no shoes on his feet and hunger his constant companion. He was struck down by TB as a youngster and again in his young adult life, the scars on his lungs eventually contributing to his death at Christmas 1996.

My father was an expert at living for the day and having a rigid routine. He ate to the clock. If it was twelve-thirty that meant lunch and five o'clock meant dinner-time. He went to the bookies twice a week, and out drinking every weekend and Sunday lunchtimes after his weekly visit to Mass. In this routine he found contentment and shelter from what was a hard life. His younger brother Paddy died of cancer in 1964, aged 36, and his wife went soon after of the same affliction, orphaning four children, my cousins. My father's older sister, Aunt Mag, brought them up as her own after that and still looked after her and my dad's mother, who was touching 80 at the time. So my father knew and understood poverty and worked hard to avoid its more extreme symptoms. Yet he never hid the fact that he hated going to work.

Though very young, I understood him. I could see that there were girls and boys my own age who'd play out all summer and winter in the same pair of canvas plimsolls or plastic sandals, minus the socks, and the same worn and blackened summer clothing, sustained from their mothers' doorsteps with sugar or HP Sauce butties which they'd eat in the street. There was a family called McNeil and every time we saw the Rag and Bone man trundling his cart down the road, we'd shout to the multitude of offspring playing in front of their house, 'Look there's your dad.' We'd then run, dodging the stones they threw after us. That was life down our end of Old Trafford: everyone scraping by, but feeling guilty about having more than some.

Old Trafford is a neighbourhood in the Stretford area of Manchester, a mere mile or so south-west of the city centre. Back then it was very much an Irish area. Everybody minded everybody else's business, the rows of terraces may as well have been made of glass, condemnation lingered in whispers and privacy was unheard of. So we hid our deepest thoughts from the world and stuck our chests out and pretended to one another that we were perfect. But we were the children of immigrants and aware that to be Irish was to be second class.

Our parents invariably came from poor Irish stock, and though proud of this, they were afflicted with the strange 'fatality' of being Irish. They bore this inheritance with stoic resignation: 'Irish and poor, Irish and emigrated, Irish and dead'. A sort of guilt also lingered in this generation of Irish that had emigrated. Their great grandparents had survived the holocaust of the great famines between 1845 and 1849. That period brought Gaelic culture and language to its knees before English oppression. The Gaelic language, the principle means by which the people of Ireland had understood and interpreted that island and the rest of the world for over two thousand years, was draining away. Who knows what wisdom and knowledge had been lost. All our great grandparents had left our parents was the purity of their religion and virtue, and memories of their hardship. And our parents had fled the difficulties of their homeland with hardly a word of its language on their tongue. So, in spite of the fact that the Irish had never invaded, conquered and enslaved other nations or committed atrocities against other cultures on their sovereign soil, a kind of shame attached itself to the Irishness of our parents.

As for us, the kids, all the jokes we heard were about thick Irish. In the Western films we enjoyed so much, the lovable, roguish and often drunken corporal in the cavalry was Irish, but not the major or colonel. In other films the Irish were always portrayed as the poor huddled masses living from hand to mouth in peasant huts and tenements, never in big houses with servants, never as the decision-makers. And to our Irish cousins, when they'd come over to Manchester or when we went over to Ireland, we were English or what they'd call 'half a Dalmation' – not one thing or the other. Even as 'English' we spoke with broad Mancunian accents, not the accents of the heroes in films or people in positions of importance or power.

On special occasions when the drink would flow, something would stir and the old stories and songs of forgotten rebels and rebellions would be sung, with us kids hanging on every word. We heard the stories from our parents of signs that read, 'No Blacks, No Irish, No Dogs'. We'd heard of that Saxon world and we wanted none of it anyway. The English were two-faced, boorish and snobbish – even on a Sunday they weren't full of grace. We were told the stories of 1916 and the brutalities in the Twenties of the Black and Tans who'd drive through the streets of Ireland's towns and villages shooting randomly at people and property. How my paternal grandmother had been a neighbour and friend of Kevin Barry's mother. Kevin Barry was an 18-year-old lad who was tortured and hung by the British in November 1920 and became the subject of possibly the most famous Irish rebel song of all:

In Mountjoy jail, one Monday morning, high up on the
    gallows tree
Kevin Barry gave his young life for the cause of liberty.
But a lad of eighteen summers, yet no one can deny,
As he walked to death that morning, he proudly held his
    head up high.

Just before he faced the hangman, in his dreary prison cell,
British soldiers tortured Barry, just because he would not tell.
The names of his brave companions, and other things they
    wished to know,
'Turn informer, or we'll kill you', Kevin Barry answered 'No'.

Calmly standing to attention, while he bade his last farewell
To his broken-hearted mother, whose sad grief no one can tell.
For the cause he proudly cherished, this sad parting had to be,
Then to death walked softly smiling, that old Ireland might
    be free.

Another martyr for old Ireland, another murder for the crown,
Whose brutal laws may kill the Irish, but can't keep their
    spirits down.
Lads like Barry are no cowards, from the foe they will not fly,
Lads like Barry will free Ireland, for her sake they'll live and die.

In alcohol our elders were proud to be Irish, descendants of warrior-poets, saints and high kings; when sober they were glad they had left a country that had little to offer them only a legacy of shame that they could neither understand nor come to terms with.

The conclusion was, the less Irish, the better your luck, so our parents did their best not to thrust our Irishness upon us. We were born in England and in the culture of amnesia in which we as immigrants lived our lives, we called ourselves English, but we couldn't escape our heritage, the cravenness of our dependencies, our fear of self-belief. It seemed that every bad habit we had was 'the Irish in us'. My mother used to say it with an amusedly resigned sigh, as if we'd been born with the mark of Cain. Our selfishness, disobedience, idleness and mithering way, but most of all our quick tempers and violence, were all to do with the turbulent sentimentality of the Celt.

A certain machoness pervaded our neighbourhood; you had to fight, and not only that you were supposed to enjoy it. The whole language we spoke as children was a series of hostile challenges to fight. 'Oi, Ginger-nut, what's your name?' ... 'What, Phillip! Thought that was a girl's name, you look like a girl, even your pants look like nickers!' ... 'Say that again and I'll knock your teeth so far down your throat you'll have to scratch your arse to brush them.' It was like a long line of gauntlets being thrown down. But it has to be said, being best buddies with Jimmy Millar didn't leave you much choice.

Jimmy's parents were Belfast Protestants with a Catholic-size family of eight kids and he was fifth in line. Oprah Winfrey would have described them as dysfunctional. I have fond(ish) memories of him as a tiny-tot terrorist with a nasty psychotic streak. Four years of age and a good two inches taller and a bit stockier than I, Jimmy Millar was an explosive and unpredictable kid. Whatever we did we ended up fighting and we both thought it perfectly normal behaviour. One minute we'd be happily discussing whether water snakes can live down grids, the next I'd feel my head being pushed violently on to said grid, imprinting a pattern of striped bruises on my face. It was a friendship cemented by pain.

I suppose to every four-year-old the world is a huge and expansively interesting place. But my world had definite boundaries – basically three streets either side of where I lived. It was as if somebody had rolled a carpet over these streets and said, 'These are yours, mess about in them as much as you like but don't let me or anyone else catch you.' Excitement lurked in every nook and cranny and the unexpected and mysterious around every corner. Looking back now it was like an Eden on earth and like the hapless Adam and Eve, we were really only interested in tasting forbidden fruits and doing our own thing.

The most forbidden of all fruits for a pre-school four-year-old is fire. We'd spend hours in the small square of wasteground we called the croft, overlooked on four sides by the backyards of terraces, collecting anything that would burn from the junk dumped there. Furniture stuffing (which we called 'ginger') made great kindling. Once the flames were going good and strong we'd roll a discarded car tyre on to the blaze, dodging the shower of sparks, and wait for the pall of acrid black smoke to rise into the air (scarpering in case a neighbour called out the fire brigade, disappointed if they didn't).

Other highlights included the ice cream van tinkling slowly down the street, with all us kids scattering in different directions on the same mission. 'Mam can I have an ice cream?'; disappointment nine times out of ten and then you'd huddle with slumped shoulders alongside the others denied their requests just behind the lucky ones who were delightedly queuing. As the last one was served we'd assail the ice cream seller through his hatch. 'Have you got any broken lollies mister?' 'Well have you got any broken wafers?'

At the top end of our street were pebble-dashed prefabs built as emergency shelter during the war. Needless to say these concrete and hardboard bungalows were still occupied, their small sizes compensated for by the huge overgrown gardens at the back. We'd run in and out of their snaky paths, narrow enough to be filled by our small feet, spying cats creeping around the undergrowth. The quietude was occasionally spoilt by Jimmy Millar jabbing a dandelion flower up a protesting nostril and forcing the victim to sniff it: 'You'll wet the bed tonight!' It invariably worked.

The problems started when young James got bored or needed an extra top-up to these everyday excitements. One by one various parents began to ban their children from playing with Jimmy and myself. We bore the strain of each other's company for what seemed an eternity, calling the other kids softies and throwing stones at them, until in frustration we'd end up fighting one another, with Jimmy coming out on top nine times out of ten.

No matter the promises he made, Jimmy could not entice the other youngsters on our street to play with us. I'd forced him to call a truce of kinds with me, but it wasn't the same lighting fires with just the two of us, and I got sick of him trying to push me off the roof of the Sharon Gospel church. I was fed up of Jimmy Millar, but there was no chance of hanging around with my big brother Tony and the older lads – that just didn't happen.

There were the McPhee twins, Brian and Kevin. They had several older brothers, mates with my big brother Tony, and all reckoned to be quite hard, so Jimmy laid off them at first. But he needed some violence to spice up his life, and sooner or later, in a one-on-one situation, he'd leave each of us sore and bloodied losers. Jimmy told us that kids who stayed in all the time (i.e., who'd been kept in off the street) were snobs and sissies, so whenever we spotted one of these imprisoned children staring at us through the glass, we'd bare our teeth and snarl at them while raising a clenched fist. Looking back this probably didn't make playing in the street particularly enticing for them. Jimmy Millar was beginning to put us all off playing out.

Like most four-year-olds, when faced with a problem I retreated to my mother for all the big worldly advice. Now I had a question for her: how could the McPhees and myself avoid Jimmy Millar 's incessant violence. My mam's answer was to begin with a bit obvious: 'Don't play with him.' But how could we not play with him, he'd just come up and join in and if we told him to get lost, he'd just beat us up. This was when I became aware of my mother's true wisdom. 'If he does that, all three of you should jump on him at once, then he'll be too frightened.' I remember some years back reading the Irish legend of Fionn Mac Uail where it says: 'Fionn got his first training among women. There is no wonder in that, for it is the pup's mother teaches it to fight and women know that fighting is a necessary art.'

The next morning I discussed my mother's plan with the McPhees who were very agreeable. We waited impatiently for Jimmy (who we'd now come to think of as an ex-member of our little gang) to show up. By the time he strolled towards us we were so full of adrenaline that we just let out a loud whoop and ran towards him. Jimmy realized that we had evil intent. He shrieked and ran, no doubt thinking we were going to lynch him from a lamppost. By the time I caught up with him, the McPhees, who were slower runners than us, were still some way behind. Still, with the confidence of John Wayne battling the Indians in the full knowledge that the cavalry are on their way, I grappled Jimmy to the ground, sat on his chest and proceeded to punch his lights out. As the McPhees arrived I let Jimmy up and he ran off home. The victory was all mine, the McPhees ... well they were sort of insurance.

Once other kids heard the news that we'd finally conquered our street's mini Ghengis Khan, they began to gingerly venture out again and join in our good times and pyromania. Sure enough Jimmy calmed down somewhat. I suspect this was in part because he was now part of a full gang of nine or ten kids, and we had found a new outlet for our aggression.

We all lived on Duke Street and around the corner on the same block was Clifton Street. We shared a dirty stinking alley-way, but as far as we were concerned, that was all. Beware the plucky kid from Clifton Street who thought he could come peddling his trainer-wheels around the corner on to our street. As Jimmy said, and we agreed, those Clifton Street kids were cheeky taking a shortcut to the paper-shop on Chorlton Road by walking down our street. One young fellow had his sherbet dab emptied over his head to remind him not to feel too lazy to take the long way round. As I learned later in my catechism, sloth is one of the seven deadly sins.

To show our ascendancy over the Clifton street kids Jimmy would suggest we take a walk around the corner to see the witch's house – a strange little shiny redbrick bungalow which conjured up visions of Hansel and Gretel and stood at odds between the terraced houses on Clifton Street and Shrewsbury Street. The witch's house was occupied by an old lady who, it later turned out, was the owner and landlady of all the houses on the neighbouring streets. That old lady was guilty in our eyes of the sins of having a bigger house than any of us, which she greedily occupied by herself; being old and well spoken; always wearing a hat; and having a pink eyepatch which lent her a somewhat sinister aspect, thus making us all the more certain she was a witch. So we'd dare each other to go and knock on her door and then scarper before she could spot us and, as Jimmy said, 'Put the evil eye on us'.

Of course, what Jimmy really hoped for by having us parade down Clifton Street with our pockets full of stones and armed with various sticks was that we'd provoke a response from the local kids who'd been previously caught or pursued on our turf. These frequent incursions into enemy territory normally involved six or seven terrors from Clifton Street throwing stones and pieces of glass in our direction as we retreated slowly back to the alleyway that ran between our street and theirs, all the time keeping up a steady barrage to cover our retreat. We'd invariably be joined by other lads from our street and a battle involving a hail of stones criss-crossing in the air would ensue. This warfare would last until a couple of combatants got hit on the head or some adult chased us off.

The Rag and Bone man was a real treat, that is if you had any old cotton clothes for him. Any kid handing over a few torn shirts or aprons cadged from their parents was rewarded by the Rag and Bone man with a bow and arrow set made out of bamboo or a balloon on a stick. Strictly speaking you had to be six to qualify for the bow and arrow. We'd been told we could put someone's eye out with them, which of course made them all the more alluring. So we'd wangle bows and arrows from the Rag and Bone man, sharpen the bamboo garden-stick arrows and fire them at cats or other kids.

★

All this fun was limited to the surrounding few streets. I couldn't go collecting frogs on Chorlton Meadows, it was a bus-ride away. I was always excited when my 12-year-old brother Tony would return with his friends from a trip to what I imagined to be a countryside paradise, carrying a collection of frogs and newts in an old paint tin containing an inch or so of murkily pungent pond water. He kept his captive amphibians in some dirty water in an old mop-bucket in the backyard, a half-brick acting as an island for the frogs who would die over the following days if they didn't escape. God knows what frogs ate, our Tony certainly didn't.

Big brother Tony – or as me and my younger brother Kevin later dubbed him, Saint Tony. He was nearly top of the class at school and would tell us stories about the Siege of Troy, the 300 Spartans and the wars between Ancient Greece and Persia. He'd tell us how brave Horatio held the bridge to Rome against the Etruscan hordes and how Hannibal and his Carthaginian army, plus assorted elephants, crossed the Alps fighting battles all the way. Tony seemed to have the answers to every question in the world (but struggled with my more complex queries like whether Superman was stronger than The Hulk or whether The Flash could run faster than Billy Whizz). His favourite subject though was Manchester United.

In the corner of our bedroom was a small, flimsy plywood bedside cabinet with a couple of drawers. These drawers bulged with Manchester United programmes dating back to 1958. To Tony it was both shrine and altar, and only the true believer could rummage through with grubby fingers, wondering at the wealth of mystery adorning the glossy pages. Tony went to every home game with his best friend George Doran and regaled me upon his return with stories of the invincible Reds, singing me the songs that rang from Old Trafford's golden terraces, describing Denis Law's goals and telling me how

George Best dribbled around all the players and was so rich he was paid £100 every week and had a Jag. We shared a bed, and in hushed tones he'd share a world of heroes from myth, legend and Manchester United until I'd fall asleep, dreaming of Nobby Stiles slaying the dragon, Beowulf scoring the winner after some tricky ball-work from Best, a flicked-on header by Achilles, who'd managed to jump that high despite Robin Hood having shot an arrow in his eye …

At the time I liked Man. United and the idea of football rather than the game itself. On TV it seemed like nothing much was happening and I'd squirm around and mess about, being told to shush up while black and white figures kicked a ball about the screen. I knew it was the World Cup because there were World Cup Willie footballs, keyrings, ice-creams, ice lollies – that little lion mascot got everywhere. But I knew for a fact that World Cup Willie footballs, which cost 7/6, were a swizz – they were really light like a balloon and soon popped.

The day of the England–West Germany World Cup Final I was thrown out of our front room (which we had the nerve to call a parlour) after about ten minutes for fidgeting about. I couldn't see what all the fuss was about: I knew England would win, our Tony had told me and besides they had Bobby Charlton and Nobby Stiles – and it wasn't even that big a game, I mean it wasn't even United and they didn't even play at Old Trafford. Funnily enough my feelings towards the glamour of international football altered little in the next 30 years.

2

Miss Roberts v. Mother Michael

Starting school was not, despite my being humoured to the contrary, a prospect I savoured. I knew life had been good up until then. I was perfectly happy to watch my older brother Tony and older sister Mary toddle off to school. They had their crosses to bear and they'd told me nothing about school that made me feel as if I wanted to go. No, I'd happily stay at home for all eternity with my little brother Kevin and light fires on the croft, search for empty lemonade bottles to return to the shop for their sixpenny deposit, hang off the back of the coal lorry, hitching a ride as it trundled slowly down the street.

When the fateful day arrived I went quietly if somewhat glumly with my mam to St Alphonsus RC primary school on Ayres Road in Old Trafford. My older brother Tony had left a couple of years earlier having passed his 11-plus exam. He'd been a model pupil, played for the school football team who'd won the local cup, and I knew I had a lot to live up to as I trudged reluctantly through those gates for the first of many times.

I was an unforgiving pupil and from the first day the drilling in ABC that they called lessons, even having to sit still, bored and frustrated me. The other kids seemed like soft mummy's boys. I'd seen some boys crying that first day – I memorized their faces and in all my seven years of primary school I never befriended any of them. I looked at the other lads who'd talk to me and wonder, how many of these are just like Jimmy Millar? Consequently if any boy looked at me funny or showed the slightest sign of hostility I reacted with what became an almost reflex form of violence. The first day in the school yard, some lad said something to me: I punched him a couple of times and looked on with some satisfaction as he crumpled and cried. I felt I might enjoy school after all.

My high opinion of myself was cooled in the classroom where other kids were much better at drawing pictures – some could even read, and we hadn't even started to be taught that yet. I felt clumsy and left out listening while three quarters of the boys and girls spoke with broad Irish brogues, never thinking that it was because they hadn't spent any time playing on the streets and so had heard only the accents their parents spoke with.

At home that evening I quizzed my mother about this school lark. How long did I have to go to school for, and why? My mother humoured me as ever with a simple reply: 'To learn to read and write and do sums.'

'And what then mam?'

'Well then you'll get a good job when you grow up.'

'But if I learn to read and write and do sums before I grow up, can I leave school then?' Somehow inside I felt that I'd won the argument.

But reading was a difficult thing and I was too slow and too bored by it. Much of this can be put down to my first primary school teacher – a relic of the Victorian Roman Catholic variety – called Miss Roberts. At least 60 years of age, she had no patience for four- and five-year-olds and seemed stern for no particular reason especially with kids she didn't like. I was that particular kid.

At least at home I knew I'd be punished for being naughty or for separating our Tony's League Reviews from the middle of his United programmes. Inside the school gates everything was at the teacher's whim. There were no clear boundaries for me in the classroom. A chance remark got me slapped with a ruler as did copying an 'S' or 'J' off the blackboard the wrong way round. Drawing a picture of a house and colouring it in red, I found myself admonished because 'well now houses aren't red are they Terence?' The rules weren't the same for everyone: some kids chatted and the teacher joked and laughed with them.

One moment stands out in that first year at school when I felt badly victimized. Miss Roberts announced she wanted absolute silence, so she could get on with some work, and handed out crayons and paper to everyone to keep them quiet. She missed me out (on purpose?) and sat down to her marking. I waited with my stomach turning over: should I sit there quietly for the next half hour and hope she doesn't notice, but then she may want to look at our pictures, and I'd be in big trouble. I decided the best policy was to speak up – besides I liked crayoning. I tentatively approached her desk and stood next to her tall stool. She continued marking, oblivious of my presence.

'Excuse me, miss ... '

Those were the only words I managed to utter before I was picked up and shaken vigorously. She planted me back down, pulled me round and administered several hard smacks with a wooden ruler to my legs, then lifted me up and dangled me upside-down by the ankles. A fairly unnecessary response, even for that era, I'd say. Threats were screamed at me and the rest of the class warned to carry on in silence as I was pushed out into the corridor to recover my senses and concoct vengeful thoughts.

I must have been traumatized by Miss Roberts' mystifying persecution. I started wetting the bed again and she certainly put the final touches to toughening me up on the outside. No child smirked in that class when I got in trouble. One thing Miss Roberts was unable to do was make me cry. All the shame, pain and humiliation I felt got bottled up inside – I knew she wanted to make me cry but she couldn't. It all stuck in my craw somewhere turning to bile. It wasn't as if I rebelled: I tried to be good, I wanted to be liked, besides I was too afraid of what she might do if I was genuinely naughty.

The reading, not surprisingly, didn't get any easier, and I wasn't great at sums either. I was still on the very first reading book while most the class were at least on book three. My weak bladder wasn't helping – I still occasionally wet the bed at home and in Miss Roberts' class it seemed as if I had to go and pee every ten minutes, a request I was invariably denied.

My mother couldn't help but see something was wrong. She noticed that although I could read some kids books from the library and I could read for her all the way through my school reading book, I was still stuck on that same book. I told her I just couldn't do it for Miss Roberts, I was too frightened of her. I was taken to the doctors and my mother spoke to him at length, particularly puzzled as to how my two older sisters, Janet and Mary, and my older brother Tony had all been star pupils yet I was seen as the class dunce.

A little while after I was back in the classroom copying off the blackboard. My writing looked neat for once. Miss Roberts came around behind me … 'That's very good Terence, oh dear look what's spoiling it, that 'J' is back to front' … I felt the tension rise up. I had a strong feeling that particular back-to-front 'J' was about to cause me a lot of trouble.

'So Terence what are you going to do about that J?'

'Erm, rub it out and write it again,' I said with little hope.

'No you're not allowed to use a rubber, I thought you'd know that by now,' and with that she wandered off.

I stared at that 'J'. I decided I'd write a thick black 'J' the correct way round over the original. It stood out on the page of neat writing like a black stain of sin on a saint's soul. My head snapped up as the classroom door opened and in stepped the headmistress, Mother Michael. I liked Mother Michael – she was an Irish nun, around 50, and had a heart of gold; she was genuinely caring and didn't seem to hold against me my frequent playground scraps and the complaints from Miss Roberts. We all stood as we'd been told: 'Good morning, Mother Michael.'

'Good morning, children.'

She wandered around the class, accompanied by Miss Roberts, looking at everyone's work smiling and giving out words of encouragement and making little jokes. Finally she came to where I was sitting.

'Well Terence this is very good work.'

The relief I felt was like one of my regular trips to the toilet, instant and profound. I noticed Miss Roberts was being very smiley, but there seemed a nervousness about her as she drew Mother Michael's attention to my extra-thick 'J'. My sin, she's letting Mother Michael see my sins!

'Oh so this is your little mistake Terence; never mind we'll just get a rubber and rub it out and write a new one in there … now that's grand.'

Ah, the satisfaction I felt as I looked towards Miss Roberts smiling benignly at her prodigal pupil. I nearly said, 'But we are not allowed to rub out', but she was the supplier of the rubber and was in agreement with Mother Michael that it did now indeed look grand.

I felt Mother Michael had come in just to check up on me and that somewhere down the line Miss Roberts had been told to lay off, and by a nun, by God really. After that things improved: I got on to book three and caught up with some of the pupils in the class. The most important lesson I learned at the time was that adults are more devious liars than kids and with that lesson came a resentment of authority which would linger into adulthood. I look back now it just makes me wonder how many bright and imaginative working-class kids, who didn't find a bit of understanding, were stifled and alienated by that sort of teaching.

This letter 'J' incident did not exactly see a Saul on the road to Damascus style transformation in me. Some bits of school were fun – I led the playground gang and relished any chance to employ Machiavellian tactics – but I still resented being prevented by school from doing all the stuff I loved. Apart from the fires, the frogs, our Tony's stories, my other favourite things were: trying unsuccessfully to catch pigeons with some bread, a piece of string and a box; our cat Percy, who ran away, and was replaced by a kitten who I demanded also be called Percy; making go-karts out of wooden planks and old pram-wheels, which we called 'bogies'; and my dad. He'd regularly take us to the Imperial Cinema around the corner on Chorlton Road.

The Imperial was another world, and while other pre-school kids made occasional visits to see Disney cartoons, our dad always took us to see action and adventure films, especially Westerns. *The Magnificent Seven, The Return of the Seven, Eldorado, How the West Was Won, Shenandoah, Zulu, Lawrence of Arabia* ... all these epics of the Sixties I saw before I'd even experienced *Winnie the Pooh* or *Bambi*. As for any trauma I suffered from the violent nature of those films, I can't remember any nightmares until our Tony took me to see *Planet of the Apes*. It was the sinister gorillas and the doom-laden ending in which the goodies don't win and the baddies are supreme. Afterwards I felt quite concerned whenever I heard stories on the news about 'gorilla fighting' going on in Africa and Asia.

The cinema was magical to me and it was the rare occasion when I could stay up late and spend time with my dad, who always seemed to be at work doing shifts and overtime. He would make us hats out of newspaper and tell us we were Irish soldiers, true Irish rebels – the best and bravest in the world who'd defeated the Romans, the Vikings and most importantly of course, the English. Despite the mice, the damp and the cold linoleum floors, it was a rich little world. And it didn't seem fair that school had to come along and take a big chunk out of it.

All of which reminds me of my late Uncle Larry. He was cheating on some guessing game and I was getting all hot and bothered.

'It's not fair,' I whined.

'Aye,' he replied, 'neither is Black Beauty's arse.'

3

Batman and Robbing

They say that football encouraged hooligan-type behaviour, but my first criminal leanings came due to Milky Way vending machines. Pocket money was meagre in our family – on Saturday we'd get threepence each and on Sunday after Mass a sixpence. One Saturday afternoon I put a threepenny bit in the machine outside our local newsagent shop. Nothing came out, the handle wouldn't turn and my threepenny bit had disappeared. Out came the owner with some keys who offered me a choice, my threepenny bit back or a Milky Way. I suddenly had a brainwave – here was an easy touch for a six-year-old to exploit.

Every evening the following week walking home from school, I stopped at every sweet shop the length of Ayres Road. With my friends waiting outside, I walked into the shop. 'Excuse me, mister/missus, I just put a threepenny bit in your Milky Way/bubbly-gum machine but nothing came out ...' It was a cinch – only parents can tell if their six-year-old is lying and I could act the innocent sweetface. Unfortunately a scam like this wasn't new and despite sending different kids in we were soon rumbled by the shopkeepers, who started moving the machines inside the shops.

At school football cards became the new currency and status symbol. The first person to collect the full set of first division players would be hailed a hero. But with only ninepence-a-week pocket money and the cards threepence for a packet of seven (complete with a stick of plastic-tasting bubble-gum) I would be hard pushed to get the full set. Luckily enough at school we played cards for keeps.

There were several different games we played with our football cards. Topsy was a game where you would alternately flick your cards against a section of wall from an agreed distance – the first person to land one of his cards on top of another won all the cards that had been flicked. Another game was knocksy, where each player would stand an agreed number of cards against the wall and, taking it in turn, would flick a card to try and knock them down. The person who knocked the very last card down won all the cards thrown. Knocksy was a test of nerve as it could often use up all the cards you owned, but the winner was always assured of a big haul.

Like golfers have caddies, a top card player would have picker-ups. This was a mate who supported you and would gather the winnings from each game – he'd be rewarded with any swaps you won – cards that you had two or more of. Of course in an ideal world when one was going for the full set, one only played with 'twicers' anyway. But necessity meant I'd risk all several times before I became the owner of that first set of football cards in our year, complete with team photo cards which had the full checklists.

I was amazed to find that the team photos were Manchester City, the current League Champions in that 67–68 season, and 1968 FA Cup winners West Bromwich Albion. To this day I remember there being player cards which were so common you couldn't give them away – there was nothing more disheartening than seeing five tatty cards of Jeff Astle or Jim

McCalliog thrown into a game of topsy. 'Go on I'll give you six Jim McCalliogs for a Bobby Moncur' – 'No chance'. Every day I lived and learned.

At this time I found the football cards far more interesting than the game itself. Going to actually see a football game was a promised future event like getting a bike or winning the pools. 'When you're seven Tony will take you' was all my mother would say. I knew it would be torture, he'd hold my hand purposely too tight, squeezing it with his long bony fingers and pull my arm half out of its socket as he dragged me across busy main roads. Call me cynical, but I knew the only way our Tony could stop me from wanting to go to every game was to make sure my first experience of a match was as big a nightmare as he could make it. Going to a real match could wait.

In the evening after school I'd take my wad of football cards out of my pocket and go to our Tony for his unbiased opinion on each player. Our Tony had seen them all in action and would regale me with his expert knowledge – or rather his severely Red-eyed interpretation. This way I heard that Mick Mills of Ipswich Town was a clogger, Ralph Coates of Burnley was a fine player, Jeff Astle was all right but Bobby Moore was crap and over-rated. And any Manchester City player, Alan Oakes, Colin Bell, Glyn Pardoe, Francis Lee, Mike Summerbee, was rubbish and dirty, ugly and lucky into the bargain (although he wisely failed to mention that these were the reasons City had won the championship above United by three points that season).

How I would memorize his every word to inform my classmates at school: Ron Davies of Southampton, good header of the ball; Allan Clarke, Leicester City, good player; Jim McCalliog, Sheffield Wednesday, hmm not bad; Emlyn Hughes, Liverpool, a whinger. I couldn't keep up with him though on Willie Morgan, who was playing according to my cards for Burnley – 'overrated'. Morgan went to Man. United for £100,000, his form as a player suddenly improving to 'almost as good as George Best' – not even the baby Jesus was that good.

In the evening after school I'd go home and get my full set of football cards out, dividing them into teams. Joe Royle, Howard Kendal, Jimmy Husband, Alan Ball, Gordon West, Ray Wilson – Everton. Wyn Davies, Iam McFaul, Jimmy Sinclair, Bobby Moncur – Newcastle United. Rodney Marsh, Ian and Roger Morgan, Tony Hately – Queens Park Rangers. George Graham, Frank McLintock, Bobby Gould, Ian Ure, Bob Wilson – Arsenal. And then I'd always get to the Manchester City League Champions card.

This Man. City League Champions lark confused me. Our Tony told me Man. United were the best team in the world, the champions of Europe at Wembley versus Benfica. (He'd even been allowed by my mother to take two days off school so he could go, while I watched nonchalantly at home on TV, never in any doubt whatsoever that the Reds would triumph. After all it's what all the adults told me would happen – United never lost – I was just surprised it took them all that time to score four and George Best hadn't scored the lot.) What worried me though was if United were champions of the world and the best, then how come they weren't on my checklists.

The very foundations of my faith were shaking. Kids in school forlornly taunted the United supporting majority that Man. City were the champions and the best and the fact that City were on the checklist lent weight to their argument ... our Tony was wrong. In the all-Red Christian household a crisis was looming: I was turning into a City fan. I began gazing at my cards of Francis Lee, Colin Bell, Mike Summerbee, Ken Mulhearn, Tony Book and Neil Young, and saying if you are truly the champions let me see. Besides our Tony was getting on my nerves and I liked City's socks with the bit of maroon around the top and the maroon stripe on their white shorts.

I confronted my brother Tony. How come City are the champions if United are the best? He explained that City were lucky and dirty and how Francis Lee was always diving for penalties and how Mike Summerbee couldn't run fast in case his nose got stuck in the ground. So who wins when they play each other? I asked ... and this is when I became suspicious: mostly United won, but sometimes, just sometimes Man. City won.

Well I was devastated. Here's God making the world and the baby Jesus and all that and our Tony had as good as admitted that City were the champions and sometimes they even won against United and now was one of those times and City were the best and they were indeed on the checklist. So I cried to the heavens and I rebelled against God, Matt Busby and George Best, as I had against Miss Roberts. From now on I would blaspheme in the presence of our Tony by naming the new Trinity of Bell, Lee and Summerbee and their mate Ringo Starr out of the Beatles (who I loved and wished as an older brother instead of our Tony).

I thought our Tony was the fountain of all knowledge but he did torment me so I wouldn't want to hang around with him and the older lads on the street. He wouldn't let me look at his United programmes unless he was there and he'd go spare if he caught me with my hand in his drawer getting the League Reviews separated from the middle of the programmes to which they belonged. And then there was last summer ...

The previous summer we'd been on holiday – a week at Pontins in St Annes, near Blackpool. Accompanying us were my mother's sister, Nancy, her husband and their two lads, Colin, who was a year older than Tony, and his younger brother Christopher, who was in between me and Tony. This trip to Pontins was going to be fun, but I knew I'd be the victim of all our Tony's torments. Even in the paddling pool, Tony, Colin and Chistopher would come in and kick water at me when it was time to get out.

Then one afternoon Colin came over smiling and put his arm round me as he spoke to Tony: 'Wow look at his muscles, and in those trunks he looks like Tarzan.' Now I was a wise old five-year-old, but I'd never had to cope with being told I was like Tarzan before, so I believed it. I flexed my biceps for Colin who called our Tony over; nor did they laugh when they said I must be really strong with such huge muscles. Colin faked an arm-wrestle with me, pretending I'd really beaten him. Hey this was good, if I was stronger than Colin now and I was only five then Tarzan had better watch for me when I grew up. Suspecting that nothing was afoot I bit straight away when they came to the point of this conversation. Pontins were hold-ing a Junior Tarzan contest for the under-sevens and not only was I to be their representative, but I was going to win. For days I kept flexing my biceps, refusing to wear anything but my swimming trunks and grimacing as only a true apeman can. This wasn't show business, this was serious – I was Tarzan.

On a sunny afternoon I was taken to the main ballroom on the Pontins site and lined up with a bunch of kids my age and younger who were all dressed in their Sunday best. I had my swimming trunks on beneath short cream trousers and a brand new light-blue short-sleeved shirt with pink and white border-ing on the collar and pockets – in fact my Sunday best. But hey, no way would it be staying on: I'd be out there under the lights, stripping off and letting out such a Tarzan-like roar that every animal in the vicinity would stop in its tracks before flee-

ing in terror. Then some over-perfumed female in a blue coat
gave me a large numbered card and I was led across the stage
with the other contestants as the announcer asked for a big
round of applause for ... 'all the children entering the Junior
Prince contest! ...'.

'JUNIOR PRINCE!' The shame of it. To my mind the very
word 'prince' meant some tarted-up ponce in a stupid suit who
played with his sisters and liked it, all dollies and tea sets, the
sort of person who appeared in our Mary's *Bunty* comics. I'd
never felt so humiliated in my life (in retrospect, the shape of
things to come) and it was one of many incidents which
fuelled my precocious cynical outlook on the world. And as far
as our Tony was concerned, deep inside I thirsted for
vengeance – my time would come.

My guardian angel was in and our Tony's out when I discovered the Typhoo Tea offer. This involved cutting out 12 picture
tokens of footballers from the empty tea packets and sending
them off for a big cardboard colour photo of a football star of
your choice. Already adorning our bedroom wall were pictures
of Bobby Charlton, George Best and Denis Law, which our
Tony had sent off for. It was after a visit to my Aunty Katy's,
when I saw that her husband, Uncle Charlie, had Typhoo Tea
pictures of Colin Bell and Francis Lee on the wall, that I determined to hijack our Tony's monopoly and get a couple of
photos of my own on our bedroom wall. Tony might think
Uncle Charlie had poisoned my mind, but he used to give us
two bob each when we went visiting and he was at least telling
me the truth when he said that City were the champions. On
the home front at least I became to all intents and purposes a
City fan.

After what seemed like years of asking my mam why she
couldn't drink more tea, I had 12 tokens to send off. After this

purgatorial phoney war my first ammunition arrived in the form of a large brown envelope addressed to Master Terence Christian. Inside, a photo of Colin Bell, the anti-Christ to our Tony. Immediately a drawing pin was demanded and Colin Bell became the first non-Man. United player to adorn our bedroom wall or any wall for that matter in the Christian household. To escalate matters I then recruited my little brother Kevin who was nearly four into the plot.

I told him how City were the champions and if our Tony was a United fan, me and our Kev would be City fans and get all the other Typhoo Tea pictures to join Colin Bell on the wall and we'd drive Tony mad. This driving our Tony mad was the whole point, especially as I wasn't even that knowledgeable about football's crazy rules. In retrospect my propaganda job on Kevin worked so well that even today, raised in Old Trafford amongst Reds of all ages, young Kevin Patrick is still as loyal and as bitter a Blue as he became the day that picture of Colin Bell was exhibited on our bedroom wall.

Now as far as Tony was concerned that wall was leased from the room's owner, i.e. him, and he made life very hard for young Kevin and myself. The fact that Kevin called football 'kick-kick' and Cornflakes 'Lorlakes' and Father Christmas 'Father Miss-miss' must have helped his painless conversion to the boys from Maine Road. Of course our Tony tried vainly to get our Kevin to do a U-turn from Blue to Red, but he was having none of it. Personally I think he was a bit frightened of that Bobby Charlton picture, and the fact Colin Bell had a full head of hair and didn't give him nightmares eased him into the trauma of being a bitter Bluenose for life.

City were over the other side of Moss Side from where we lived, and 90 per cent of the lads at school were Manchester United fans. So I became a City fan at home to annoy our Tony but at school I would carry on being a Red (with a sneaking silent regard for City). At this point Tony got worried, changed tack and started trying to get into my good books. He said he would take me to a proper football match.

We walked from Brookes Bar the half-mile or so to Old Trafford. It was only when I said there didn't seem to be many people around that Tony explained it was a reserve match with all the players who couldn't get into the first team. 'So who are United playing?' I asked. 'Netherfield Town,' I was told matter of factly. Now I was a collector of football cards and I'd heard of a lot of first and second division football teams from the results on TV but who the hell were *Netherfield* (apparently big in the Northern Premier League at the time and based in Cumbria I've since discovered). To be fair there were a few United players I'd heard of playing in that game: John Fitzpatrick who was coming back from a broken leg, Willie Morgan, David Sadler, Francis Burns and Shay Brennan. But the star player that evening under the Old Trafford floodlights was a ginger-haired, slightly dumpy Italian called Carlo Sartori. The first in a long line of 'the next George Bests', he never quite made the grade but he did score the only goal of what was a very dull game indeed. I suspected that City or even City reserves would be preferable to this.

A few weeks later on a Saturday afternoon I was taken to see United reserves play against Liverpool reserves. I looked at my Liverpool football cards before the game – Ian St John, Ron Yeats, Tommy Smith, Roger Hunt, Peter Thompson. Needless to say none of them were playing but Brian Kidd appeared for United, as did Alan Gowling and Johnny Aston (who was making a come back from a broken leg or something). The match was a boring 1–1 draw, but it was plain to me with all the broken legs knocking about that it was a man's game. In the street after school every night we played with a burst football. I barked instructions at Jimmy Millar and the McPhee twins like a film director: 'Right when you get tackled you have to pretend you've got a broken leg'. So we hopped about on one leg trying to kick the ball. If there was one thing more glamorous than being George Best, it was being George Best with a broken leg. I often wonder what it would have been like if Bryan Robson had been playing for United then – three broken legs, a dislocated shoulder and a dodgy collar-bone. Now that would have been something challenging for us to ape.

Football cards it seemed, were on the wane. The biggest most unmissable programme on TV was *Batman* and Batman cards were the new currency. Part one of *Batman* was on Saturday night followed by part two on Sunday. Besides the Batman Cards, you could buy Batman masks – that looked nothing like Batman; a whole Batman suit – that looked nothing like the caped crusader's outfit; Batman and Robin figures with detachable cloaks – though the figures didn't punch as they had their hands resting on their hips; and Batmobile cars courtesy of Matchbox – which went as fast as you whizzed them. If you were rich there was a decorating shop on Moss Lane West that even sold Batman and Robin wallpaper.

At school kids were loathe to play topsy's with me for Batman cards, such was my reputation, and despite the wide range of available merchandise, Batman cards were the only Batman thing I had. Wearing duffel-coats to school we'd take our arms out of the sleeves, fasten the top toggle up and put our hoods up – hey presto, an instant batman outfit! Then we'd fight with pretend punches that inevitably ended up with someone being whacked in the nose for real – then Batman would have the other Batman in a headlock, punching upwards without saying 'POW!' or 'ZAP!' (hood up or down optional).

As with the football cards, I did well collecting the majority of Batman cards, the backs of which when you had the whole set made a huge jigsaw puzzle. One rainy afternoon I sat on the cold oilcloth in our backroom, surrounded by my toy soldiers and broken fort, showing our Kevin my re-enactment of the Siege of the Alamo. Grim-faced on the battlements Hawkeye, Robin Hood, various cowboys, bedraggled members of the US cavalry, a Roman standard-bearer and a machine-gunner from the British 8th Army were repelling a massed attack by the Red Indians, Household Cavalry, Confederate infantry, medieval knights, Zulus and red-coated mounties – all of whom died in order of how much paint they had left on them – when there was a knock on the front door. It was Jimmy Millar, who said that his brother Stephen, a year our senior, had loads of Batman cards like me, and that we could go to his house, and play topsy (not for keeps though) and try the jigsaw puzzle. Lying on the lino-covered floor playing topsy and attempting the puzzle, my cards got mixed up with Stephen's and after a free-for-all fight in which I ended up in a headlock for an eternity. I went home minus half my Batman cards.

A few years ago, just after I'd finished working on the first series of *The Word*, the Channel 4 show I presented, I was down my local in Old Trafford with some friends when I bumped into Jimmy and Stephen Millar. They greeted me as a long-lost friend while I warily tried to cover my shock at seeing them, as I couldn't remember the last time they'd both been out of prison at the same time. In fact they'd both just finished a long stretch for armed robbery, which was at least a fairly respectable and honest crime, so I was on my best behaviour. I was doing the 'I'm still the cheeky kid you grew up with' when Stephen chirped in conspiratorially, 'Eh, Terry, remember when you used to come to our house and play with those Batman cards?' Now it was Jimmy who was my friend back then and that was the only time in my life I'd ever spent more than ten minutes in Stephen's company. Perhaps it was the beer talking or a wish to connect with my roots but I laughed and put an arm round Stephen and said to him.

'Oh aye yeah, and you two went and nicked them all off me, mugged me for my Batman cards and didn't even bother to wear a mask that time.'

Now Jimmy laughed, but Stephen, well his eyes hardened and the smile froze on his face before he growled, 'We didn't nick your fuckin' Batman cards.'

Here I was aged nearly 30 and I'm in that same Old Trafford predicament – I can't back down, even though nobody in Old Trafford would want to tangle with Jimmy and Stephen Millar. I floundered but kept smiling.

'No I didn't mean you really nicked them, remember you won them off me playing topsy and I was whinging that I didn't know it was for keeps.' An anxious glance in Jimmy's direction and relief when he backed me up. Holy nearly shit my pants, Batman. 'Er anyway ... do you want a drink?'

4

Confessions of a Red

I was a confused young boy, and took a perverse pleasure in being contrary. My split personality was the crowning glory of this awkwardness: the Red Dr Jekyll at school, and the Blue Mr Hyde at home. Out of eighty-odd kids in my year at school there were a mere half dozen or so claiming to be City fans. Even better was that all the clever and funny remarks our Tony made to me with regard to supporting Man. City, I'd then use mockingly at school, ingratiating myself even further with the United fans.

I know City supporters perpetuate this myth that in Manchester itself as many if not more people support City and United are merely for the tourists. This really is fantasy football. In all my years at school City fans were always outnumbered three or four to one by United fans. In fact those City fans I did meet in largish numbers later in life all seemed to come from the Stockport area, which makes their accusations against United of being Stretford Celtic a bit rich really.

Perhaps it's because I attended Catholic schools that United fans were always the most numerous. Manchester United were labelled as a Catholic club and even at that young age I knew that Matt Busby, Brian Kidd, Paddy Crerand, Shay Brennan,

Nobby Stiles, John Fitzpatrick and Tony Dunne were Catholics. I even remember my late Uncle Jack stating years later that the only reason he thought Frank O'Farrell, Wilf McGuinness and Dave Sexton were employed as managers at United was through the Catholic connection. As for Busby, he was a devout man who often attended Mass at our local church, St Alphonsus. But bigotry was something that Busby, brought up in a sectarian Scotland, had learned to hate. The transformation at the club (which previously was in the shadow of City) that he brought about in the Fifties and Sixties had little to do with religion.

There is no legacy at United that compares with Celtic or Hibernian in Scotland (or indeed the now-defunct Belfast Celtic) – but there are historical reasons (apart from more recently the Busby factor) for the Catholic association. Manchester United was founded by railway workers, many of whom were Irish, Scottish and Welsh and there was talk in the early days of naming the club Manchester Celtic. As I've described, Old Trafford was home to a large number of Irish Catholic families (although less so nowadays).

The area of Trafford was originally owned and named after the Earl De Trafford, whose family had been English Catholics since the Reformation and who were in turn very welcoming to the early Irish Catholic immigrants. Although those early immigrants were mainly educated people training to be doctors and lawyers, this laid a welcoming foundation for the waves of Irish Catholic immigration during the industrial revolution, when thousands came to find work digging the Manchester Ship Canal (the original navigators or 'navvies').

The city has long been characterized by a high proportion of outsiders. The 1851 census of Manchester and Salford pointed to the fact that out of 400,000 people, 220,000

claimed to have been born elsewhere. There were strong anti-
Irish prejudices voiced at the time with even the purportedly
liberal *Manchester Guardian* reporting:

> The extensive immigration of poor Irish has inflicted a
> deadly blow upon the health and comfort of the working
> class. They are a most serious evil with which our labouring
> classes have to contend.

The author Fintan Vallely, describing the character of the Irish
just after the potato famines, was more sympathetic but no less
damning:

> The present Irish character is a compound of strange and
> apparent inconsistencies; where vices and virtues are so
> unhappily blended that it is difficult to distinguish or sepa-
> rate them. Hasty in forming opinions and projects, tardy in
> carrying them into effect, they are often relinquished before
> they have arrived into maturity, and are abandoned for
> others as vague and indefinite … The virtues of patience,
> prudence, and industry seldom are included in the compo-
> sition of an Irishman; he projects gigantic schemes, but
> wants perseverance to realise any work of magnitude; his
> conceptions are grand and vivid, but his execution is feeble
> and indolent; he is witty and imprudent, and will dissipate
> the hard earnings of today regardless of tomorrow; an appeal
> made to his heart is seldom unsuccessful, and he is generous
> with an uninquiring and profuse liberality.

Our religion often blended with our nationality. As Irish we
were a scattered, tribal nation. The mayo folk stuck together, as
did the people of Donegal, Tiperary, Cork, Galway, Clare,
Kerry and Dublin; eyeing each other suspiciously across
centuries of oppression, forced emigration and an almost
conditioned subversive resistance to Anglo-Western world
conformity. We were non-conformists in most ways except

when it came down to religion. All the colour and pageantry in our lives came from the church, the candles, flowers and ornate statues that adorned the altars, the clean smells of incense, wax and polish, the holy water, the brightness of the stained-glass windows and the priests' robes. Who needed a purely functional church like the Methodists or the Presbyterians? We had enough spartan functionalism at home with our discoloured oil cloths and shabby mis-matched furniture. Religion was our hope, the poor inherited the earth or were loved by God or however it was referred to in the Bible. So in the end, we'd win.

Our Catholicism made us feel special, but we considered ourselves Mancunians first and Irish Catholic second. We knew that there were people who didn't like Catholics or Irish and when we'd attend the Whit walks it was obvious that Catholics marched on a different day to the local Protestant churches and always had the more spectacular banners, pipe bands and floats. We were a minority in England, but in world terms we were the biggest Christian club, the biggest tribe. Likewise Manchester United reviled by the fans of other teams in Britain, were the most supported football team on the planet and we felt United was our club, the outsiders' club.

As a young lad brought up in the Church, I knew in terms of fights and disobedience alone I was two thirds the way to being the Devil's disciple; bung everything else in I'd done, like the Milky Way scam and I was on the Hell express, one way. Now I did go to Mass every Sunday and that had probably saved me so far, but it worried me. There was a glimmer of hope on the horizon of heaven. We were to make our first confessions and cleanse our dirty heathen six-year-old souls, ready to receive the body and presence of Christ at our first communion.

The Catholic Church made great demands on its young

sons and daughters. Mass every Sunday lasted an hour and involved getting dressed up in something invariably uncomfortable and itchy. The rosary every night in October with its joyful, sorrowful and mysterious mysteries; church on All Souls' Day to pray for the dead to get into heaven; all those holy days of obligation; and the rites of passage like confession, communion and confirmation and wearing rotting discoloured shamrock which would be sent in the post from our relatives in Ireland every St Patrick's Day. My parents were particularly devout, and due to the profound grief they felt after the death of my oldest sister Janet at the age of 11, they wanted us all blessed with the grace and protection of God. But this grace and protection business was a drag at times.

I was heading for my first confession. I'd learned all the lines. All I had to do was go to church on a Saturday and spend a few minutes kneeling in front of the altar examining my conscience while waiting for my turn in the confessional box. When my turn came, with eyes downcast and hands joined as in prayer I entered the box. In the darkness of the Cubicle there was a small square of light coming through a grill. The priest greeted me from the other side and I started.

'Bless me Father for I have sinned, this is my first confession and these are my sins. I have been disobedient, I have been fighting, I have been telling lies, I have been stealing; these are all I can remember, Father.'

Absolution was swift and my due penance handed out: 'Say five Hail Marys and five Our Fathers. Go forth and sin no more.'

I was relieved of my burdens, determined to sin no more and stay full of grace, and I have to admit that being six, going on seven, it's not that difficult. I would be as good as gold. The big problem was the next time I went to confession I had nothing to confess. How could I walk in and face Canon

O'Donnel or Father Carter two weeks later and say, 'Sorry Father, nothing to report but a new halo.' So like every other self-respecting, self-abusing and self-deluding Catholic through the ages I made some sins up, so at least that covered the lies part.

It's only when you know how imperfect you are that you'll make up sins for the confession box, and it's then that you properly understand what guilt is and feels like. Perhaps it's only when we are convinced of our innocence that we are truly guilty. But this was difficult when we were young, as we were told every day that we were sinners. We had a bible story every morning in class and a fairy-tale in the afternoon. A lad called David Fallon could never quite grasp the metaphysical concepts when cross-examined by Miss Roberts on Adam and Eve's fall from grace.

'Well, miss, Adam and Eve are in this big garden and this witch gives them these poison apples which they eat, then they're dead and then Jesus and these dwarves come and bring them back to life again and chop the witches head off with an axe ...' And he thought it was all true. Despite being unsure whether it was a sin or not to be amused at David's Gospel according to Hans Christian Andersen, I felt holy enough to laugh. Even today it still tickles me and I often imagine young Mr Fallon as an evangelical preacher quoting bible passages – 'In my Father's gingerbread house there are many mansions and a few wicked stepmothers'. We heard stories of saints and martyrs who suffered gruesome and painful deaths, being shot full of arrows, crushed under doors by heavy boulders, stretched on the rack and eaten by wild beasts. Piously, we imagined ourselves walking with no fear to be a quick snack for a lion, in the knowledge that it was a first-class ticket to heaven and that Sam Peckinpah may well buy the movie rights.

When our local priest from St Alphonsus church came

visiting once in a while he'd make us laugh and be a refreshing change from Miss Roberts' overbearing dourness. We'd chuckle at his jokes and he'd talk to us about football and the school team; in fact just about everything would get a mention except God. We always laughed at the priest's jokes even if they weren't funny; it was a good idea to stay in his good books as from the age of eight lads were eligible to be altar boys – and everyone knew altar boys could make nearly ten bob, even a pound, in tips serving at weddings on a Saturday and at funerals.

The teacher gave out little cardboard boxes to us at school. 'These are your St Joseph's penny boxes, so if you put all your pocket money in over Lent it will be sent to children who live in poor countries around the world so that they can have regular dinners, school books and learn about Jesus.' I took my St Joseph's penny box home, but as I didn't really get much pocket money, I tried to get my mam to fill it and paraded it out when various uncles and aunts visited. I saw my Uncle Jack put in the two bob he'd normally give to me. The box was sealed so I tried to get it out by tipping it upside down. I knew God and the baby Jesus would see this, but so what, I'd have something true to tell the Father or Canon O'Donnel in confession. The slot was too narrow.

I waited until Lent was over and kept my now empty St Joseph's penny box. Led astray by some sinful advice from friends at school I took the box around some of the houses on our street. 'Er it's for the baby Jesus and God and children who don't have any dinner.' Together with my meagre bits of pocket money and some birthday money, I managed to scrounge together about nine bob. I spent six buying myself a tortoise from the pet shop on Moss Lane West. It was all very well looking after Godless children in far-off lands but you couldn't put them in a cardboard box with newspaper in and make them hibernate for the winter.

Religious holidays or holy days of obligation where atten-
dance at Mass was compulsory meant a day off for us Catholics
that the Protestant kids didn't get. All Saints' Day, All Souls',
Pentecost, the Feast of Peter and Paul, the Annunciation, the
Ascension ... we were forever saying prayers and being grate-
ful, which we indeed were, especially when granted a day off.
It was around this time I decided that, if I didn't develop the
dribbling skills of George Best and get paid £100 a week as
well as the Jag, perhaps the priesthood would be a good move.
Sure it wouldn't be the same in terms of glory or glamour, but
you'd be important and respected in the community and those
collection boxes looked full every Sunday and all our priests
seemed to have cars like the doctors did.

One time when the whole of our school was seated in the
pews for Mass on Ash Wednesday, the priest gave us a sermon
about the significance of Ash Wednesday, about life and death.
He told us a story of a February day in 1958 and a Manchester
United team, the greatest ever, and a plane crash on an icy
runway in Munich, a city in Germany. He talked of those
young men, with great talents that were God-given, yet they
too had been taken into heaven to be with God and all the
saints, because no matter who we are, we all belong to God and
will ultimately join him. And all the while all I could think of
was a plane in flames and Duncan Edwards and the other players lying on the tarmac, just ashes.

We all sat there through this riveting sermon, mouths open
in fear and wonder until at the end of the Mass we went up to
the priest to have our foreheads anointed with ashes and to
hear him say, 'Remember man that thou art dust and unto dust
thou shalt return'. I couldn't help wondering if this meant that
God was a United fan too, and he so loved those players that
he wanted them for a special team up in heaven. I pondered
my mortality and prayed that God wouldn't want George Best

and hoped the fact that Best was a Protestant might keep him out of God's Select Heaven 11.

In class a few weeks later I asked the Father if you could play football in heaven, and he said you could do whatever made you happy. 'But what if your side gets beaten and you're picked last for the team after all the other boys like John Mulvaney, then you'd be sad.' The Reverend Father agreed and then said you could play football in heaven but every game would be a draw and everyone would get picked at the same time. This perplexed me: if every game was a draw and even crap footballers like John Mulvaney in our class got picked, why did God want all those great footballers off United who would suffer the humiliation of drawing with the likes of Oldham Athletic reserves or a John Mulvaney not-so-select 11. Further questioning along these lines would prompt that greatest of answers all clerics resorted to: 'Well my son, it's a mystery'.

Our priests would even take the mickey mercilessly out of the few City fans in the class and would refer to them along with Protestants as 'that other lot'. Yes even God mocked the Blues. Heaven demanded I support United and the only devils the Catholic Church loved were the Red variety. My mother was dubious though when I told her I'd be a priest.

'You have to be very clever to be a priest.'

'Oh.'

Despite the priests' football punditry and my trips to the reserve matches, I didn't feel able to let our Tony off the hook that easily. I enjoyed winding him up too much. After endlessly cajoling my parents into drinking more and stronger cups of tea, I at last added Francis Lee to Colin Bell on the bedroom wall.

The following year at school we found ourselves in the psychologically more comfortable surrounds of Miss O'Brien's class. She was a young and rather fetching auburn-haired woman who was very kind and had a habit of examining her stockings for ladders throughout the day. I was seated next to Richard Behan, one of the biggest lads in the year. Richard was a very friendly and intelligent kid and well liked by the teacher, and thanks to his outgoing nature we were made milk monitors for the class. This involved going outside into the yard everyday and bringing back two and a half crates of small milk bottles and handing them out to our classmates. The perk of this job was that we had first claim on any spare bottles, although these extras were invariably donated by Miss O'Brien to the five or six children in our class who hadn't had any breakfast.

I can still recall those pupils all sitting together at a table, slurping their milk through a straw and sharing a packet of ginger biscuits the teacher had culled from the school tuck-shop. We thought these kids were lucky getting this special treatment and we'd whisper over to them, 'Oi, Burkey, give us one of them Ginger Nuts you greedy git.' Of course, we knew all the stories: 'such and such a boy hasn't got a dad' or 'Steve's dad spends all his money on beer so his mam can't buy him any Cornflakes'. We'd force these kids to relate all the gory details of their tough home life to us in the yard. Then, if the teacher was telling one of them off we'd interject on the accused's behalf saying, 'Sean had to stay at his nan's house last night and she hasn't got a bed for him and he had to sleep in the chair and that's why he's tired.' We did feel quite protective of our more unfortunate classmates, but much of it was just that innate nosiness nurtured in our terraced streets. In fact we bullied these kids for the stories of their poverty and problems, which we feared – we reproached them as if it was their own fault.

The Polish kids came in for some bullying too. There were usually about six in each year, and they were guilty of many sins in our eyes. Firstly, we suspected many of them of living in semi-detached houses up the posh end of Old Trafford and there was evidence to suggest piano lessons, changes of clothes nearly every day and having lots of toys, new bikes and the like. To be fair they didn't brag too much, but they were always well behaved and good at reading, so we preferred the skinny, undernourished, snotty-nosed kids who were thick as planks and poorer than church mice.

Maybe we were emotionally hardened by all this but I don't think so. Old Trafford was nowhere near the worst area of Manchester to grow up. But there were big differences and contrasts and our family was somewhere in the middle. One time, the caterers at the town hall who usually made the school dinners went on strike and we had to bring our own sandwiches. This exposed genuine inequalities. We loved the novelty of bringing sandwiches in but were at the same time haunted by the sight of kids like Kevin Leary, a forlorn, unloved kid with big dull watery eyes that blinked constantly over a permanently runny nose. We'd heard his dad was a Pakistani and had never married his mother or seen young Kevin.

He walked around in plastic sandals with no socks, wearing the same torn stripey T-shirt, with its neck pulled to his razor-blade shoulders, and thin cotton shorts, summer and winter. He was the kid who always got the ginger biscuits with his milk at break-time because, as he put it, blinking and stuttering painfully, grabbing at every word as if it might be his last, 'M-m-m-my-er-er-mam w-w-wen-er-er went to the shop for milk and it was shut'. Always the same excuse, the same story. The school dinners were off, so Kevin Leary went hungry, scuffling his plastic sandals and matchstick legs around the playground, asking if he could have a bite of a sandwich. We'd have a whip round until he was facing a mixture of banana and sugar, corned beef, brawn, spam and cheese sandwiches. Somehow it was important and natural to us that we shared what we had.

Don't forget we were none of us well off, so being generous to the Kevin Learys was our equivalent of driving a Jaguar or having a flash house, a way of asserting superiority. After a few days the dinner ladies who patrolled the yard began to feed the hungry kids.

Nobody wanted to sit next to those kids, nobody wanted to befriend them. If you went hungry, smelled because you weren't washed or bathed and had no change of clothes you were therefore smelly and had fleas or nits and were a bad reflection on all of us. As young kids we could be kind but we unconsciously blamed them for their own misfortune and bullied them. We feared them and their poverty in case it rubbed off, knowing that one simple twist of fate could reduce any of us to that state. I saw it happen to one of our group when his father died a few weeks before his tenth birthday. Sometimes at night I'd pray to Jesus and St Francis for these kids, made an effort to mock those lads who in turn mocked Kevin Leary.

When it had been raining I'd often be the first kid out there in the street when the drops had stopped, dragging my feet in wellington boots through the puddles formed in the broken tarmac, past the terraced houses of my streets – all virtually identical to a casual passer-by, infinitely varied to the curious young local. There was No. 158 with its dirty orange and cream faded paintwork and freshly scrubbed and stoned step, then lower down, the frosted glass door behind which lurked the local bulldog and then, around the corner on Croston Street, the front door which boasted a large crystal-glass doorknob. We imagined the doorknob to be a huge diamond and the woman who lived there to be rich. In fact she was the Republic of Ireland-capped footballer John Sheridan's Aunt Julie. But the house had a more fascinating football lineage.

It once had been the abode of the Manchester United and England winger George Wall. George Wall was from County Durham and played for the first ever truly successful Manchester United team. He made over 250 appearances for the club between 1905 and 1915. During this period, United won promotion from the second division in the 1905–6 season, the first division championship in 1907–8 and 1910–11 seasons, the FA Cup in 1909, and the first Charity Shield in 1908. He also went on United's first ever European tour, that of Austria and Hungary in 1908, which included two cele-brated victories of 6–2 and 7–0 against Ferenczvaros, who had conceded only one goal in their league all season. The second of the two matches was the one that made headlines, for the hostile crowd reception the United players received. George Wall scored two of the goals. It was what happened after the game that had United's first famous manager, Ernest Mangnall, vowing that United would never go to Budapest again. As the team left the field they were attacked by the crowd. Harry Renshaw, the *Manchester Evening News* reporter, wrote:

Everybody made for the gateway through which the players must pass on their way to the dressing room ... Harry Moger was struck across the shoulders by one of these rioters with a stick. Stacey was spat upon, Picken and Charlie Roberts struck, in fact nearly all the team were given a reminder. Then the police charged the rioters, and fully twenty were arrested and dragged into one of the club rooms which was utilised as a police station. Even in the dressing room the team were not safe and a shower of heavy stones let in more air and daylight.

The players left the ground under police escort and were

on their way back to their hotel in a row of coaches when the rioters attacked again.

Particular attention was paid to the last carriage and a huge stone knocked me down and cut my head. Then Alec Bell was hit behind the ear, and Picken received another. I was then hit on the head again. It was so sudden that the players had no time to raise the hoods of the carriages. Mr Mangnall was hit and Thomson caught it badly in the neck, with Wall and several others. Many arrests were made and the police were compelled to draw their swords.

George Wall would make history again, playing in the side and scoring the third goal in United's very first game at their new Old Trafford stadium on 19 February 1910. Unfortunately United lost that day to Liverpool 4–3, despite leading 3–1 at one stage. Wall took part in the first players' strike in 1909, aimed at abolishing the maximum wage, when Manchester United's footballers became known as the Outcasts FC. The strike's main instigator was the best player of that era, a footballing legend then at Manchester United and a good friend of George Wall's – Billy Meredith. Those footballers fought for a players' union and a fair wage, perhaps the most important contest players from Manchester United ever took part in. George finished his time at Old Trafford playing in front of up to 60,000 people every home game.

And his reward for all those honours, medals and battles of his career? Not £30,000 a week, or even George Best's famed £100 a week and a Jaguar motor car. No: they gave him a job on Manchester Docks and a terraced house on Croston Street, down the Brookes Bar end of Old Trafford, with a large glass doorknob that little kids in the area said was a diamond.

5

Fire in the Melting Pot

For the kids of Old Trafford the two biggest events of the year were Christmas Day and Bonfire Night. I loved the story of the Catholic Anarchist Guy Fawkes, who attempted to blow up the King and the Houses of Parliament. The fact that most of the youngsters on our neighbouring streets were Irish Catholics didn't dampen our enthusiasm for making Guys and getting out there and hustling. The end of September was a good time to start collecting a 'Penny for the Guy'. Mind you, any tight-fisted individual who only tipped up a penny was roundly and vociferously ridiculed as a skinflint. 'What's he going to do with a penny, mister, stick it up his arse and have a race?'

Our Guy was a work of art: a pair of our dad's old trousers and a shirt or pullover stuffed with newspaper and sewn together, a head made of more rolled-up newspaper in a brown paper bag with a face painted on it, and our Tony's Man. United scarf wrapped around its neck as an added selling point. And, of course, an old trolley or baby buggy to wheel it around in. Owning the Guy meant the majority of any money collected went to you. Our parents may well have voted Labour and my own father was a shop steward for 25 years, but at that age I had no qualms about entrepreneurial ruthlessness.

It was important to have a crew. First of all to clear those pesky Oxford Street kids off a prime site and then of course to reach as many punters as possible. Thursday evening was the best – all the blokes were in a good mood as it was pay day and they'd be walking round with pockets full of change from the paper-shop. We had to suffer the odd lecture off some old geezer who'd tell us that Penny for the Guy was like begging. We never quite cottoned on to this as we thought beggars were old men with ragged trousers and no shoes who asked for pieces of bread while sitting in the road. Strangely enough, back in the Sixties, with all the terraced houses and lack of bathrooms and inside lavatories, we had never actually seen a genuine beggar.

Penny for the guy was lucrative but it was important to pick your crew carefully. You couldn't have any kid who was known for giving cheek to the local grown-ups ... this ruled out the McPhee twins. Also it was no good picking a kid who was too tough and would start arguing about getting a fair share of the money ... so that definitely ruled out Jimmy Millar. The selected crew for Penny for the Guy was my little brother Kevin and two young kids of West Indian descent, Richard and Rennie Samson. This was a particularly good move business-wise as a lot of West Indians lived on our street. These were mainly young single males working in Trafford Park and several actually lodged at Richard and Rennie's house and they were very generous, often tipping up as much as two shillings a time.

The Samsons were the nicest, politest and in some respects the softest kids on the street, and good fun to be with. Richard and I were the same age and first met when a gang of us, led by Jimmy Millar, chased him and his brother Rennie off the street to the front of their house. Richard and Rennie were the first black kids of our age to move on to the street and had only just moved in, so we pursued them with violent intent. I can still picture them knocking urgently on their mother's front door, shouting through the letterbox, frantic to be let in before we caught them and gave them the obligatory treatment for … well for being darker skinned than us and as a kind of welcome to the neighbourhood.

I had a large pebble in my hand and in the flush of the chase I threw it at Richard's head from an angle that meant, if it didn't hit him, it would hit the side panel of the house's bay window. He ducked and with a sickening feeling I saw the glass shatter and tumble. As we split to scarper in different directions, Richard's mum flew out the door like a whirlwind and snatched Brian McPhee and started to interrogate him. As I sat breathlessly in my mother's kitchen there was a loud, urgent knocking at the door. Mrs Samson was there with Richard and Rennie. I was a shambolic set of excuses.

'Why were you chasing them?'

'Er, we were just playing … pretending.'

'Why did you break the window?'

'Well he threw a stone at me [I lied] so I threw it back and I was aiming for his head and he ducked.'

There was no escape from my guilt and my dad was none too pleased when he had to pay for and install a new window in the Samson residence. My dad hated doing jobs around the house and wasn't too even tempered when, after working a 12-hour shift, his short amount of leisure time was disturbed. I was hit with his belt as punishment, which may seem harsh but seemed to be the law with regard to every kid in those days and understood as such.

What I could never get over was the dexterity of Richard's duck. My stone had been well aimed and was going straight for his head and he only saw it for a split second, I was impressed ... he was a decent kid.

After that we started hanging out together, but it was when my younger brother Kevin started palling around with Rennie, who was the same age as him, that trouble started. Because Richard never went anywhere without his brother Rennie, I had to let Kevin hang out with me. It put a dampener on being able to mess about with the McPhees and Jimmy Millar. Our Kevin was too small to run fast enough to escape the clutches of angry grown-ups. This stopped us climbing on to the roof of the Sharon Gospel church on Chorlton Road, or climbing on to backyard walls and sitting on the roofs of outside loos, or knocking on doors and running away. The only thing our Kevin and Rennie were good for really was Penny for the Guy.

The deal was this: Richard and myself stood with the Guy and trolley outside the newsagent's window on Chorlton Road, accosting the punters as they came out with the change still warm in their hands, while Kevin and Rennie worked the bus stops further up the same busy main road. All the money collected was to go on fireworks, and as Richard and Rennie weren't allowed fireworks, they'd be fobbed off with a portion of cash and enjoy the odd stick of liquorice or a few penny chews to keep their spirits up.

One particularly cold, dark Thursday evening at around five-thirty we were raking it in like bent stockbrokers. Bonfire Night was almost upon us and I'd saved nearly a pound over the past few weeks. As it approached our six o'clock curfew I turned around and there was no sign of our Kevin or Rennie. I was concerned as Richard and myself jogged along Chorlton Road pushing the trolley with our Guy's head flopping around worryingly as we flew over the cracks in the pavement. We looked around ... nothing, no sign of them. Retracing our steps back towards the paper-shop my fear mounted ... they'd taken a lift from strangers, they'd wandered off too far and got lost in the dark near the Whalley pub, or one of them had been knocked down and was lying bleeding by the side of the busy road, their cries for help drowned by the din of the traffic.

But then I was frightened of something which in a way was much worse and as we neared the paper-shop the full horror dawned on me. Kevin and Rennie were coming out with their hands and pockets bulging with sweets, lucky bags and toy soldiers that cost sixpence each. I'd never seen so many sweets outside a sweetshop – over seven shillings' worth of goodies. Apparently at my sibling's suggestion they'd hidden, waited until they saw Richard and myself head towards the bus stops in our misguided search and slipped past us into the shop. Now the bottom line as far as I was concerned was that it was my Guy and my money, so after administering a good thumping and forcing them to hand over the majority of their purchases, we ordered Kevin and Rennie to stop crying and say nothing to our mams. I have to admit that after that I had a sneaking admiration for my younger brother, in many respects he reminded me of me!

The build-up to Guy Fawke's Night was an occasion for great excitement in our area. All the local teenagers from the neighbouring streets would compete to have the biggest communal bonfire. Around that particular end of Old Trafford and neighbouring Hulme and Moss Side were streets full of condemned houses awaiting demolition. They were full of large wooden rafters, floorboards, abandoned furniture, even the thick planks of wood used to board up the doors and windows before the corporation got round to bricking them up. These boarded-up houses were raided first for the copper boilers and lead flashings which would be wheeled on prams by the older teenagers to Albert Quixall's scrap-metal merchants on Stamford Street. (Albert Quixall was a former

Manchester United player, a record transfer buy from Sheffield Wednesday at £45,000 just after the Munich air crash of 1958.) Once those valuable items had been stripped and sold the gangs then set about plundering anything flammable.

This bungy wood as it was called would be stacked to a height of over 20 feet in a huge tepee shape on our croft, the wasteland bounded by the houses on Croston Street, Duke Street, Chorlton Road and Ayres Road. This operation was in many ways the most exciting time of year for us younger kids. The older lads talked to us and acted as supervisors, organizing us into foraging parties. We'd be told to guard the stack of bungy wood on our croft and raise the alarm if any gangs of rival youths from Oxford Street and Clifton Street came raiding. Meanwhile the older lads would also form raiding parties to steal wood stacked on the rival crofts, even going as far as Hulme on their forays.

Those left to mind the bungy wood would build little dens in the middle of the stack, scraping our bare legs on rusty nails and getting some of the nastiest, dirtiest and biggest wood splinters you could imagine. We were constantly told by our parents that making dens in the stack was dangerous and we'd hear how the wood had collapsed and crushed other small children. Of course knew it to be perfectly safe as none of us had ever been crushed and although bits of the den wobbled precariously from time to time we were still in one piece. The only worrying story was that once some lads had set fire to a bonfire with paraffin while some young kids were inside and some of them got badly burnt. We took notice of this and set sentries at all the entrances of the croft to warn us of any impending threat, especially after we heard a local lad bragging how one year they'd torched Oxford Street's bonfire a few days before 5 November. As Bonfire Night got nearer several of the older youths in our street would stay up all night guarding our bungy wood.

It always worries me when I read that the first sign of a serial killer is a childhood fascination for lighting fires. It was one of our biggest thrills. That whole period of Bonfire Night was like the spirit of the Blitz. Everyone pulled together whether teenager or toddler. We were Duke Street kids, cocks of the area. We'd watch the older lads throw bangers at the girls and laugh at how annoyed and aggressive they'd become. We'd shriek and run like the clappers when Robert Porter, wearing a leather glove would hold, light and aim a Roman Candle at our retreating figures. When Jimmy Millar got hit on the leg with a Roman Candle, it scorched a bit, he said, but only like when we'd leap bare-legged in our shorts over a fire we'd built. We watched our elders and imitated every trick.

Unfortunately Richard and Rennie didn't enjoy fireworks. Mainly because, as the only black kids of that age in our street, they were seen as moving targets by the likes of Robert Porter. Also their mother kept an eye out for them, as did all the lodgers who stayed at their house, whom Richard and Rennie called uncles. So they were always being spotted and reported and kept in. Bonfire week was my opportunity to renew my acquaintances with Jimmy Millar and the McPhees and hang around with the older lads. Living on Duke Street was a bit like the X-Files; the truth was out there somewhere. But we knew from an early age that the first rule was to keep stumm, know nothing and deny everything.

We continued hanging around with Richard and Rennie, although they were nervous of both Jimmy Millar and the McPhee twins, and with good reason. The McPhees had an 11-year-old brother called Brendan who we all looked up to. He was sarcastic, saying things that sounded hard and funny at the same time, and he was the best fighter of his age in the area and a fantastic footballer. However, despite Brendan's best friend at school being black, he voiced concern over his younger twin brothers playing with darkies.

The real trouble came when Richard and Rennie had two older cousins from Jamaica move over to live. There was Raymond, a big, stocky light-skinned 11-year-old, but built like a 14-year-old and his mentally retarded 15-year-old brother Darren, who though a good six foot tall was just a bag of bones with a gormless expression.

Although we were four years younger than him, Raymond played in the street with us. He didn't understand football, so we'd dribble rings round him or stick him in nets. And although he was brilliant at cricket, he'd bowl underarm for us when we batted so we could hit the ball. Just the fact that an 11-year-old acknowledged our existence was a big deal to us, and he didn't seem to mind when we took the mickey out of his broad patois. What was even more unbelievable was that Raymond had never heard of Manchester United or George Best, so using my football cards I educated him in the intricacies of football – as I did subsequently with many kids straight from Jamaica.

All the black people in our street were Jamaican, along with a few mixed-race families where the fathers were Jamaican and the mothers Irish. But their kids, the half-caste kids we used to call them, were still a bit too young to play out on the street. The majority of the Jamaicans on the street were either young couples with very young children, like our next-door neighbours the Reids, or older couples with 15 and 16-year-old offspring who were out at work. Basically there were no black kids playing out on our street over the age of seven, and as they'd just grown up with the rest of us, any name-calling or bullying was just that and nothing to do with any sinister embryonic racism. Yes it's true they would invariably end up playing the Indians in games of Cowboys and Indians; and they'd inevitably have to be baddies in games of Batman; and they wouldn't dare go nicking apples out of the back gardens of the big houses in Whalley Range or we'd have the local dibble on to us in a flash; but to us they were just mates with brown skins. It's just difficult to love your neighbour when you've been made to hate yourself.

One day, as we played cricket with a bat and tennis ball against a chalked wicket on an end-of-terrace wall, a football came arcing across the road in front of us, bouncing up. Raymond caught it and held it, looking around. Brendan McPhee arrived followed by the Porters, Billy Millar and assorted older lads. Brendan marched up to Raymond and immediately knocked the ball out of his hands, shoving him violently in the chest and demanding to know why Raymond was trying to nick his 'fucking ball'. Turning to the others for some kind of moral support, Brendan appealed for witnesses who'd seen the 'sambo' nick his ball. 'He just caught it,' I said – Brendan was getting on my nerves. He told me I shouldn't be hanging around with thieving nig-nogs and that I'd get a kick up the arse if I didn't shut up.

All this time Raymond didn't react, but merely insisted in his strange musical patois that he'd just grabbed the ball to kick it back to where they were playing. He didn't back down or apologize, he just seemed mystified as to why Brendan should be so annoyed. Brendan, who wasn't quite the height of Raymond but stockier, continued pushing him in the chest, calling him sambo, nigger, coon, telling him to get back to the fucking jungle, to get back on the jam-jar label with all the other golly-wogs, topping the abuse by punching him hard in the stomach and then kneeing him in the face as he doubled over, leaving him in tears on the hard and unforgiving pavement.

There would be no let up for Raymond and his brother Darren. They lived next door to the Porters, next door but one to the Millars, at the end of the street where the older kids congregated. Consequently Raymond stayed within sight of his aunt's front door, ready to run for his life at the slightest sign of trouble. One day, as we all hung around by the corner of Croston Street and Duke Street, Brendan McPhee came over again. This time we all implored him to leave Raymond alone but to no avail. He grabbed Raymond and told him that he'd been warned not to hang around the street and then kneed him in the stomach. As Raymond lay writhing on the ground, McPhee started on the older brother Darren. Darren was very tall and gangly, as skinny as a famine victim, with buck teeth and hooded eyes that were half crossed – he had the mental age of a four-year-old and Brendan mocked him callously.

'Give us a kiss, gorgeous.' Then, turning to his audience as usual, he said, 'He looks like a fuckin' monkey. With those teeth if he gave me a kiss he'd probably take a chunk out of me.'

Darren remained gazing indifferently, no expression on his face, a gormless and innocent victim. Richard bravely interceded, saying that Darren was simple. Brendan McPhee casually turned around and thumped Darren viciously in the stomach, then, spitting on the ground, he swaggered off with his head down, beckoning the others to follow him back to the part of the street where they'd been playing football

Nobody had to tell me that this was wrong. When you are a kid you understand fair play, you crave a kind of justice in the world and see everything as clear cut, right and wrong, black and white. Later on, as a grown-up messing about with lawyers and solicitors, you realize there's no such thing as justice, only the law, and not even that on Manchester's council estates. Had it been any of the other kids who'd done it, like Billy Millar or even the Porters, we'd have told Raymond to fight them, but Brendan McPhee was an out-and-out scrapper, and no one in the area would go near him looking for trouble.

I remembered the summer evening when Brendan McPhee had fought Billy Millar. Despite Billy being two years older and having a reputation as a scrapper, Brendan had annihilated him, finishing off by throwing an old bicycle wheel at his head as he lay prostrate and bleeding on the ground. Now Billy Millar, even to our young minds, had it coming; but not Raymond or Darren. I felt sickened by what I'd witnessed and just couldn't see the fun in bullying in that way. I suppose I thought life was like the films my dad took me to see and only bad guys got beat up. I felt like fighting Brendan McPhee myself just to prove a point, I felt Raymond's humiliation and shame in a way that I'll never forget, especially as Brendan McPhee was a sort of hero for us younger kids.

Although we didn't quite appreciate the irony then, this 'get back to where you come from' attitude was rich coming from the assorted second generation Irish of Old Trafford. We lived down the Moss Side and Hulme end of Old Trafford which was one of the first areas to have significant numbers of black people moving in. Nowadays most of the Irish who lived in Old Trafford have moved out to Stretford, Urmston, Flixton, Davyhulme and Chorlton. A lot of those people have said over the years how Old Trafford used to be a nice area until all those blacks moved in and made it rough. My memories of living in Old Trafford stretch back over 30 years, and I can honestly state Old Trafford was always rough, and as the Raymonds and Richards and Rennies can testify, it was rougher still when you're skin was dark. It wasn't that smooth a ride even when as a white Irish kid you belonged to the dominant group in the area.

In a way I wonder whether Brendan McPhee and the other lads felt jealous that at least those immigrants like Richard and Rennie had brown skins to remind them they weren't English and would struggle to fit in. Those older lads would have had

a sense that to live in that area then, with such a steadily growing proportion of black people, was a reminder that we
belonged on society's bottom rung with them. It didn't do to
be different or think differently, but even then I think I felt
intuitively that those black kids were just like us, just as poor,
just as vociferous in speaking their minds, just as full of hopeless dreams and desires.

6

The Summer of '69

Jesus Christ, the Virgin Mary, the Holy Ghost, George Best, Albert Quixall, George Wall and Jimmy Clitheroe. These were the celebrities surrounding us in Old Trafford. Albert Quixall had been a star player for United in his day but the local lads like our Tony, old enough to have seen him play, weren't impressed. 'Good at taking penalties,' Tony said, and for him about a United player that was a very damning verdict. So Mr Quixall didn't figure as a role model.

As for George Wall, footballers back then wore stupid long shorts, huge boots and had daft haircuts (the Seventies hadn't been inflicted on us at that point ...) so apart from the fact that he was dead and had left behind a glass doorknob, Mr Wall didn't exactly sum up the Swinging Sixties for us.

Comedian and comedy actor Jimmy Clitheroe was on the TV on Saturday night and the radio on Sunday lunchtime, which we'd listen to avidly as my mother stalked endless amounts of spring cabbage and peeled mountains of potatoes. When I discovered he wasn't really a kid I felt a certain distaste for him. Mr Clitheroe was actually the ill-tempered passer-by on our street of a Sunday, when he'd visit his aunt on Croston

Street and make his pilgrimage to the Shrewsbury pub on Shrewsbury Street. Once my 11-year-old sister Mary and some of her friends approached him wondering how he could be on the radio one minute and walking down our street the next and he told them to 'bugger off'.

Which left, apart from the mysterious Catholic icons, and above all other mortals (except perhaps John Wayne), George Best. George was the most glamorous person in the whole world, the best footballer the world had ever seen. All our big sisters fancied him (along with Elvis and Paul McCartney) and everyone knew he was rich. George wore shirts with button-down collars and smart leather jackets, Chelsea boots with zips up the sides. He owned posh clothes shops and later would own a nightclub. On the pitch he could do things with a ball no one else could and every time he was on TV on the Sunday match we'd look on in amazement and talk about his exploits on the street later.

In our Tony's League Review magazine that came with the United programme there was a top ten voted by female foot-ball fans of the most attractive footballers and George Best was ahead by miles. This is a list from the 1968/69 season:

1. GEORGE BEST (Manchester United)
2. GEORGE LEY (Portsmouth)
3. JIM BAXTER (Nottingham Forest)
4. EMLYN HUGHES (Liverpool)
5. EDDIE GRAY (Leeds United)
6. WYN DAVIES (Newcastle United)
7. TREVOR HOCKEY (Birmingham City)
8. JON SAMMELS (Arsenal)
10. IAN CALLAGHAN (Liverpool)

There wasn't one of us who didn't want to be him – he was a cult and religion all of his own. We'd also seen on TV where he'd grown up in Belfast and it looked just like the streets round our way, and now he was somebody. To every scuzzy little ne'er-do-well on our street he was a sign that you could be someone even if you weren't well spoken and rich. And that if you were rich, you didn't have to be well spoken and poncey.

Manchester City were to play Leicester City in the 1969 FA Cup Final. There was a lot of excitement about this at school for several reasons. Despite 90 per cent of the school supporting United, Manchester City had knocked a very good Everton side out in the semi-final thanks to a goal by their young centre-half Tommy Booth. Now we knew this Everton side were good because they'd had the barefaced cheek to knock United out in the quarter-final. The City–Everton semi was the very first football match I listened to and followed on the radio, and I admit I was willing City to win so then I could see them on TV in the final.

What had really captured everyone's imagination though was Manchester City's new second strip. Red and black vertical stripes and black shorts. I'm not sure that Man. City didn't choose it just for that match as a dig at United, as it was virtually the same as the first strip of AC Milan who had just beaten Manchester United in that year's European Cup semi-final. Man. City, managed by Joe Mercer, had been in the European Cup that year too (qualifying as League Champions, while Man. Utd qualified as holders of the European Cup) but had been knocked out 2–1 on aggregate in the first round by Turkish no-hopers Fenerbahce. So much for City coach Malcolm Allison's boast that City would terrorize Europe.

> Who's that knocking at the window
> Who's that knocking at the door
> It's Joe Mercer and his mates
> They've got Turkey on their plates
> and they won't be going to Europe any more

But back to that red and black kit of City's. It was a huge seller, every kid at school seemed to appear with one, despite the majority of them being United fans. We'd watch the older lads at school troop down in pairs to Seymour Park for football on a Tuesday afternoon, swinging their boots by the laces, wearing that red and black shirt under their pullovers, to compete for the school team. This would be step one for me next year.

Suddenly it was cool to like City. In the classroom the teacher no longer had us drawing Saturn rockets and Apollo landing modules in our news books – now we wrote bogus football reports of Man. City v. Leicester. At home in the evening I'd reference my football cards with our Tony, checking up on the merits of the Leicester City team. 'So what about David Nish?' 'He's a good player.' 'What about Allan Clarke?' 'He's brilliant.' 'What about Peter Shilton?' 'The best goalkeeper after Gordon Banks and Alex Stepney, fantastic.' 'What about Peter Rodrigues?' 'Welsh international, he's superb.' Basically our Tony was saying City had no chance. 'So how come Leicester City have just been relegated then!?' What a wind-up merchant he was.

The match itself on TV on a Saturday was different. Our Tony actually stuck up for City, so did my mam and dad. City pressed with Mike Summerbee playing a blinder on the wing, but once Neil Young stuck City's goal in Leicester started pouring on the pressure and it was Harry Dowd in the City goal who had to show he was the brilliant keeper. Though City won 1–0 it was Leicester's Allan Clarke, soon to sign for Leeds in a £165,000 record transfer, who won the Man of the Match award. In the post-match interviews I remembered we all laughed when Mike Summerbee, on being asked what he was going to do next, grinned and replied, 'Go and get drunk!'

★

As a warm spring turned to summer, out came the beige cotton shorts and a new pair of baseball boots (price: 9/6, or 47fi new pence) from Woolworths. Everybody knew new baseball boots made you run faster, indeed any new shoes had this magical effect on the recipient. Twenty of us racing across the yard – Billy Heffernan touches the wall first – it's a miracle we think – 'Billy's got new shoes on,' Joe Mahon says – we nod sagaciously – no further explanation needed. Every breaktime now at school we played football. Twenty aside, no throw-ins, no corners. To get round a player, like in five-a-side, you'd play a one-two off the wall. Tackles came in from all angles, shirts and jumpers were pulled into a variety of shapes and buttons lost into the asphalt black hole of the school yard. Elbows, fists, feet – it always ended up in a punch up when we'd lose track of the score at 35–29 or something.

Now we knew all the technical terms and rules – throw-in, offside, dead ball (we *never* said 'goal-kick'), free kick, penalty, corner, handball, foul (if someone started bleeding, otherwise we'd say it was a shoulder-barge) and 'dirty bastard'. On the street at night we'd play 'three and you're in' – the keeper would throw the ball out (with eyes closed or back turned), the rest, every man playing for himself, trying to be the first to score three goals, who would then have to go in goal.

Another game was 'knockout': again you were all, every man for himself, trying to score past the same keeper but this time in the first rounds you had to score one goal to go through to the next round. Any player not scoring when everyone else had was out and so on until three players remained. Then it was the first two players to score two who would go into the final and then it was the first player to score three goals who would win. In the summer heat knockout was often a gruelling test of stamina and tactics, an exhausting game and there was nothing more disheartening than dribbling the ball past an opponent in the final with the scores at two-all, aiming your fiercest shot on goal, only to have the keeper parry it out and your opponent score on the rebound. Then you'd start all over again from scratch. The best tactic in the early stages was to just hang around the goal area and dispossess some kid as he fought his way through the pack and bore down on goal, or indeed get your foot to a rebound. Then there was 'Wembley': each player took turns to cross the ball from the corner and you had to score with a volley or header (i.e., without the ball touching the ground).

Like ancient crafts and folklores, nobody remembers when these games were first played. Games that children play are passed down from school generation to generation by word of mouth like some druid's code – the oral tradition of the school yard, the freemasonry of infancy.

Football shirts were a rare thing, certainly new ones were, and in the main the property of the over-nines, who also had football boots with screw-on studs if they were lucky and played organized football in the park. Our break-time football games were a confused kick-and-rush affair with much shouting and calling for the ball. This made it perplexing for even the most composed players, given the preponderance of Irish names – 'Give it Sean/Paddy/Mike/Ged!'

In my next class I sat next to James Martin. A small lad like myself with rosy-red cheeks, jet-black hair, a wide pug nose and big brown eyes. Well didn't the girls in our year love him. He was a brilliant footballer and a dribbler in the George Best mould. Girls never told tales on Jimmy Martin, instead they plied him with sweets and crisps, and invented games of 'catch a boy, kiss a boy', only inviting James and Mike King to play. The only reason James and Mike could get away with these suspiciously sissy activities was due to their prowess at both fighting and football. James Martin was also something of a crooner and was often brought out to the front of class by the teacher to sing a rather odd version of an old Irish rebel song.

> I looked up to the sky and saw an Irish soldier laddie:
> He looked at me quite fearlessly and said,
> 'Will you stand to the band like a true Irish man
> For tonight we fight the forces on the field.
> We will march with O'Neil to an Irish battlefield
> For tonight we go to free old Wexford town.'

> As we entered through the town in the Sabbath of the
>   evening,
> All our banners flying low in the memory of the dead,
> Well I looked up to the sky and saw that Irish soldier laddie:
> He looked at me quite fearlessly and said, etc …

In fact his vocal performances impressed the teachers so much that he'd be sent to sing his treasonable ditty for other classes, often returning from Mr McLoughlin's class next door with a bag of salt and vinegar crisps, the jammy bastard.

James Martin was supposed to be one of my best mates at the time. He was obsessed by the American TV series *The Untouchables*, which starred Robert Stack as Elliot Ness. This show unfortunately came on at my bedtime, eight o'clock, which gave me some grounds for a subconscious resentment. He'd casually swing his school chair backwards until it was balanced on its hind legs and, pretending his pencil was a ciga-rette, draw deeply on it, blowing imaginary smoke out of his mouth while flaring his nostrils and addressing me in a phoney American accent as 'pank' (not 'punk'!).

I suppose he was the ultimate lad at school – great foot-baller, not too clever at lessons but worldly wise, cheeky yet loved by the teachers. He was allowed by his parents to stay up late to watch Frankenstein and Werewolf films and always had money for sweets and crisps, which he was only too happy to share. All the girls loved him, he was a bit of a pop star, quite a tough kid; and he went to every single Man. United home game with his older brother and his father. More importantly he was my friend; and secretly, I hated him.

James Martin's trouble was that he was just too perfect; and I began to realize that we love each other for our imperfections, and loathe those we wish to be like, especially when we suspect they have no wish to be like us. I'd moan at my mam, why couldn't I stay up and watch *The Untouchables* and Frankenstein films? Why didn't we have a record player so I could listen to Irish rebel songs and learn them off by heart and sing them in front of class to be rewarded with bags of crisps by the teachers. Most of all, why was I only ever taken to the odd reserve game at United. At this rate I'd be eight before I ever got to see them play, and our Tony had gone to his first game when he was only six.

My mother would gently mock me, which made me furious inside. 'Early to bed early to rise, makes a man healthy, wealthy and wise' was her pat answer. 'James Martin must be falling asleep in class,' she'd say. 'We can't afford a record player, and besides when it comes to football, how can Tony take you to Old Trafford when you're telling him you're a City fan?'

'But Mam, James Martin isn't tired and he's better than any one in our year at football and he's as clever as me [which wasn't saying much for him at the time], he was also really good at football cards and was one of the first kids in class to collect both sets, so he must be wealthy as well as wise.' Alas my arguments fell on deaf ears and the frustration that I was not born into the same tolerant opulence as Jimmy Martin and others nagged at my young mind.

My only comfort was that I was holier than James Martin, I knew it when we made our first communion. We met that bright sunny May morning in the school yard. Our parents were already in the church and us kids were to meet up and be taken into the front pews by Sister Elizabeth. I was dressed in my very best clothes. A pair of charcoal-grey shorts, white shirt with a navy-blue and red St Alphonsus school tie (the only time anyone really wore anything approaching a uniform), a pair of long grey socks and some shiny slip-on shoes. First communions were a big deal to us. We'd been told to purify our hearts and our thoughts and invite Jesus into our lives and when that piece of communion wafer went on your tongue that was the baby Jesus, and you left him there to melt. You could under no circumstances chew the baby Jesus or you'd end up in hell like all those proddy dogs.

In the school yard as we lined up James Martin spat out a pink Bazooka Joe bubble-gum. We weren't allowed to eat for an hour before communion, and Master Martin was a sinner. 'It only counts if you swallow something,' he told me. I wasn't at all sure about that. There were all sorts of horror stories concerning the consequences of misbehaviour in church. We were told by some Polish kids that Adolph Hitler used to spit in church, and look what happened to him. One nervy girl in our class was sternly told by a visiting nun that if she whistled in church it made the Virgin Mary's lips bleed. The girls, even the poorest ones, were decked out in new white communion dresses replete with veils and white socks, while us lads looked a more motley crew, with the poorer ones wearing discoloured white shirts, white plimsolls and regular school trousers, some with thinly disguised patches on them.

St Alphonsus church was packed with the broad-shouldered Irish fathers, straining to burst out of the jackets of their suits, thick red necks spilling over their tight shirt collars. The mums were dressed in various shades of polyester and terylene, and sported monstrous hats. The whole church smelt of Brylcreem, cheap perfume and incense.

The Mass proceeded with hymns we'd learned at school, moving from a regular one-hour long Mass into something of a mini-series. Eventually, we marched slowly and solemnly from our pews to kneel along the altar rail to receive the sacrament. 'Body of Christ ...' and then flick your tongue out and feel that communion wafer stick to it, that mysterious white disc which we'd always wondered the taste of. Was it really the same as manna from heaven and had Jesus really magically sent it down into the priest's little cabinet on the altar.

Well I was choking and red-faced as I made my way solemnly back to kneel in the pew. The communion wafer had stuck to the roof of my mouth and I was frantic about breaking the body of Christ in two with my tongue. It tasted a bit like a wafer, the broken wafers we'd beg the ice-cream man for. It concerned me that at this moment when I should be full of grace and filled with the body of Christ, that I was thinking about ice-creams and how the hell I could unstick baby Jesus from the roof of my mouth without breaking him in two.

The best thing about the first holy communion was the money. Most of the kids expected at least a pound all told from relatives and parents. I knew my Aunty Nan and Aunty Katy were there, surely good for two bob each and then there'd be money on their next visits from my Uncle Jack and Uncle Peter, who may even go up as high as five bob each. So I wouldn't quite make a pound, but I'd have over ten bob, or so I reckoned. I wasn't sure about this, as my parents always had ways of economizing. When I tugged and pulled at my first loose tooth and shoved it under my pillow, the tooth fairy left sixpence. When I put the next under my pillow ... nothing! So I didn't hold out too many hopes of a huge windfall from my communion, especially after I'd shamefully tortured the transubstantiated body of Christ on my sticky palate.

In the end I received a total of 8/6 (42fi new pence) in cash for my first communion. Other kids, who my father once again assured me 'only had jam butties for their tea', got five quid at least. But then I was closer to God than they were as after all wasn't the baby Jesus poor and wouldn't he have bit someone's hand off for 8/6, especially when for two bob he could go and see Manchester United play at home.

So far there had been several sets of football cards released and thanks to my skill at topsy I'd collected the whole set. Had you been Prince Edward or some rich kid, you may have had the set before me, but not much. Then problem time ... instead of football cards some bright spark brings out a 'soccer stars in action' series of paper stickers. Now this caused me extreme concern at the time. First, it cost sixpence for seven of these small paper pictures of soccer stars. They had a thin strip across the top so you could stick them in an album containing all the first division teams and there were spaces for fifteen players from each team. The stickers album cost 2/6 and then you had to fork out for glue as well. This was a damn cheek really, it was going to cost what we considered a small fortune to get the whole book full, but we persevered.

Now in my life I've met lads into football from across the full economic spectrum, from the very rich to the very poor, but I've yet to meet someone who managed to complete the album full of those soccer stickers. I can imagine Paul Getty's son getting van-loads of stickers delivered to the back door of his mansion, going through every packet searching in vain for Colin Sugget of Sunderland and Colin Viljoen of Ipswich Town, surrounded by hundreds of spares of Paul Reaney of

Leeds United. I once met a lad in London who had a very affluent upbringing who proudly showed me his football sticker book from this era and there were still four blank spaces – players who were as elusive as rosary beads in Ian Paisley's house.

So there were two Neils that mattered during the glorious spring and summer of 1969. Young, FA Cup Final goalscorer, and Armstrong, the first man on the moon. (I remember drawing pictures in my news book of the lunar module on the surface, being fired at from behind a rock by a little green man with antennae sticking out of his head, holding a rather nasty looking ray-gun, and Neil Armstrong holding a machine-gun and firing back, saying 'Take that pank'.) Is it a coincidence that Man. City won the Cup the year that man first landed on the moon? Many predict next time they win that trophy we'll be landing a man on Mars.

It was during the long summer holidays of 1969 that I attended my first ever Manchester United first-team game. My cousin Danny had married at 16 and moved from Dublin to Manchester, where he worked at Kellogg's in Trafford Park while living with his young wife in a one-roomed flat in Moss Side. Consequently when Danny's younger brother Philip, who was 13, came over to see him that August, he stayed at our house, stealing my newly acquired bed and forcing me to share once more with my brother Kevin.

The good news was that Philip wanted to go and see United play. My opportunity to see Law, Best, Charlton and co. in the flesh had arrived at last; after all I could hardly be refused if our Tony was taking one of the cousins.

With the 1970 World Cup due the following summer, the 1969/70 season kicked off early, on 9 August. Manchester United took on newly promoted Crystal Palace at Selhurst

Park. United's goalkeeper, Alex Stepney, was injured at the time, so Jimmy Rimmer was deputizing. I'd seen Jimmy Rimmer in the reserves for United on those forgettable occasions our Tony had treated me to. The United team struggled against Palace in that opening game, drawing 2–2, with their goals coming from dashing Scottish winger Willie Morgan and the stalwart Bobby Charlton.

Now their first home game was against Everton on a Wednesday night, 13 August, a match which exposed that pessimistic streak all us true United fans carry deep in our hearts.

If you were poor, football even then wasn't cheap. It cost 2/6 for juniors to stand in the Stretford End Paddock, which was where the Stretford End curved round on to what we called the Cantilever Stand with all the executive boxes (now called the South Stand). Basically the Paddock was the Stretford End for kids and people who didn't like relative strangers urinating down the backs of their legs or threatening to steal their scarves or Wagon Wheel money. It was a 7.30 kick-off and by six o'clock we were amongst the massed ranks of United supporters singing their hearts out. I feel sorry for youngsters now who have never seen or heard over 60,000 standing spectators in full voice.

To the tune of Al Jolson's 'Mammy' we would sing 'Oh Denis, Denis, I'd walk a million miles for one of your goals, oh Denis ...' To the tune of 'Gin Gan Goolie', 'We've got Willie, Willie, Willie Willie Morgan on the wing, on the wing', then there was also 'Champions of Europe,' 'You're going home by F.....ing ambulance,' 'We don't carry bottles we don't carry lead, we only carry hatchets to bury in your head, we are the great supporters and that is everyone, we only hate Man. City, Leeds and Everton.' And to the tune of 'Land of Hope and Glory': 'We hate Nottingham Forest, we hate Liverpool too (and Leicester), we hate Manchester City, but United we love you'. And of course the tune the Cockneys nicked for 'Maybe It's Because I'm A Londoner': 'I get a funny feeling inside of me, when I see United score, Maybe it's because I'm from Manchester, where the King is Denis Law.'

The crowd around us swelled and we could hardly breathe as the ground filled with more and more people. We were down by the wall and tried to climb up and sit on it, only to be shoved off by the stewards. Standing on tip-toes I could see the players from what seemed like the legs up, before the weight of people from behind caused me to duck suffocatingly beneath the mass of bodies. My cousin Philip seemed most perturbed. He didn't like big crowds or wide open spaces. He caught his asthmatic breath and looked around him nervously, the sweat shining off his face, accentuating his teenage acne. (My Aunty Mag later said that Philip was both claustrophobic and agoraphobic and there's only one thing worse than agoraphobia ... and that's going out.)

From the scoreboard end the Everton fans were chanting, 'Everton ... Everton ... Everton...' In the gaps the United fans shouted 'Shit! ... Shit!' My shoulders were squashed inwards, my feet were suffering cramp from standing on tip-toes. Would I be able to see over this wall when Bobby Charlton scored? As the teams came on to the field, choruses of 'Kiddo, Kiddo' rose up from around the ground, hailing United's 20-year-old striker and, more importantly to the United crowd, local boy made good, Brian Kidd.

The Everton team in their royal blue shirts were full of big names: Howard Kendall, Alan Ball, Brian Labone, Ray Wilson, Colin Harvey, Jimmy Husband, Joe Royle, Gordon West. Our Tony nervously pointed out that there were so many internationals in that team. Even worse United were without international defenders Nobby Stiles and Tony Dunne, and first-choice keeper Alex Stepney ...

I gazed at that sight under the Old Trafford floodlights with an awe which I can almost taste at every match-night still. When the teams came on to the pitch my senses were assaulted by an explosion of primary colours – I'd never seen grass so green, shirts of such bright red or such royal blue, and the brilliant whiteness of the players' shorts and the trims on collars and cuffs were an icing of almost eucharistic purity. It was a magical communion of over 60,000 and their chanting turned to enchantment as I strained for a better view of this long-awaited event. It was almost as if it was one degree removed, as if the players in front of me on that pitch were in a different dimension like holograms and the real Charlton, Best and Law were sitting at home. It was pure magic.

The magical enchantment turned to a certain disenchantment from the moment of kick-off. The match took on a familiar pattern – Everton seemed to be first to every 50–50 ball, and Alan Ball was everywhere. United may have been the best team in the world, but on this particular night Everton made them look second rate and the Goodison school of science made my first trip to Old Trafford an unhappy one. The final score was Man. United 0, Everton 2. I had seen my first United game at Old Trafford, but it was to be some time before I could understand what our Tony had got so excited about when it came to the way United played. As for Everton, it remains a mystery to me why, with that particular team, they didn't dominate English football for years – they were simply awesome.

Still, I'd seen all those players from my football cards in the flesh; it meant a lot to me. And the way some of the players in the United side performed left me in no doubt that I could and would one day do much better when it was my turn to pull on that red jersey in front of 60,000 people and hear my name ringing from the terraces.

Our Tony was glum after the game. 'They should never have had Wilf McGuinness as manager and let Matt Busby move upstairs to general manager, if Nobby Stiles and Tony Dunne had played we would have won, and if Bill Foulkes had been left out we would have stood a chance.' Tony's vitriol poured on the veteran Bill Foulkes – he was past it, United needed a new centre-half – and Denis Law who didn't look fit. I walked silently, hurrying in our Tony's footsteps in the night air. He'd already called me a jinx and said he'd never take me to another United match again – to this day he's been as good as his word.

No wonder everyone is starting to support City, I thought silently and defiantly. This could have been a truce between our Tony and me but it would have to be war, pure attrition. The next day collecting the Typhoo tokens I got my mam to send off for a picture of Mike Summerbee – I'd show him.

'No you have to be Pelé, Eusebio, Clyde Best, Paul Reaney or Stan Horne.' I couldn't seem to get Richard and Rennie to understand that they couldn't be George Best because I was him, or Bobby Charlton because he wasn't black. The only black footballers I knew were Clyde Best of West Ham, Paul Reaney of Leeds United, Stan Horne of Man. City, Eusebio who played for Benfica of Lisbon, and of course Pelé. In the end Richard said he'd be Pelé and Rennie said he didn't care and he was going to be Denis Law. There was some argument between the McPhees meanwhile as Kevin McPhee wanted to be Denis Law ... if he couldn't be Denis Law he'd be Willie Morgan ... but his twin brother Brian had already bagsed that.

Football violence wasn't confined to the terraces that afternoon in the sunshine of Seymour Park. Our Kevin was the one who pointed out that, as Kevin McPhee with his pink eye-patch was playing in goal, he couldn't be Willie Morgan anyway, but he could be Gordon Banks who was the best goalie in the world. Richard then observed if he and Rennie couldn't be Best and Charlton because they were the wrong colour, Kevin McPhee couldn't be Banks because he only had one eye and wore glasses and Gordon Banks had two good eyes and wasn't a speccy four-eyed little gink. It was eventually decided that Kevin McPhee could be Gordon Banks with a sty in his eye and that anybody could be anybody and let's get on with the game and stop sitting on my new ball or you'll put it out of shape and it's three and you're in and I'm winning two-nil.

Football was the most fun we could have together, so it was serious. Nothing else compared – well, only going to see something really good at the pictures, like *True Grit* starring John Wayne (who incidentally in that film wore an eye-patch, but not a pink one like Kevin McPhee). I don't know what it was but we were always arguing, especially when Jimmy Millar wasn't around. When Jimmy played with us we just did as we were told, and at least we'd get on with the game – even if that meant biting our tongues when he'd shoot well over the anoraks and jumpers we laid on the ground as goalposts and claim a goal. 'In off the post' – nobody argued with Jimmy.

Now Seymour Park was a fair old hike from where we lived in Brookes Bar, but I felt it added an authority to our games as it was where all the older lads at school played their organized games on a Thursday afternoon. It was no good in Hullard Park anyway, there were too many flowers, old ladies, young toddlers and mothers pushing prams, plus you couldn't see the older boys coming at you through the rhododendron bushes to thump you in the stomach and steal your ball. Seymour Park was basically just a flat expanse of grass with a few trees, but bigger than Hullard Park and unlike that flowery fenced-off garden it didn't smell of horse shit.

We played until the sweat burned dry on our faces and our bones felt weak and rubbery, then went home and drank about eight cups of water (or 'corporation pop' as my mother called it), ate our tea, then played on the street until the pigeons were roosting noisily in the high chimney-pots. Football fever – it was serious to us, there could be no rest until we could all earn £100 a week and have a Jag. If only we knew then what we know now (who, of our little group, would end up with the top-of-the-range cars and through what shady enterprises – certainly not from anything as respectable as playing football). We knew nothing about cars really, but we knew that an E-type Jag was something out of the ordinary, something you saw in American films and TV series.

We probably didn't think it was an English car because we loved all things American, especially Westerns and Western TV series like *The Virginian*, *Wagon Train* and *Bonanza*, and we longed to have BBC2 so we could watch *The High Chaparral*. We hated Blue Peter and well-spoken, upperclass kids in TV dramas and we loved the *The Beverly Hillbillies*. We were born in England, but felt more akin to the Americans, who didn't seem to look down their upper and middle class noses at us or speak in accents that made us want to switch the TV off. They seemed a fairer bunch all round.

This determined 'sod off' to English middle-class superior-ity was in our case probably down to being not just Irish and working class but Mancunian. Manchester's a city with little or no old money, the social hierarchy is perhaps less manifest than in some cities and it's always had this undercurrent of aggres-sion. The abrasiveness can be detected in the way we speak, the outspoken bluntness, and in the expressions we carry on our faces from childhood that try desperately to say, 'mess with me and I'll paste you'. We were outspoken, anti-authoritarian, tribal and were often judged harshly by outsiders.

★

Tuesday evenings in the summer holidays, the Sharon Gospel church had their six o'clock club. One night I quizzed the kids coming out and it sounded like a good *craic*. Free orange juice and chocolate biscuits plus cartoons like Woody Woodpecker shown on a screen, and the obligatory bible stories. Annoyed that I'd missed it but excited at the prospect of joining up, I asked my mother's permission – what the hell, I'd even offer to take our Kevin.

'No you can't go. It's a sin to go into a Protestant church.'

'But they give you chocolate biscuits and show you cartoons, I mean Jimmy Millar and Richard and Rennie go and so do the McPhees and the McPhees aren't Protestants.'

'I don't care what they do, you're not going, it's a sin and that's that, now stop mithering me.'

There was a big box of chocolate digestives and jugs of orange squash on a long table as we walked in. An old West Indian lady told us we could have two biscuits each and poured us a paper cup full of orange juice, directing us to some collapsible wooden chairs laid out in rows, which were filling up quickly.

An oldish man with glasses and an oversized suit told us to sit down and be quiet. Next to him was an old lady in a voluminous brown-coloured flowery frock. Once we were all settled the man told us we were good children and tried to crack some jokes.

'When's Woody Woodpecker coming on, where's the film being shown,' I whispered to a rather taciturn ginger kid called Philip who lived at the top of our road.

'We have a story and some singing first, and then they have a white screen that comes down.'

'Well, we've got some cartoons for you soon children, but first lets talk about …'

After talking about Samson, which I'd heard before, and sins which I knew all about, the fat lady in the brown dress went to an organ and started playing and we were to sing 'All Things Bright And Beautiful'.

We murmured along to the song, impatient for the cartoons to start, only for the old lady to stop playing, and the man with the glasses informing us at length and with more than a hint of annoyance that there would be no cartoons that evening unless we sang more joyfully and raised up our voices to God.

The Sharon Gospel church's Tuesday Club was reminding me far too much of school for my liking. Nobody told me that it was all singing and bible stories, and voices being raised up joyfully to God, Protestant ones at that. I knew then that this could be a sin. The dirty dusty floorboards, the fusty smell, the Spartan wooden benches and chairs and décor: God wouldn't want to live in a little church like this, no wonder he didn't like the Protestants.

Finally after what seemed like a purgatorial length of time listening to the man with the glasses, the cartoons were announced to a great cheer. A small screen of what looked like white paper was wheeled out and a noisy projector at the back started up by another adult who'd been making sure we sat still. In the darkness of the room, watching two rather duff, unfocussed cartoons, I had a revelation! Now I'd been to our local cinema lots of times, and I knew they had a projector, but I thought the films were on a big TV, but in colour. This experience in the Sharon Gospel church made me think that perhaps the cinema was just a projector shining on to an even bigger paper screen. I made a mental note of this and thought I was the cleverest boy in the world.

'Don't dare say anything to Mam.' I held my clenched fist under our Kevin's chin next to his throat. We'd committed a sin, I knew. I'd go to confession and add 'I went to a Protestant church' to my usual list. I wouldn't say I'd eaten Protestant biscuits or drank their orange squash or I might not be allowed to go to communion. That night I dreamt of the devil making noises like Woody Woodpecker. I'd been lead into temptation, and all for a couple of ropy cartoons and some chocolate digestives.

7

The Imperial Experiment

Playing football in Seymour Park I bumped into a lad from our year at school called Gerard Murray. Ged was one of the best footballers at school and an even bigger United fan than James Martin. He bragged that he'd been going to United matches since he was three and now went with an older lad, a neighbour who was 11. He lived nearer to Old Trafford than I did, just off Seymour Grove near Trafford Bar, and if I wanted to go to United's next home match on Saturday against Southampton I could go with him and his friend. Not only that but they were going down to the ground really early to get all the United players' autographs and bagsy a good position by the wall in the scoreboard end.

Saturday 16 August was very sunny with a cool wind. I called round to Ged's with two bob in my pocket and waited in the living room while Gerard got his coat and his father finished a fry-up while he listened to the radio. I wondered what it would be like to live up that end of Old Trafford, so near the ground and within spitting distance of Seymour Park, and then shrugged – some people it seemed were born lucky. Seymour Grove held a glamour for us. It was posh once you got away from the Trafford Bar end but even there the council houses had front and back gardens. Seymour Grove was near where our school football team played their home games, and was the road which had been lined with thousands of people when the coffins from the Munich disaster were transported from Manchester airport, before being laid in state at Old Trafford. It was my yellow brick road as a kid, and led to a happy life and Manchester United.

Wearing shorts, the wind whipped a chill around my bear legs, but wearing my one and only coat and our Tony's knitted United scarf, my face felt too hot and sweaty. I decided scarves were as itchy and uncomfortable as balaclavas, but it was more than my life was worth to lose it by taking it off.

There were a few hundred people already hanging around outside the stadium and it was just gone eleven in the morning. We wandered into the Man. United souvenir shop, to discover that everything was totally unaffordable. We only had enough to get in the ground, but anyway even the cheapest items seemed to cost as much as the admission price. This was the beginning of one particular lifetime's resentment. The Man. United souvenir shop had nothing to do with football or our team, in the same way the statues and icons in a church have nothing to do with God or faith. The souvenir shop and the megastore are hawkers in the temple, and although raised a Catholic, somewhere there's a puritan inside fighting to get out.

We waited patiently in the wind and sunshine for the United coach with the players in it to arrive. I felt nervous about this autograph-hunting lark and my hands were sweaty and uncomfortable holding the small bookie's pen I'd taken from my dad and some paper from my mam's writing pad. As the coach arrived and the players alighted they were rushed from every side. Bigger kids and stout teenage girls knocked me aside and elbowed me to the edges of the clamouring mob.

I dived back in only to be knocked back again as Paddy Crerand barged through the crowd face fixed ahead. Francis Burns knocked my pen out of my hand as I closed for his signature by swivelling around to sign someone else's book. As I knelt in the throng to recover it George Best just walked through me, knocking me sideways to the ground, where I was trampled by the most expensive feet in European football. I struggled to get to my feet and tried to mouth the words 'Excuse me can I have your autograph, please' when the rough screaming teenage girls came ramraiding through the crowd shrieking 'Georgie' and crying with hormonal hysteria.

Back on my feet I managed to join an orderly queue away from the frightening teeny-boppers for Brian Kidd's autograph and Bobby Charlton obliged, as did Jimmy Rimmer, Shay Brennan, David Sadler and Willie Morgan. who scrawled W.I.L.L.I.E right across my other autographs.

It wasn't turning out to be an enjoyable day. I was hungry, thirsty, cold, hot, too small to even be noticed by most of the United players and a fair hike from home. We hung around outside the ground talking about what we'd buy from the souvenir shop if we had the money and discussed whether we should bother trying to get any Southampton players' auto-graphs as they arrived. Ron Davies was Southampton's star player at the time, a Welsh international and high-scoring centre-forward, the best header and best player in the air in British football, we'd heard. 'No one jumps higher or heads the ball harder,' Gerard Murray told me conspiratorially.

'So is he better than Denis Law?'

'Is he 'eck, but he scores loads of goals.'

Gerard Murray, aged nearly eight, should have given United their team talk that day instead of Wilf McGuinness.

As soon as the gates opened we went in, straight down to the wall behind the goal at the scoreboard end. I felt like a recruit in the Foreign Legion dying of thirst in the desert, only this was Old Trafford where the cheapest drinks on offer were plastic cartons of weak, warm orange squash at sixpence a throw that spotty teenagers carried around the perimeter on little trays along with Wagon Wheels and crisps. Everything may as well have cost a hundred pounds because we didn't have a penny between us, so we just stood next to that wall in the sun waiting the full three hours before kick-off tortured by hunger and thirst as the crowd behind us began to swell steadily.

Soon I was squashed between Ged, his older friend and a large teenage girl and her father who were pressing in relentlessly behind me. This teenage girl kept leaning her elbows on my head and shoulders, trying to get me to move from the small section of wall I was wedged against. I turned round to her and pleaded rather feebly, 'You're squashing me.' She looked down, sneering with disdain and pulled a cod-sympathetic 'Aw diddums' face and then continued chewing her gum and pressing her elbows into me. Every time we tried to escape the shoving, pushing mass by jumping up and scrambling to sit on the wall, a steward came along and told us to get down.

With my eyes just about at pitch level and craned on tiptoes I gasped for air and pondered my misery. All I could think of was what I could have spent that two bob on instead of coming here for this. Two trips to the pictures on a Saturday afternoon, an unheard-of indulgence; 24 Refresher chews or eight lucky bags; or a Superman comic; two lucky bags and a small bottle of Tizer and I'd get threepence back on the empty bottle; or even eight packets of football cards. Any of these options seemed preferable to being buried up to my neck in a crush of human quicksand beneath that blazing sun in Old Trafford with our Tony's scarf itching and scratching amongst the sweat pouring down my young neck.

As luck would have it, the match itself turned out to be the worst thing about the whole day. Manchester United were slaughtered. Southampton were playing toward our goal at first – a crossed ball came over from our right, the Southampton left, courtesy of their winger John Sydenham, Ron Davies met it with his head, his whole body moving through the air and crashing into the back of the United goal a split second after the ball. In fact Ron Davies scored all four that day, and every goal looked like an action replay of the last. Final score: Manchester United 1, Southampton 4.

On the way home Gerard's older friend merely hung his head, spat nonchalantly on the ground, hands in pockets, fringe in eyes, and said, 'Bill Foulkes is shit and Brennan and Burns were hopeless.' Then looking at me and turning to Gerard, 'I reckon your mate's a jinx.'

I was at Old Trafford again with Gerard Murray and friend a couple of weeks later for a Wednesday-night match, walked up Stretford Road by our Tony and walked home again after. We were playing Newcastle, and this time the danger man, as Ged pointed out, was Wyn Davies. A Welsh international centre-forward, brilliant in the air and scored loads of goals … somehow the story had a familiar ring. Again, hungry, thirsty, squashed and sweaty, I watched uncomfortably as a 0–0 draw unfolded.

Outside the ground the silent, long-fringed 11-year-old spat on the ground. 'If Denis Law and Nobby Stiles had been play-ing we would have won them easy. At least Bill Foulkes wasn't playing, mind you that Ian Ure bloke looks shit too.'

In the street the following day I spoke to Jimmy Millar and the McPhee twins, trying to make my fringe look long and keeping my hands in my pockets and head slouched down, I spat on the ground. 'We'd have won them easy if Denis Law and Stiles had played, mind you that Ian Ure bloke looks shit too.' Oh I was learning all about football.

So far it didn't look as if United were going to have much of a season. Stiles injured, Law injured, Stepney had just come back. We'd played six, drew three, lost three and it wasn't even September yet. Meanwhile Man. City had played five, won three, drew two. I had to see City play and sooner rather than later, but how?

I'd seen City often on the Sunday afternoon match on Granada. They were a hard-tackling athletic side with more than their share of skilful players. Our Tony would always knock them, basically for being Man. City, which in retrospect was fair enough, but they always seemed to be winning and in a convincing fashion. I suppose my life was full of restrictions in terms of behaviour and full of people bossing me about – to be a secret City fan was the only form of rebellion open to me. The truth is I liked City, flirted with them, conducted a secret affair which dragged on for years. City had a winning side while United interspersed their greatness with ugly, lanky nobodies like Paul Edwards, Alan Gowling, Don Givens and Steve James; and prima donnas like Carlo Sartori and Jim Ryan who looked like world beaters in the reserves with their dribbling skills, but in the first team failed to impress.

Despite all these doubts, at heart I was wedded for life to the glorious boys from United. Nothing could quite match up to their legend and magic. City had good players like Lee, Bell and Summerbee, but United had all-time greats in Charlton, Law and Best. But hey, I was allowed to doubt – the least they could have done was win the odd game.

Things brightened up as I witnessed Man. United win their first game at home to Sunderland on a dull overcast Saturday afternoon. Goals from Brian Kidd, young Irishman Don Givens (in for the injured Denis Law) and Best saw

Sunderland off in fine style. But, and it was a big but, I was finding it hard to extract the entrance money from my mother. Football was, like everything else in our house, 'too expensive'. 'We can't afford it' was an oft-used phrase. Electricity, gas, Sugar Puffs, lemonade, a pair of football boots, a bike, a lucky bag ... every request was met with the same phrase until it became a mantra.

Feeding and clothing seven of us was a constant strain on our mother who'd often suffer from migraines which lasted for days on end, so we learned not to ask for stuff we knew was a luxury. This meant my trips to Old Trafford went on hold for a while and, despite my tender years and self-centredness, I still felt the anxiety bred by our fragile household budget. Looking back there was a heroism about the unselfish way those working-class mothers sacrificed everything for their kids. They had no social life, never had new clothes or complained. Yet to me they had more vigour, strength and personality than any number of high-flying career women I've met – a raw and unblemished goodness that gave of everything they had, receiving little in return and expecting nothing. They worked all day at home, did cleaning jobs or worked on school dinners to fit in with the kids' timetable, and lent a dignity to what was to all intents and purposes a life of unpaid slavery.

My father worked all the time, 10 and 12-hour shifts, six days a week. The occasional evening at home ruined by a visit from the priest who would sit there drinking tea out of my mother's best china, trying to get my parents to give money to the missions or for church funds. My father always became sullen and quiet when the priest came round, the TV would be turned off and he'd leave all the talking to my mother. I think his view was, he went to Mass every week, tipping up a few bob into the collection plate, and confession every month, so why on earth should the Vatican invade his house, mithering for money and bringing discomfort to his leisure time. But he never voiced these opinions.

He would tell us how as a boy in the Liberties of Dublin he'd stand in his bare feet outside the cinema with a man who'd been friends with his late father, watching the priests slink into the matinee. The man he stood with was a well-known communist and ex-docker who'd mock the priests as they rushed in the swinging glass doors for their fix of the latest Cagney movie, chocolates in one hand and cigarettes in the other.

'I can see you there, Father, sneaking into the pictures with your black magic box.' The *double entendre* was not lost on my father or his young friends, who looked up to this guru of the Dublin streets, who thought priests, like the bosses on the docks and business owners, were only interested in robbing from the poor.

Added to the financial worries was the big question of where we would be rehoused. My father was working at Esso in Trafford Park, so we couldn't move too far from where he worked; also none of us kids wanted to change schools. But the fact was the house I'd been born in was to be demolished along with the rest of the street. The fortunes of the Christian household were reflecting the up-and-down season Manchester United were struggling through.

There was one other way to spend winter Saturday afternoons. And Saturday afternoon pictures at the Imperial was a bit of a rough-house. Kids would be fighting in the queue, having their money stolen off them by older kids, shouting, pushing in, all kinds of bullying going on. The first lesson we learned was never, ever sit right at the front of the house.

Everything for sale in the pictures cost a minimum of sixpence and the one thing you could buy at the cinema kiosk which wasn't available elsewhere was Vimto Jubilees – a frozen rectangle of Vimto in a waxed cardboard package that was almost impossible to open. Kids who could afford it bought them and sat on the back rows sucking away until all the Vimto had disappeared and they were left with a pinkish coloured block of ice. This was then hurled towards the front rows, aimed hopefully at the back of anyone's head.

In the darkness of the cinema everything was thrown forward – half-sucked gobstoppers, frozen Jubilees, ice-lolly sticks, chewing-gum, semi-chewed nougats. In a happy coincidence we would usually get money for the pictures when it was raining, so we'd sit in the warmth of the cinema with our anorak hoods up throughout the programme to deflect the worst of the missiles. It wasn't uncommon for someone sat behind to misaim a punch through the darkness into the side of your head. It was bedlam. Going as a posse was always the best way, then the other kids had better watch out.

One particular rainy afternoon, as our Kevin, Jimmy Millar and I called for the McPhee twins, something in my memory glimmered. The Sharon Gospel church had shown those Woody Woodpecker cartoons on a paper screen, so what if the Imperial cinema had a paper screen too ...? Soon we were bending over with discarded crisp bags, filling them with earth from the yard of the Unitarian church on the corner of Ayres Road, and then mixing this with water from the puddles in the gutter. We couldn't help but feel excited by our forthcoming experiment.

More often than not at the Imperial on Saturdays there was some sickly Children's Film Foundation effort which we hated. At the time I kind of preferred the pictures in the winter to going to the match, but, win, lose or draw, the match never made me feel alienated. There was always something extremely annoying about these ugly posh kids who acted in English children's films. The very thought of the *Railway Children* or *Swallows and Amazons* and all those thin-lipped, pasty-faced, Post Office savings account stamp-collecting, plummy-voiced, Famous Five types got right up our hooters. We wanted American films and serials and you could hear the collective groan run through our local cinema when the tell-tale opening titles came up.

With filthy hands and mud dripping on to our trousers and bare legs we joined the queue at the Imperial. Handing over mud-encrusted shilling pieces we made our way down to the very front row of the cinema, always the last to fill up. Our necks were craned looking upwards when about 15 minutes into the opening film – about some toffee-nosed kid with a speech impediment, sent to his aunt's for the summer, who befriended other toffee-nosed kids with similar speech impediments and obligatory pet dogs – we began hurling our mud-bag missiles at the screen.

I watched as the mud trickled down, obscuring bits and pieces of the celluloid magic in front of us. Suddenly the house lights came on and the film stopped. We started up from our seats and looked down the aisles to see the man who tore our tickets heading towards the front. We were frozen to the spot, not accustomed to the sudden brightness. Before I knew it the man had me, our Kevin and Brian McPhee, not so much red handed as mud handed. Pulling us off the floor by the backs of our anoraks, he frog-marched us to the entrance and threatened us with the police, the fire brigade, the wrath of God and worse, our parents. Money was mentioned and our Kevin and Brian suddenly started crying.

'But it wasn't us mister, it was these two big boys who ran away and said they'd batter us if we didn't help them honest … I don't know where they are now, I'd never seen them before, but they had plastic bags with mud in them and said if we didn't throw them they'd stick them in our faces and on our clothes and then our dad's would belt us.'

Despite fast talking and being backed up by our Kevin and Brian, we were ejected from the cinema and told we were banned from ever going again. Outside I pretended I was glad, taking off those plummy kids – 'I say you rotters I shall tell your papa and mama what mischief you've been up to'. For a moment we laughed in the rain, then the cold damp of doubt crept in. Where could I spend those cold wet Saturday afternoons in the future. The rain lashed down, soaking through our anoraks. There was no way we could go home now; our parents knew how much we loved the pictures, they'd never believe we'd just come home of our own accord. Besides the whole point of them giving us a shilling each to go to the pictures was to get us out and away from under their feet.

We wandered around aimlessly on Chorlton Road and Ayres Road, looking vainly for any sight of Kevin McPhee or Jimmy Millar. We weren't expected back until five o'clock, so we were stuck in the freezing rain and wind for over two hours. We sheltered at the bus stop ... there was absolutely nothing to do. We walked in the freezing palls of drizzle which numbed our faces and legs, socks squelching with every step, until we reached Hullard Park and hung around the drenched and deserted playground. We tried to go and look at comics and picture books in the Old Trafford Library but the librarian threw us out for being filthy and wet and getting the books filthy and wet. We hung around in the park shelter listening to the roar of a large excited crowd drifting and echoing across the houses from the direction of Old Trafford. We tried to guess who'd shot and missed and who had scored by the crowd reactions. It was one of the most miserable afternoons of my life.

At quarter to five we started off home. It was God who'd done this to us – he sees everything and punishes all sinners.

We'd thrown the mud at the screen, we'd lied to the man in the pictures, we'd planned to lie to our parents and we'd never be able to go to the Imperial again as long as we lived. In the dark damp dreariness of our street and our house, my life seemed particularly grey that Saturday afternoon and the guilt I felt seemed to penetrate every pore of my body. But as we knocked on the front door the ethereal quality of that noise from Old Trafford, that had stopped us mid-conversation in Hullard Park gave me a warm glow inside.

Mam was furious at the state we were in – our shoes and every stitch of clothing was soaked through. We were hit, given our dinner, our Saturday-night bath and sent to bed. Through the bedroom window the backyards, rooftops and alleyway looked as bleak, grim and forbidding as I felt inside and I let myself drift off. The memory of the echo of the Old Trafford crowd sounding the only comforting whisper in my young head as I finally sank away. A home victory that day for United; another home defeat for us.

8

The City Kit

'Mam, can I have a knife?'

'No you can't, they're dangerous.'

'Well Jerry's got one.'

'Well you can't, you're too young.'

'But he's got a Scout knife.'

'Well when you're a Scout you can have one too.'

'Well when can I join the Scouts then?'

I enquired at school. No way could you be a Scout until you were 11, but you could join the Cubs, and the Cubs went camping outdoors and stayed in tents like the Red Indians. So I joined the Cubs, or I should say we joined the Cubs. There was safety in numbers, so I immediately recruited Richard Behan and Mike King, my best friends at school. The local Cubs were based at St John's church hall on Ayres Road. It was a Protestant church, but my mam didn't seem to hold the same objections to this Higher Anglican landmark as she did to the Sharon Gospel church's Tuesday club or the idea of me wanting to join the Boys' Brigade (to get a bugle like the US cavalry).

We already knew how to light fires; now we'd just get off into the woods, live in a tent and maybe start with something small like a penknife and work our way up to maybe a sword. I'd never been to the country. I'd seen a few cows and a bit of countryside from the train when we travelled to Blackpool and to Holyhead in Wales to get the boat to Ireland. But woods, rivers and streams, knives and tents, this would be something else.

The Cubs, well they looked a right bunch of narnas in those daft green jumpers and little schoolboy caps and those woggles, but we didn't have any uniform because we'd just joined, so that was a relief. We crowded into the hall and were given pieces of paper saying how much the uniform cost. I was a bit taken a back by this as I thought, as did my mother, that the uniform was free. Then we said ... prayers. We looked at each other; this was looking bad. Then we sang a song called Michael Finnegan, which we'd sung at school. 'There was an old man called Michael Finnegan, he grew whiskers on his chinnigan, the wind came up and blew them in again, poor old Michael Finnegan begin again' and on and on. Cubs was proving more boring than school already.

My Scouting days were over before they really began. In the second meeting I set off a fire extinguisher in the hall and abused the Scoutmaster or whatever you called him. I didn't want any Michael Finnegan, dib-dib-dobbing or gin-gan-goolieing or things that were the same as school. There were no repercussions at home for any of us – was a whim and a silly one really. Being excluded from the Cubs saved our mams sixpence a week and all we really wanted was a knife and to go camping, but not with that shower of sissies.

'I've been to football matches and you haven't been to any, and you're supposed to be a City fan.'

I taunted our Kevin mercilessly, which was a mean tactic because he was a good-natured and unselfish kid. Even when he was four he'd never argue to get the last biscuit or the plastic toy in the Cornflakes packet. I remember one Christmas morning waking up to find two pillow-cases at the end of the bed full of presents. By this time I no longer believed in Father Christmas, but our Kevin did. I went through the parcels on my side of the bed in the cold darkness of the room, feeling them. There seemed to be a disheartening number of books and annuals in mine, which meant there wouldn't be much to play with on Christmas Day.

I rummaged as silently as possible through our Kevin's pillow-case – there was a large parcel. I peeled some of the paper away and slid the box out carefully. Inside was a Western wagon and horses with cavalry men and Indians. I slipped it back into its wrapping and put it in my pillow-case replacing it with one of my annuals. A fair swap I thought.

'Hey, Kev, Father Christmas has been. Look.'

Bleary-eyed he joined me at the end of the bed, furiously ripping open his parcels in the darkness. As he threw aside a *Look and Learn* book, I attracted his attention to what Father Christmas had left for me.

'Look, Kev, a wagon with cavalry and Indians just like *Wagon Train* on the telly, we can play with it after.' Such magnanimity, but then it was Christmas.

Later in our front room I trundled the wagon and its escort of cavalry across the lino on to the mat in front of the fire where the Indians were waiting behind the surround in ambush. Our Kev wanted to play too.

'Just wait until after,' I said.

He went to tell our mam that I wouldn't let him play with my wagon. Mam came in from the kitchen where she was preparing dinner.

'Where did you get that,' she said accusingly.

'Father Christmas left it me,' I replied, knowing full well that she knew that I knew there was no such thing as Father Christmas, but I'd been warned on pain of death not to spoil Christmas for our Kevin and Sheila by sharing this recent revelation with them.

'Yes well Father Christmas must have made a mistake, because that was supposed to be for our Kevin, not you.'

'Father Christmas doesn't make mistakes like that though.'

'Well he did this time, that *Look and Learn* book was for you, and that was for Kevin, now stop annoying him and me and give over acting the goat.'

The only thing that had stopped the situation being worse was that Mam probably thought Dad had got the parcels mixed up, but I was none too pleased ... 'Hey, Kev, I know a great game to play with a wagon train.'

Kevin had to learn read between the lines quite quickly, and a fair bit of my worldly wise cynicism rubbed off on him. But he was our mam's blue-eyed little boy, cute, fair and chubby, and in many ways angelic. He didn't want all the time like I did, so invariably my mother would go to great pains to get him what he did want on the very rare occasion that he asked for it. So if I wanted to go to see City, it would have to be achieved with some intercession from Kevin.

'Just imagine, Kev, you can see Colin Bell and Francis Lee, but you'd have to ask Mam to ask Dad to take you.'

It was a cold Wednesday night, 29 October 1969. We waited at the bus stop for the No. 53 to take us to Maine Road. On the bus we went straight upstairs so my dad could have a cigarette. The upstairs of the bus was a thick fog of tobacco smoke which burned my eyes and lungs. The journey seemed endless as the bus trundled behind a queue of match traffic up Great Western Street in Moss Side.

It was mission accomplished as far as I was concerned. My dad hadn't been to a football match since the Busby Babes played at Old Trafford and that was only a couple of times. Before that it had been when United played City at Maine Road in 1947. He was doing his fatherly duty, and I'm sure that he wasn't too pleased about taking us out on a cold autumn night after a 12-hour shift at work and another to come the next day.

We went in City's scoreboard end. It was the League Cup quarter-final, City having already knocked out both Liverpool and Everton in the previous rounds. City's opponents were second-division Queens Park Rangers with Rodney Marsh playing for them. Unlike at Old Trafford, City let the youngsters sit up at the wall and it wasn't as crowded or claustrophobic. This was actually a comfortable way to watch a match and Dad had bought us a packet of Opal Fruits each to eat on the bus.

As the teams came out we started cheering as we saw the players wearing the familiar red and black City second kit; then there was a huge roar as Man. City ran out wearing their sky-blue shirts and white shorts … now this was confusing to Kevin and myself as it appeared QPR were wearing Man. City's away kit, which indeed they were, right down to the socks themselves. Perplexed by this we settled down to watch the match.

Rodney Marsh was QPR's most famous player, but he didn't make much impact that night as City, with Bell, Lee, Summerbee, Oakes, Doyle and Young, took the West Londoners apart. It was easy, the most one-sided game I'd witnessed so far. Final score: Man. City 3, QPR 0. Our Tony could lie all he liked, but truth and football should go hand in hand. Nine times out of ten the best team won, and the team that won the most was the best. So little else in life was as inspiring in its purity and honesty ... and City seemed to win often. I'd have to see more of this.

Meanwhile I continued, whenever I could, to go to Old Trafford with Gerard Murray on a Saturday. If the first team were playing away we'd watch United's reserves as it only cost a shilling to get in and it was somewhere to go on Saturday afternoon. But to be quite truthful, I longed to be taken to Maine Road and see the hard-battling Super Blues. They'd gone on to knock United out of the League Cup semi-final, winning at Maine Road 2–1 and drawing the away leg at Old Trafford 2–2, and at Wembley they won the League Cup Final against West Bromwich Albion. On top of that they were also in the final of the European Cup Winners' Cup against Gornik Zabzre of Poland. That cup run had also been an exciting affair. A particularly tricky European tie against Athletic Bilbao had been drawn 3–3 in Spain, City winning in fine style at Maine Road 3–0 with a 35-yard screamer from Alan Oakes amongst the goals.

United's season, which had promised much after a shaky start, concluded in a third FA Cup semi-final replay at Bolton Wanderers' Burnden Park, after three marathon games against another hated enemy, Leeds United. The Reds were dogged by bad luck in every game and finally and undeservedly lost 1–0. Two cup semi-finals and no glory. It was City's year in Manchester again. When my eighth birthday came I asked my dad to get me the Man. City red and black away kit. This way I could pay my homage to City and my favourite football kit, annoy our Tony and still keep my self-respect with the lads who were United fans at school, but themselves wore Man. City away kits for five-a-side games in the park.

Football kits even then were expensive, and the kit really meant the socks and shirt, as I already owned some white shorts, but City's away kit had black shorts and I wanted the full kit. Lunchtime on my birthday and I was in the school yard. We were to play five-a-side in the park after school. I'd brought my boots and I was wearing my white shorts under my grey school shorts and a pink-red United shirt I'd inherited from our Tony. My dad turned up at the school fence on his bicycle. He was working nights at the time, and he had a parcel under his arm. I rushed with my friends to the gate to meet him. He handed over the brown paper package. I opened the parcel and with a mixture of horror and delight found myself looking at and breathing in the brand-new smell of sky-blue City shirt and socks with a maroon trim.

'Oh,' I said, faking bitter disappointment and surprise to my friends, 'it's a City kit. Didn't they have any red and black ones.' I could see the annoyance, hurt and anger on my father's face and suddenly stopped. 'Thanks Dad,' I said, immediately sorry and guilty for what I'd done. It was a big thing for my dad to carry a City shirt all the way up to the school just so I could wear it for football in the park. He obviously thought I'd be thrilled, as I secretly was, and wanted to see my delight – the way he always loved Christmas Day for the same reason. I hope I didn't break his heart that day, but I often think of that moment. If I could live my life over again and go back and change just one thing, that is the moment I'd choose, just to make that journey for him worthwhile and be able to show him how pleased I was. I've thought about that incident a lot, especially on the freezing-cold, wet-sleet day soon after Christmas 1996 when he was lowered into a grave that he'll share for eternity with my 11-year-old sister Janet Margaret.

Wilf McGuinness was replaced as manager of United by Frank O'Farrell, a quietly spoken Irishman who'd managed the Leicester side that had lost to Man. City in the 1969 Cup Final and seen his side relegated the same season. He made a few good early signings for United: notably Martin Buchan from Aberdeen and Ian Storey Moore, a player whose skill and pace in his better moments reminded us of George Best. Of the two though it was Martin Buchan who would go on to carve his name on the hearts of United fans as a captain of renown.

Some players as a United fan you just take to, and they are all different. Best was simply magical, yet strangely shy and modest. Cantona was aloof to the press but down to earth and accommodating to the fans, and an inspiration on the pitch, but Buchan ... well to all intents and purposes he was a bit of a stiff, a goody two-shoes, but what a player, what a man. He stood in as captain in only his second match for United. He would be one of the greatest central defenders the British game has seen and played for Scotland through two World Cups.

He wasn't tall, but he was quick, a good tackler and passer of the ball, and crucially he could organize the players around him. Off the pitch he always wore a suit and tie and never had a hair on his head out of place. He was just as immaculate for eleven seasons, most of them as captain, in United's central defence. But he had some charisma too – once, asked by a reporter after a game for a 'quick word', he casually replied 'Velocity' before heading off.

There were times under Frank O'Farrell when United looked to be really on their game. In one particular match against Crystal Palace, United overran the visitors with Best on one wing and Ian Storey Moore on the other. The opposition were not up to much, granted, but the spectacle that day of what at times looked like two George Bests will always stay with me. Ian Storey Moore, Law, Charlton and Gowling were the scorers as Palace were annihilated, the 4–0 scoreline flattering them.

We'd started brilliantly and were top of the table by five

points with Christmas approaching. But then Best was always in the headlines for the wrong reasons and things went downhill towards the end of the season. After beating Coventry away 3–2, United then lost to Liverpool, a 3–0 humiliation at home. Things never seemed to pick up for United after that. Gerard Murray blamed moaning fans like me. 'Everyone picks on United, no one gets behind Gowling and we missed playing at home early in the season because of the knife that was thrown on the pitch last year.'

It was true we didn't like Alan Gowling, but that's because he wasn't Denis Law or Brian Kidd, and as for having to play our first two home games against Arsenal and WBA at Anfield and Stoke City's Victoria Ground, well we actually won both those matches (and it was quite cool to support a team whose fans threw a knife on the pitch). Still we were as ever in awe of Mr Murray's match analysis.

Defeat at Leicester was followed by a 3–1 humiliation at Old Trafford by Manchester City. Oh it was hard to be a United fan then. It seemed every derby game City would romp home comfortable winners. I suppose it always meant so much to them to beat United, as it always has to every team in the country, but more so. The difference was of course that back then those other teams, especially City, were, unlike United, winning trophies. For the third season on the trot United finished way off the top (eighth) without winning a thing, and I thought it couldn't get any worse, paying good money to see dregs like Steve James, Paul Edwards and the woeful Willie Watson scuppering our defence … it did.

9

The Stretford East League

Proudly I placed the daffodils and blue flowers I'd picked out of our garden in front of the Statue of Our Lady in the classroom, adding to the floral half-circle which was replenished every day in spring. It was only the second time in my short life I'd done such a thing; the first time wouldn't count up in heaven as I'd picked the flowers from Hullard Park, so it might have been considered stealing. I walked back to my seat with a swagger which told the other kids, 'Yeah we've got a garden now.'

We certainly did and at no little pain.

That dreaded day had come when the council rehoused us. I'd watched each day as family after family moved out. Richard and Rennie had moved three streets further up Ayres Road to Stamford Street. I'd watched as, supervised by their ferocious mother and helped by their older cousins Raymond and Darren, they'd wheeled the heavy furniture round the corner on two old prams. Wardrobes on wheels, chairs carried, tables carried between two and armchairs balanced on the frail-looking prams. No removal van for them as they showed the shabby contents of their home to the neighbourhood.

Jimmy Millar's family had moved on to Ayres Road almost directly opposite my primary school, and I lived in fear that with my final year at school looming on the horizon, I'd be forced to move further away than the rest and leave not just friends but the school behind. Fortunately we were moved to a three-bedroom council house on a street just off Seymour Grove, around the corner from Gerard Murray and within roaring distance of both Old Trafford football and cricket grounds. The house had an inside loo, a back garden, a pebble-dashed front and was decorated in cream-painted woodchip. I honestly thought it was the poshest thing I'd ever seen.

It was one of those 1920s corporation houses and sat next to a large bakery and soya mill, the noises rumbling comfortingly in through our bedroom window every night. More importantly for me it was right on the doorstep of Seymour Park, which when I'd lived in Duke Street was a long walk through alien territory. My world seemed brighter if somewhat disarrayed as my mind concentrated on two big worries: getting into the school team the following year, and passing my 11-plus.

The 11-plus exam was like a religious icon to my mother. She was one of eight children who'd emigrated to Hulme in Manchester in the 1930s from Dublin. At school she'd been a bright pupil and passed her 11-plus, only to be denied a place at Loretto Convent School because her mother couldn't afford the uniform. Her father, an Irish man with a fierce temper and a fondness for whiskey, was unable to work as he had been gassed twice on the Somme in 1916, before being taken prisoner of war, then subsequently released by the Germans because he was so ill.

He'd been a regular soldier in the British army and had served all over the world with his regiment, including India, before coming a cropper in the mud and blood-soaked fields of France and Belgium. An invalid, with only an army pension, he spent his days in isolation, drinking, and never spoke a word to my mother or her three sisters in all the time he lived. He died when my mother was 11, having clearly suffered deteriorating health since the mustard gas poisoning. After his death his widow, Bridget Cullen, was denied his pension because the board of doctors and army people said that, despite the fact he'd been coughing up pieces of lung and blood daily, his death was not due to his being gassed in the war. My mam says her mother had to go and stand in front of this tribunal, but wasn't allowed to speak, everything being discussed in front of her with the family doctor, as if she didn't exist – her dead husband, her poverty, her nationality – leaving her mute and invisible. Ten shillings a week she was given to bring up a family of eight kids, who were subsequently pushed out of the door to work as soon as they were of an age to leave school, at 14. As far as my mother was concerned, we had to pass our 11-plus, it was her mission in life.

I was determined to pass for Mam and so I wouldn't be seen as the family failure. My older brother Tony had passed, going on to St Bede's Catholic Grammar in Whalley Range and so had my sister Mary, who attended Loreto Convent in Moss Side. My problem though was that I felt in no way anywhere near as smart or grown-up as my older brother and sister, who had been model pupils.

In fact, my schoolwork had already begun to improve and I'd gone from being one of the least promising academically to a respectable position on the middle tables. This had been thanks mainly to one of those fickle twists of fate. At home I'd always been envious of how much my older brother and sister read. Then a stint in hospital to have my tonsils removed and the subsequent two-week convalescence forced me to realize my own love of books and stories. This was due in no small part to one of our Tony's friends, a Ukrainian lad called Roman Sedegento, who lent me what looked like a mountain of American comics. I spent two weeks dreamily deciphering Superman, The Flash, The Green Lantern, Caspar The Friendly Ghost and Captains Marvel and America. So this had improved my appreciation of the written word.

Now, the inspiration to achieve academically came in the shape of a six-foot, four-inch heavily built Irishman from County Mayo called Mr Fallon. He was a fearsome sight, with a roar that struck fear into the cheekiest 11-year-old, turning knees to water and idle hands into quivering jelly. Nobody dared even whisper in his class and he wasn't the type to patronize, humour or indulge children. Mr Fallon forced us to learn through fear, and yet looking back he wasn't too hard on kids who weren't that bright and wanted to try.

As for me – well I suddenly found my powers of concentration improved in direct proportion to my fear of getting on his wrong side. And that fear was such that I finished top of the whole year, first out of 88 children, much to my surprise and everyone else's. I looked a safe bet to pass my 11-plus the next year, but at the same time I was sadly aware that the majority of my friends would be going to St Mary's Catholic secondary modern in Stretford. Even worse my friends who were also safe bets to pass the 11-plus, like Peter Burgess, Richard Behan, Mike King and David Lindsay, had all put down to go to different Catholic grammar schools to me. In fact there were only three other pupils in the whole school who'd opted to go to St Bede's, and I wasn't bosom buddies with any of them.

It would be a wrench because that last year at St Alphonsus was one of the happiest in my life. The main thing was getting in the under-11 football squad to play in the most senior side in the school. I'd got my first pair of football boots over two years before, second hand of course, and I was still growing into them. (In the meantime kids in our year were sporting George Best's Stylo Matchmakers with the laces up the sides and the white boots, as worn by Pelé and Alan Ball, with their screw-in studs.) But I'd been a member of the team of under-10s who'd played half a dozen friendlies the year before, drawing two games and winning four. I'd also been in our year's winning five-a-side team. I was primed and ready now to play the serious stuff, which was in the Stretford East league.

Thursday afternoon we played organized football in the park, members of the school team squad staying behind for extra training, mainly in shooting and diving headers. We trained with a heavy leather casey which must have been in the school since the 1940s. It seemed to crush your head into your shoulders, juddering and rattling fragile necks and numbing our brains every time we headed it, especially on a wet day. I was fairly skilful and very combative, a little Nobby Stiles or so I thought, with occasional stints on the right wing.

The fixture list for the Stretford East league was up and running, and we approached each new school we played with some foreboding – especially schools like Seymour Park, Lostock and Old Trafford school where 90 per cent of the kids were of West Indian descent and built like 14-year-old basketball players.

We needn't have worried. Seymour Park, who fielded more or less the same team as they had against us the year before in a hard contested 3–3 draw, were given an 8–2 drubbing. Old Trafford school were dismissed 4–0 at their ground, then 10–1 at ours; Moss Park were soundly beaten 4–0 home and away, as were St Teresa's; and Kings Road school looked miserable and sore as they walked off shamefaced after losing by double figures.

The jibes our friends who were not Catholic and went to some of these schools received from us hurt. A particular friend of mine, and Mike King's next-door neighbour, John Sullivan was an excellent footballer. He went to a small Anglican primary school called St Hilda's on Warwick Road South. He bragged that St Hilda's had beaten Kings Road and drawn with Moss Park and Gorse Hill. The last of these had burst our bubble of runaway victories, losing to us only by a narrow 2–1. I remember Mike King and myself worrying unduly about this St Hilda's game as we approached the cosy little football pitch behind their school

It was sunny and not too cold. Playing in our now-feared red and white stripes (Sunderland kit – if only they'd had our success!) we lined up against St Hilda's in their navy blue and gold trim. They looked smart, and as the school was in the posher part of Old Trafford, not far from Longford Park, all their mams and dads had turned out to cheer them on.

When the twelfth goal went in their net, John Sullivan, a big strapping lad and a bit of an all-round sportsman and tough-nut, burst into tears and was so inconsolable he had to be substituted. 16-0 we beat them, and Mike King at the final whistle went straight over to John and put a comforting arm around him. 'I told you we'd hammer you, you big sissy,' I said, empathy not high in my list of attributes.

It was the fear that drove us on – everything about football was serious and stomach-churning. We played to win because we didn't want to be like John Sullivan crying, didn't want to be substituted or dropped and miss out on being one of the lads. In every part of our lives we seemed to be surrounded by the trappings of failure and exclusion. The one way we could be anything that counted and was respectable, and be acknowledged as such by infants and adults alike, was football. And the way you played. To have another kid's dad come up to you after a match and say 'You played a blinder today, son' was like that feeling on Christmas morning. But more than this, the elation for us came from knowing that in this at least we were not failing.

In the freezing cold the ground was rock hard and we were playing the quite useful Gorse Hill again. With my rubber moulded studs I was slipping and sliding all over the place, got a twisted ankle and was substituted by Paul O'Byrne. In pain on the touchline I watched a close game as Gorse Hill wanted revenge for that earlier 2–1 home defeat. We won by the same margin again, but I couldn't play for two weeks, and as a result was frustratingly relegated to the subs bench.

'But sir, I'm all right now. It's boring being substitute, I'm better than Paul O'Byrne and Brendan Moody.' I was almost in tears. I thought they'd been picked over me as they were bigger. The only really small player on the team at that time was James Martin, who was the star player and top scorer. I couldn't believe I wasn't getting a chance to get back in the side and had to stand around with a flimsy anorak covering my football kit as I watched my friends trouncing the opposition each week. I felt so left out.

At night I included prayers for Man. United to get on a winning streak and for someone, anyone in that St Alphonsus team to get a verruca and lose their place in the team to me. After water into wine and feeding the five thousand with a few loaves and fishes, I imagined one or two strategically placed verrucas would ensure my future and God wouldn't begrudge me that.

'You can be the match reporter as well as the substitute,' Mr Fallon informed me one Friday afternoon – it wasn't so much a friendly suggestion, as an order. The next day I sat with hands numb from the biting wind, pencil in hand, as the team thrashed Old Trafford school 15–0. In the rucks of players around the goal-mouth I couldn't work out who scored what and when ... it was hellish. Each week they'd run out winners by an avalanche, and all the match reports, which Mr Fallon now expected as a part of my homework were put up on a noticeboard in the corridor every Monday morning, often three and four pages long.

I began to experience the power of the press and my school chums would clamour for a mention or start moaning about any criticism. 'Paul O'Byrne isn't very good at tackling and surely there are better players at tackling than him, he didn't play well really because he said he had a stitch and was trying to run holding his side when that big coloured lad from Seymour Park scored their first goal.'

Despite my misuse of power to try and regain my place in the side Mr Fallon brought in the top players from the year below us. My chances of regaining my place in the team dwindled to nothing. Then came the cups. In the borough of Stretford there was the Bates Trophy and the Fearnhead Shield, the finals of both to be played at Longford Park stadium. All the teams in the Stretford East league went into the hat with those the Stretford West league, and that meant coming up against the invincible St Anne's Catholic Primary School in Stretford and St Hugh of Lincoln Catholic Primary School, both of whom had reputations as good as ours.

In the Fearnhead Shield, St Alphonsus were drawn at home in the semi-final against St Anne's. There was a buzz about this match. St Alphonsus claimed to be the rightful parish of Manchester United, and we did indeed play in red and white (albeit stripes), where as St Anne's played in royal blue and were the actual parish that Old Trafford football ground was in. We'd demolished all opposition in the early rounds, but these had all been Protestant schools and we thought we had God on our side. But now it was the battle of the Catholic giants and God may well have to sit this one out.

Then disaster struck. Our goalkeeper and seven of our best players were out with flu (or forced to go to Polish school – a Saturday school where history lessons were given and films were shown in Polish) and we were in dire straits. So dire in fact that I was actually going to get my first game for ages, though I'd been told I still had to hand in that match report.

The game was a travesty. We lost 6–3 and to add insult to injury the local paper, the *Stretford and Urmston Journal* reported the score as 6–2. We would never visit Longford Park stadium and pick up a trophy, though we knew in our hearts we were the best, the Old Trafford elite and runaway champions of the Stretford East league with a 100-per-cent record. I remember glumly writing that match report, singling out the special contribution of one young man who'd played very well, despite lack of competitive matches and having to play in second-hand boots that were too big for him with moulded studs.

After our school team matches on Saturday I'd walk back with Gerard Murray. I could listen to Ged for hours when he got started on football and tactics. He'd kind of look away as if having a vision before relaying his thoughts. Other times he hardly spoke and when anybody spoke to him he would pull a kind of face that made you wonder if he actually liked anybody. It was like he was silently saying to the world 'show me' and if he hadn't been a little overweight and slow on the pitch, he would have been made captain of our school team. As it was he acted and the rest of us responded to him as if he was. Hanging around with Gerard Murray made me feel grown-up.

Then, 'Hiya Mam, I'm home, we won eight-nil', up stairs wash my legs, hands and face, if I'd been playing, down to the mini-market, queue up in Bebbington's the greengrocers, back home, bolt down a dinner of sausage and chips, and then, 'See you Mam, I'm going out to play.' Ten minutes later, on the streets near the ground: 'Excuse me, mister, do you want your car minding?'

Easiest ten pence I'd ever made. There were about a dozen of us who did the stretch, the Slatterys, the Mulvaneys, the Minihans and the Riordans. We had to tip up most of it to the older lads and share the rest out. I'd end up with 45p usually, sometimes as much as a quid, but not all the drivers paid up.

'I'll sort you out when I come back.'

'If there's any marks on this car when we get back I'll rip your head off and shit down the hole, now f★★★ off out of my way.'

'I'll fetch the police you cheeky buggers.'

Nowadays the young kids who do it have more of an aura about them: you know they would definitely let your tyres down, scratch your paintwork or smash your windscreen.

'Get lost, I don't need you to mind my car, I've got a Rottweiler.'

'Oh yeah, is it any good at putting out fires?'

Back then we genuinely just suggested we minded their cars, not that we would. Oh no, we'd be off spending the takings to get into the match, splashing out five pence on a programme and buying Wagon Wheels and diluted orange squash in plastic containers with straws off the youths with faces like adventure playgrounds for young dermatologists who circled the pitch before kick-off and at half-time. We honestly couldn't give a fig if every four-wheeled vehicle in a ten-mile radius was hijacked and burned to a blackened shell.

Mickey Riordan was the biggest business brain amongst us. He'd go to the match, but leave ten minutes or so before full-time and get some of the drivers to pay up twice or get some drivers who'd parked up late on their way to the match and had escaped our net. He never said that he was leaving early for that reason, but we knew it just the same. Everything he did was about money – I suppose he was ahead of his time. Although only 13 he kept his thoughts and actions to himself. It was one of the Mulvaneys who told me that when Mickey's family had moved house, he'd robbed the gas meter in the old house the very next day, before a new family moved in. He also liked to squeeze up behind people at the turnstiles and get in for free, using the money he'd saved to buy an extra programme for the token; and he would never miss a reserve game when they were giving out tokens on the two-pence teamsheets. (These tokens enabled you to get tickets for the big fixtures – in the same way now some clubs give priority to those who have stubs from previous match tickets.)

Once when we were older we had a whip-round and offered Mickey 87p to eat a piece of the round blue soap out of a urinal in the toilets at the ground. To our disgust he did. As a big joke I then offered him 20p to eat a squashed chip off the floor covered in all kinds of crap and filth. Amazed when he did, I was reluctantly offering him my 20-pence worth of change when he pushed my hand away. 'It's all right, Tezzer, that one's on the house.'

Car minding itself was considered by us kids to be fairly innocent, but if I spotted anyone who knew my mam going to the shops on Seymour Grove or Skerton Road, I'd dive behind a car double-quick. My mother would have slaughtered me, even though I was sure car minding wasn't a sin. The best payers were usually the visiting fans, even the threatening looking ones who didn't wear scarves or show team colours. They'd park their Bedford or Volkswagen vans at the top of our road, and often hand over 50p with just a 'behave now lads'. Sometimes older teenage kids would ask us if we knew any cars that belonged to the Spurs/Coventry/Derby/Everton fans, but we wouldn't say and we'd even deny we were minding cars in case they wanted to nick our money.

However, like a good Catholic, I became less certain that car minding wasn't a form of extortion, and what my mother always said about what goes around comes around was forever in my thoughts. 'If you steal sweets or comics you won't enjoy them.' She was always saying things like that to keep us on the straight and narrow in an area where thieving from shops was so common we used to refer to it as 'five-finger discount'. Living in Old Trafford was like living in a goldfish bowl and many's the time I'd think, if only the people who lived there had five-second memories like goldfish. I was getting the money for matches from a dubious source, and God punished me for it and indirectly punished United. Believe me, it's true.

Apologies to the likes of Leicester City, Crystal Palace, Norwich City, Notts Forest fans and the rest whose teams have been up and down the divisions like a ... er, well like Notts Forest, Norwich, Crystal Palace and Leicester ... but had I wished to experience that despairing rollercoaster, I could never have idolized United. They were the only good, pure and all-inclusive thing in our world, the great symbol of triumph for our tribe, and through my sins I was pushing them inexorably into the second division.

It was still the summer holidays before that last year at St Alphonsus when I went to the first match of the season. My legs were stiff from the football training in the park organized by Gerard Murray, a regime that would have shamed Don Howe and Tommy Docherty, aimed at getting us all in shape for the crucial season ahead. With our ill-gotten gains we paid our 20p to get in the Stretford End Paddock. I bought some chips, some Bovril, a programme, some warm orange squash and a Wagon Wheel. I should have been in football heaven;

instead my sinful consumerism lead me to witness United lose at home to Ipswich Town. Even a Denis Law goal couldn't save us as a 2–1 scoreline flattered to deceive. Never mind said Gerard Murray, Ipswich are our bogey team. So that season were Everton and many others.

The world was turning upside down, United were looking old and tired, and I hardly missed a match at home. All our luck in relying on no-marks had run out and now the ship looked increasingly shaky with United only scoring four goals in their first nine games. Would we be relegated? It was November before United notched up their third win in the league that season. The opponents were Liverpool, at the time not quite the hated enemy they were to become but still big rivals, one of the very best teams around and the eventual champions that year.

Liverpool had been unbeaten for 18 games and as we trudged through the crowds, surrounded by the smells of horse manure, cigarettes and last year's dried urine, mixed with the aromas of the hot-dog and burger stands, we were anxiously picturing what kind of humiliating defeat United would face. We'd already lost to Liverpool 2–0 at Anfield. There had been some strange United sides that season with Willie Watson being revived and Tommy O'Neil and Ian Donald as indifferent as Tony Young in shoring up a leaky defence.

But we had hopes: United had bought the ex-Newcastle player and Welsh international Wyn Davies from Man. City for £60,000 and then splashed out £200,000 for Ted MacDougall from Bournemouth. Davies had scored on his debut in a 3–0 win over the previous year's champions Derby County, and MacDougall had scored in our 1–0 win over Birmingham City. Then, however, despite Davies scoring one and MacDougall huffing and puffing alongside, United had been slaughtered 4–1 at home by Spurs. And Liverpool were a much better side than Spurs.

It was a strangely subdued crowd that day, and not quite a sell-out. There was room down by the wall and six of us squeezed up. We always had faith, I mean you had to, but we couldn't see how United could do it. They battled hard and had Liverpool on the back foot in the opening minutes. It wasn't flowing football and Liverpool probably thought this would be an easy game for them as they soaked up United's early running. But United's confidence grew and when Wyn Davies latched on to the ball at the far post, behind Tommy Smith and Ray Clemence, to slot in the first goal the release of tension in the crowd took the roof off.

The Stretford End was in full voice for the rest of the game and the whole ground became a huge banner of scarves held aloft in triumph as United sang their version of the Kop anthem, 'You'll Never Walk Alone' – 'You'll get a kick up the arse and you'll never walk again'. The only comparison at today's games would be United's big European games like Juventus and Bayern Munich with the volume cranked up quadruple. United fans had the will to win, though at times the team played as if they didn't. Ted MacDougall scored the second, despite not looking the best player in the world, but what the hell did we care. United needed to win and to beat Liverpool on a frosty November afternoon was all we could ask – from now on, we had no doubt, United would go from strength to strength.

The following week was the big game for us: Manchester City at Maine Road. I didn't wear a scarf and went to the game with Gerard Murray (who I insisted leave his scarf at home before we got the 53 bus) and two of our mates from the flats who supported City, David Lindsay and his friend Kenneth. We sat with all the City fans in the Platt Lane End on the smallest, narrowest seating I've ever experienced, like perching your bum on a ruler. Still the view was good, you could stand on the plank and it only cost us 20p for the tickets which David had got for us using his dad's spare tokens.

'Right then Dave, if United score me and Ged will just clap politely so we don't get our heads kicked in and if any City skinheads start on us, tell them we're City fans because you and Ken have got scarves on.' All our pre-planning went out of the window as we screamed abuse at the City players and at David and Kenneth after one dirty tackle after another flew in on Best and Storey Moore with Buchan, O'Neill and Sadler doing the same to Bell and Summerbee. It looked like a fight was going to start at one time with Best and Donachie squaring up, but it was an uphill struggle for United from the start. The crowd were hostile, spitting at United players as they took throw-ins. There were chants from the City fans of 'City reject' aimed at Wyn Davies and 'What a waste of money', which we silently agreed with, at Ted MacDougall. Colin Bell, surely the greatest player to wear a City shirt in that era, indeed ever, was gifted a goal early on after a mix-up between Alex Stepney and Tony Dunne. Close to tears we watched as he slotted in a second and then a third, which hit Martin Buchan before leaving Stepney stranded and me and Gerard Murray in no mood to clap politely or hide our allegiances.

'That MacDougall bloke is shite, he's the one who should have been substituted not Willie Morgan, I mean how come Kidd's sub when that spakker is playing.' Gerard Murray was outraged. It hurt, and despite MacDougall and Davies scoring one a piece the following week against Southampton, we couldn't really see the use of either of them.

One of my favourite football stories concerns Wyn Davies. He treated professional soccer as if it was still a hobby, and every summer while he was at Newcastle United, rather than going off on holiday at the end of the season for three or four weeks, he'd go back to Wales and work nights in a factory.

When Newcastle won the European Fairs Cup (now the UEFA Cup) in 1969 they were to have an official reception up in Newcastle. He told the people at Newcastle that he wouldn't be able to go as he had to be at work. At the time he was one of the biggest stars at Newcastle United and the team's leading goalscorer, so his bosses at Newcastle said they would arrange for a car to take him straight back to Wales as soon as the reception was over and before the players' party started. Davies then asked his foreman at the factory if it would be OK if he was a bit late arriving for his shift the following night as he had to go up to Newcastle for the official reception and presentation. A bit mystified as to why he'd bothered to ask, his foreman agreed. So the dutiful Welsh international centre-forward worked a night shift, went home and got changed, travelled all the way from Wales to Newcastle, went to the reception and then left, travelled back to Wales and went straight to work on the night shift without sleeping in between. Can you imagine Duncan Ferguson or Alan Shearer doing that ...

'United are rubbish, City are miles better,' I goaded our Tony. His loyalty to United was 100 per cent, but blind; for God's sake he even tried to make out that MacDougall was a good player. I wanted him to hurt like I hurt. I mean if he hadn't brainwashed me with United when I was younger, I might have been a City fan, and then I could watch Colin Bell and sit down in the seats for 20p instead of witnessing Ted 'What's-that-round-thing-called' MacDougall and paying 25p to have my ribs crushed against a whitewashed wall.

Come Christmas we'd only won five games, we were bottom of the league and the unthinkable was facing the glorious Reds. Then suddenly Frank O'Farrell was sacked after we'd lost 5–0 to Crystal Place, who were struggling themselves. Tommy Docherty was announced as the new boss. He'd been managing Scotland and steered them to the World Cup finals in West Germany; now we hoped he'd make some good buys and steer United to safety and onward to triumph. But the bad news got worse when we discovered that George Best had been transfer listed by O'Farrell and then had resigned.

It was the blackest day I can remember since the Beatles split up, it was as if someone had died. George Best had carried us through the bleakest days of our childhood, the glamour boy for the girls, an idol for us and the match-winner for everyone. He'd always been there, our role model transporting all our hopes and dreams in every mazey dribble. He gave us a sheen and aura of glamour that other clubs lacked. I'd seen Best win matches on his own at United. He'd salvage victory from defeat with a couple of moments of brilliance. Six goals against Northampton Town after a long suspension and defences from Liverpool to Lisbon left in tatters by the greatest feet to ever grace a football field. He'd had his times of unpredictable behaviour before, but he couldn't ever leave us, not for good. To us George Best was United and when we sang 'We all live in a Georgie Best World' to the tune of the Beatles' *Yellow Submarine*, we were proud that there was only one player in the history of football like him and he was ours. We all knew, even back in 1968, when watching George Best, that we would never see his like again. Without him Old Trafford would be a sad and gloomy place.

Docherty was known to be ruthless as a manager, and it was obvious to all us United fans, young and old, that his first job was to clear out the old guard and any players he didn't fancy. He had built a reputation for being hard at Chelsea in the mid-sixties, when they were, alongside Manchester City, the fittest team in the league. That Chelsea team were ten years ahead of their time – a team full of running and stamina. They never stopped for the full 90 minutes, with great movement off the ball, but most of all they were a team who fought tooth and nail, and it was this battling mentality Docherty brought to Old Trafford

United drew with Leeds two days before Christmas. The chant throughout the game was 'We all fuckin' hate Leeds', which though not overtly imaginative, at the time certainly summed it up. It's a chant and tradition which is upheld to this day by many a United fan. Leeds were a good side and not averse to getting stuck in but United matched them foul for foul and kick for kick, and in between played the better football. MacDougall scored for United and Leeds had to come out and attack, with United pushing for a second and tragically unlucky not to get it. The game seemed to drag on, we waited for the final whistle to blow with even Mickey Riordan stopping until the end. With a minute left Leeds scored thanks to their record signing Allan Clarke, possibly the most hated of the Leeds players besides Billy Bremner. We couldn't believe it; I thought I was going to be sick.

'What about Sadler, he's playing like a crock and so are Charlton and Tony Dunne,' said Gerard Murray, the best manager United never had. So if he could see it why couldn't Tommy Docherty. United were second from the bottom. In the press Tommy Docherty joked that, 'United can only go up, if we get any lower we'll fall off the pools coupon.' We weren't laughing.

Docherty spent money. George Graham from Arsenal's double-winning side came in for £120,000 and another Scot, Alex Forsyth, a full-back from Partick Thistle, was bought for £100,000. Things got worse with United continuing to lose games and then Sammy McIlroy, touted as the new George Best, was so badly injured in a car crash that the fear was he'd never play again. More players were bought. The big signing was Lou Macari from Celtic for £200,000, then yet another

Scot, Jim Holton, a lumbering giant of a centre-half bought in from Shrewsbury Town. United were MacUnited with only full-back Tony Young, Bobby Charlton and Alex Stepney in the team who were English.

United fought their way back from the brink with our tartan army and it wasn't always pretty to watch. Certainly Macari had a touch of quality and class about him which was more than we could say for George Graham, who looked as if he was just watching the game. 'Oi, Graham you jock twat, you can join in if you want' is one of the more memorable assessments of his contribution. Jim Holton was a battler and Forsyth had a great shot from set pieces, even though he was never pacey in the way that Tony Dunne had been at his best, or for that matter a great defensive full-back.

United performed a feat of escapology worthy of Houdini with a string of decent results at the end of the season, having flogged MacDougall off to West Ham for £150,000, and not before time as far as we United fans were concerned.

Bobby Charlton retired at the end of the season, going to Preston North End, taking with him David Sadler and, via Southampton, Francis Burns. Middlesbrough took Nobby Stiles, and Tony Dunne, possibly the best United full-back until Albiston, went, prematurely many of us felt, to Bolton Wanderers.

That year the old guard disappeared from Old Trafford, United finished eighteenth in the league, and St Alphonsus won the Stretford East league. One Terence Christian, would-be footballer and junior reporter, moved from one side of Old Trafford to the other and prepared for a dreaded liaison with a posh grammar school in Whalley Range. Things were never quite the same again.

10

School of Hard Knocks

That summer of 1973 in between schools was, thankfully, a long one. We huddled together that holiday for comfort, knowing we were all off to different schools, no longer there to watch out for each other or the Kevin Learys of the world. There'd be 105 lads in the year at the new Catholic grammar school. They had a first team and second team, all I could think about was whether I'd make the first team.

'No! Let's not play cricket, let's play football.' I suggested this every day as we gathered in the park. Practice makes perfect, keep myself sharp for a new season at a new club. When I went to the shop clutching a list and a big empty shopping bag for my mam I'd run there and, straining with the weight of purchases, jog home. If I went to get a paper and cigarettes or to the bookies to put a bet on for my dad, I'd run. I wasn't James Martin, I couldn't be George Best, but in my mind I could run all day and tackle and pass. I could be Nobby Stiles, and surely going to school with a bunch of what I thought would be posh kids, I'd be straight in the first team, no worries.

It was a cruel trick the Catholic school system played on us back then. We went to co-ed primary schools until we were 11 when of course girls got on our nerves; and then as soon as we started to take an interest in them around 12, we found ourselves unceremoniously segregated from them. True, the novelty of being in an all-lads school at the age of 11 proved to be interesting for the first term, but after that it was sheer hell.

I felt a genuine and profound sadness about leaving my old primary school. It wasn't just a case of moving up a year, everything would be different. Kids don't like change, and derive comfort from routine and familiarity. As Old Trafford lads we all had too much in common with each other to adapt well to strangers and people with different upbringings from ours. We were conservative with a small 'c', with a set of values and a way about us that could easily be misinterpreted by outsiders. I suppose in some respects we were hard to get along with.

The grammar school I was going to took pupils from all over the Greater Manchester area. From as far south of the city centre as Wilmslow and Macclesfield, as far north as Saddleworth, and Widnes and Glossop, west and east. It was a huge melting pot of kids from different backgrounds, with Lancashire, Derbyshire and Cheshire accents mixing with north and south Mancunian. Sons of doctors, dentists and lawyers mixing with sons of lorry drivers and labourers. It was a great ideal, but from the first day it was nine times out of ten a case of us and them.

You see it's all very well believing in equal opportunities when you haven't got it shoved down your throat every day. The headmaster told us how privileged and lucky we were to go to an educational establishment such as this and that we had this chance to knuckle down and better ourselves, improve ourselves. He told us that if we didn't, we'd end up failures, working in factories or on building sites. Well, when Mam talked about bettering ourselves, she'd never referred to my father, who was an unskilled worker, as a failure, but here was a school doing just that.

The place aspired to the English public school system, and brought with it a heavy burden of Catholicism which dogged our every step through its dusty yards and corridors. Imagine *Goodbye Mr Chips* meets *Portrait of the Artist as a Young Man*, and it would begin to paint a backdrop of the type of school it was. Every morning in class we were told 'how lucky you boys are'; in our four periods of religion we'd be told how unworthy we were; and when homework wasn't up to scratch and attention flitted across dark cloudy skies through a classroom window, we'd be pulled up short and asked, 'Do you want to end up spending the rest of your life digging the road like some navvy?' Digging the road, factories, manual labour, equals … failure – that was the message being pumped into my 11-year-old brain. It took me all of a week to loathe the school and dislike anyone who liked it.

It's a shock to go from being in a well-established pecking order, like the top year at a primary school, into a school where you are in the youngest year and nobody bar three other pupils knows you. Reputations have to be built from scratch. People misunderstood all my little ways. I'd spent years perfecting the Gerard Murray 'show me' look, which many pupils and teachers misconstrued as being cocky. And I was loathe to change to fit in with a different view of the world to the one I'd grown up with.

The first day as we assembled in the yard, several long-haired second years baited us, three of them picking on me as I was amongst the smallest kids in the year. 'Oi turd.' This mystified me as I'd been called a lot of things in my life, but never heard the word turd. On the way to class I asked what a turd was. 'It's a piece of shit.'

At break-time: 'Oi it's that turd again, the one that looks like a chink.' The same group of second years were gathered in the toilets grinning and spitting on the floor. Two of them were big, and I do mean big for their age, but it was the stocky one, only two or three inches taller than me, who, as is ever the case, had the most to say. It was him I addressed.

'I'll see you later, it stinks of shit in here.'

As I proudly stepped to walk away the smaller one spat on the back of my blazer.

'Right, me and you after school tonight, I'm gonna kick your head in.'

I could see he wasn't comfortable with the idea; he grinned and started joking with his friends. 'Should we start the fight like this then?' He screwed up his eyes and holding his hands together, as in a Chinese greeting, bowed and said, 'Ah so.'

'Yeah do that and I'll just kick you in the face.' I wanted to kill him. I wasn't a bad-tempered kid as such, just unforgiving – still am. I'd been at a new school for two hours and I was already lined up to fight a second-year pupil outside the school gates at four o'clock. The word spread like wild fire. Lads in the fourth year came up to me at lunchtime.

'Are you the turd who's having a fight with Bertie Mulhearn?'

'I'm not a turd and it won't be a fight, it'll be a massacre.'

They seemed to find this funny. 'Well you want to watch out for him, he plays for the rugby team.'

This meant nothing to me – it was like watch out for him he's got a new Chopper bike. If they'd said he did karate or boxing or was known to bite during a fight it would have meant something, but I'd fought bigger kids. The whole afternoon everyone was saying how stupid I was having a fight with a second-year and doubts began to creep in. The rugby team trained with weights and were strong, someone's brother in the second year had a fight with this kid and had been beaten up, blah, blah.

I'd felt the pre-fight fear before, the tightness in your stomach, the shakiness which you try to hide from your voice as you spout brave words, the light-headed adrenaline rush. You have to launch yourself at your opponent, like jumping into a cold swimming pool. Never test the water with your toe, because doubt creeps in and then your finished. I fought the fight mentally all afternoon, at times building my opponent up into a cross between Mohammed Ali, Bruce Lee and Jimmy Millar. Four o'clock couldn't come quickly enough.

The whole school seemed to have turned out. I felt my legs shaking as I took my blazer off and laid it on my new briefcase. He seemed smaller, more annoying, but unsure as he stood there grinning, surrounded by his mates on what was to be our pavement arena. He couldn't win: if he beat me, so what, he was a second-year; if he lost, well he'd be mocked, beaten up by a turd. I'd had enough. I just launched into him landing with three or four good punches before I really opened my eyes to the situation. He backed away as if he was running. Then he started hitting me and he hit hard. My eyes watered and I felt our heads clash, my nose went numb. We closed and I grabbed his hair, swinging wild punches with my left hand, but couldn't seem to get any real weight behind them. Suddenly an irresistible force grabbed me and I was pulled back, my feet leaving the ground.

'What the bloody hell do you think you lads are doing?'

It was Mr Robinson, a maths teacher who was on bus stop duty that evening. He'd seen the crowds and had come over to stop it. He asked our names and forms and made us shake hands.

Inside I was burning up. Bertie Mulhearn was tougher than I thought but I felt the fight was about to swing back my way when it was stopped. I'd been hit but there was no pain, just a strange, elated feeling as all the day's tension evaporated. Satisfied that the fight was over Mr Robinson wandered off, no doubt thinking boys will be boys. I suddenly became surrounded by willing cornermen, all third and fourth-years. 'You were having him when it was stopped!' 'He's making out to everyone he had you, you're not going to let him get away with that are you.'

'No I'm bloody well not.' I ran towards where he was walking away, screaming his surname – he turned just as my foot kicked heavily into the side of his knee and my fist smashed into his face. He flailed weakly as I set about him; he'd thought it was all over, but not me. All day had been a mental battle with fear, now it was fun – the blood pounded in my ears and the adrenaline gave me extra strength. We came to grips and he was strong, maybe stronger than me, but he was just defending himself. I knew he wanted to stop, I'd only just started. As I held his neck and went to kick him for the second time in the face, I felt my ear tugged almost from the side of my head. It was Mr Robinson again.

'This is your final warning, if I find you two fighting again I'll have you up to the headmaster's office tomorrow, and you lot go home, all the excitement's over. Now shake hands.'

I was still frustrated – I knew he'd try and claim a draw, but he'd been beaten. I smiled, with my new grey jumper torn at the neck and my nose numb with a dull eye-watering ache that smelt like sharp metal, I gathered my belongings and headed off to walk the two miles home. In my narrow world I'd succeeded that day, I'd bought myself some time and some respect at a new school, but my weary thoughts reminded me what the headmaster had told us that day: 'We must start as we mean to go on.'

By the end of my first week at school I'd had four fights and the dubious privilege of being one of the first two boys in our year to be sent to the prefect of discipline; the other was the boy I'd been fighting.

★

Father Nolan was a six-foot-tall solidly built Jesuit priest who seemed to float silently around the yard in a huge black cape that reached the floor. The white dog-collar at his throat signalled that his wrath, when it descended upon, was of the Old Testament variety, not that liberal, wishy-washy, forgiveness-and-love Jesus bloke. An eye for an eye and a tooth for a tooth was the gospel in the confines of his frosted-glass office where he administered punishment on the wicked with an 18-inch-thick leather strap with a split going halfway through it. All the pain was in the first strike on each hand, like they'd been burnt with something right from the tip of the middle finger to the wrist. He'd stretch your palm out tight and any movement resulting in an extra whack. Three on each hand and the pain was bordering on the unbearable and lasted for hours. The perversity of it was we had to say 'Thank you Father' afterwards.

'Thank you, I'm not worthy, son of a failure, disobeyer of rules. Fuck you Father and your tight-arsed snobby school and all the scabby two-faced sly scheming middle-class spiritless twats that attend it with their tanned legs from their summer holidays abroad and their Kevin Keegan boots with the screw-on studs and giggling excitedly like schoolgirls about learning Latin and their state-of-the-art pencil cases with the full set of felt-tip pens protractors rulers and rubbers and their clever fathers doing their homework for them picking them up in shiny cars after school.'

'Father, how come at this school we have to learn Latin yet we don't do woodwork or metalwork, like some of my mates at secondary modern do?'

I knew asking this question was a golden goad. Father Doyle was a rulebook man with a sadistic streak when it came to ridiculing pupils. I had been a bit annoyed at learning how *Puella fundat lacrimam* or *Nauta amat puellam* when my mates in Old Trafford at the secondary modern were making coffee tables and baseball bats and taking them home.

'Christian, what's the name of this school?'

'St Bede's, Father.'

'What's the name of this school Christian?'

'Er … St Bede's Catholic School for Boys, Father.'

'No … what's the name of this school.'

'Errr …'

'I think the word you are missing is "grammar". "St Bede's Catholic Grammar School". The word grammar explains it all. At this establishment we are in the business of teaching young boys such as yourself grammarian subjects like English and Latin so that you may go on to university. We are not, Christian, in the business of churning out blacksmiths and joiners.'

My face went red as the laughter started. It was bad form not to laugh when the teacher was singling someone out for ridicule and the teachers encouraged it and thus encouraged the whole bullying mentality of the school. I hated them and their stuck-up ways and patronizing view of the working man. 'Priests work too you know, Christian.' If it was so obvious why did they have to say it. You never hear a docker, road-sweeper or miner emphasise the fact he or she is a worker. 'Oh a coal-miner is a worker too you know.'

My dad always hated his various jobs from rivet-heater and spot-welder to navvy (on every one of our birth certificates my dad has a different occupation). My mother a school dinner-lady, hardly a great topic of conversation, but she was very intelligent, like my dad. But the opportunities for them, their class, their ethnic origin, were always lacking. Nobody was as honest, hardworking and self-sacrificing as my parents, yet certain types of people, invariably ones with money, thought they could look down their noses and sneer at them. When my dad got his job at Esso in Trafford Park, the foreman told him he didn't like Irish men, but he could have the job anyway. The gall of it: a kind of, 'Oi, Paddy, want to do something menial for a living? Then eat this shit sandwich first.'

At night, lying in bed, I'd secretly wish my parents hadn't sent me to grammar school. The school wanted us to become middle-class and conform to their way of seeing the world. The random way in which punishments were doled out crushed our spirits slowly but inexorably. 'If any boy steps out of line I'll thrash him within an inch of his life.' This had been our welcome speech on the first day from our form master. Eleven years of age and bright, but I had no reason to believe that this wild-haired middle-aged man wouldn't do just as he'd threatened.

We had another teacher who would pick a scapegoat for the beginning of each lesson to be the one punished by detention or the prefect of discipline should any other boy step out of line. This teacher revelled in the fear the randomness of his choice sent through the classroom, wallowing in the sycophancy as certain boys painfully ingratiated themselves to become favourites and acolytes. Those teachers tried to stamp out any spark of individuality.

I used to wonder how educated people who came from working-class backgrounds could stand to work in a middle-class environment and get on. Were they traitors to their class, covering up their accents, origins and political beliefs? But I think now that you just slide into that middle-class world little by little, a square peg forced through a round hole. At first you live in two worlds, consciously holding on to your identity as you go down a new road ... and one day you're there, coming out with all the same trite and anodyne opinions and all you've learned is how to take the blows and keep your mouth shut. Yet deep inside you scream rebellion.

11

Pride and Prejudice

I was acting the cocky little bastard at school because I'd had more fights than anyone else in our year, and now I was a target for anyone trying to get a reputation. There's nothing as good and completely screwed up as an all-lads school except for the lads who go there. 'Start as you mean to go on.' The head-master's words certainly carried weight in my young mind. I couldn't spend everyday acting as cock of the year; I didn't have the ability, and I didn't want to have to hang out with Peter Hodgson, the hardest lad in our year, even though he was a decent bloke – he'd attracted a coterie of sycophants and bullies.

This was the big world now, and I knew that decisions taken here would genuinely effect the rest of my life, so I tried to be just another pupil. But violence was endemic at an all-boys' school, especially one with teachers that encouraged a bullying mentality by using it to keep discipline in the classroom. It was also an era of the most fashionable violence ever. It was the time of kung fu films and football hooliganism. In Old Trafford kids were making rice flails as used by Bruce Lee in the film *The Big Boss*.

Football violence had always been there, but now it was

135

being noticed more and reported thoroughly. It was the era of the boot-boy and the 18-hole cherry-red Doc Marten, which many lads wore to school with their dark-blue blazers and a United scarf around their necks. In the youth clubs kids wore black barathea blazers and talked about Richard Allen books like *Skinhead* and *Suedehead*, which revelled in violence, racism, and under-age sex. At school everyone read those Richard Allen books, even the well-to-do kids from suburban Stockport wanted to be terrace terrors.

Porn magazines were kept in briefcases – kids at this new school of mine seemed to have money to burn. It was porn magazines which led to the first expulsion in our school. Any lost property was handed in to the prefect of discipline, Father Nolan, the uncompromising Jesuit with the thick leather strap. Poor old Robert Piggot had only been at the school for a couple of months when he lost his bag. Father Nolan opened it to find out the name and form of its owner only to discover amongst the Geography and French homework a ten-pack of Player's No. 6 and half a dozen hardcore porn mags, which involved various four-legged friends as well as gratuitous sex. Funny how an 11-year-old was sent on his way so quickly for showing a healthy interest (ahem) in the female form (and zoology), yet later in school pupils who threw metal chairs at and assaulted teachers and each other were merely suspended.

It was ridiculous really: lads who'd be picked up from school by their mothers in posh cars and driven back to leafy suburbia aspired to be football hooligans. They became the first kids to start smoking cigarettes and later marijuana, because at the end of the day they could afford it all. Designer violence and designer vice, all so reassuringly consumer oriented. No matter how hard I tried I never fitted in at that school and the warning signs were all there in that first week.

All I had in common with many of them was my devotion to Manchester United.

'OK, today I'd like you to just relax and write me a story about how you spent your summer holidays and where you went.'

Father Richards, our English teacher, read out the best stories; one lad, the son of a doctor had been to Canada for four weeks, most had been to Spain or France. Me, well I'd been to United's two opening games of the season at home – a dull 1–0 victory over Stoke City and a scrappy 2–1 win against QPR. I'd noted in my story that although I liked our new centre-half Jim Holton, I wasn't overly enamoured of ex-Arsenal player George Graham, who was over the hill and seemed like he was never trying, strolling around the pitch. Nor was I struck with our new Irish player Gerry Daly who seemed to dash about a lot. This was not a team that was going to win the championship, although we felt they'd do much better once Ian Storey Moore and Brian Kidd got back in the side.

Father Richards wrote at the bottom of my essay, 'Quite Good, but this is what United did in the summer, not what you did.' Which kind of missed the point: the reason I loved United was that other than their results and dabblings in the transfer market, everything else in my life stayed pretty much the same.

Living where I lived in Old Trafford, going to grammar school meant you were a pouff. I would walk two miles home from school in my blazer that was big enough to fit Giant Haystacks, a school-tie and carrying a briefcase loaded down with textbooks needed in order to do my homework. 'Oi, give us a kiss and I'll carry your handbag' was just one of the many taunts I'd suffer from kids who a year earlier knew better. One of the school's many well-thought-out and useful rules: you must keep on full school uniform after school, even when walking home after football practice through Moss Side in the dark.

On a regular day, it'd be quarter to five by the time I'd got home. Soon after we'd have tea and then my mother gave out the chores. I had to wash up three nights a week, and in a household of seven people that ends up being a lot of washing up. I'd watch some TV, do my homework and go to bed. I was effectively cut off. On football practice nights of a Thursday it would be gone six o'clock by the time my aching limbs humped two bags all the way home. Life was turning into a drudge for me.

Our house seemed always too noisy and crowded. There was nowhere really to do my homework, except in the kitchen after I'd washed up, but it was always cold. I was a daydreamer. I dreamt that I'd have my own bedroom and a bike so I could cycle to school every day; a paper-round so I didn't have to mither blokes to mind their cars and then tip up most of it to the older lads for the privilege of being allowed to operate on 'their patch'. All of this would have been bearable had United been having a decent season or if my dreams of becoming a footballer had seemed any nearer to fulfilment, but nothing could have been further from the truth.

United were suffering. Tommy Docherty had cleared out the old guard, we were beaten away from home consistently and at Old Trafford after the scrappy wins I'd witnessed, we then lost to Leicester City, despite a rare goal by Martin Buchan and the reappearance (though short-lived) from long-term injury of Ian Storey-Moore. The school team was too competitive and too hard to get into. These so-called posh kids could really play and I found myself struggling to hold a place as substitute on the second team, until I wearied of Thursday night practice and gave up my dream. After all if I couldn't hold down a place in the school second team I'd have no chance of playing for Man. United.

It had all gone horribly wrong for me. I'd fancied myself for

a while as a hard-tackling midfield dynamo, but ended up playing full-back. At half-time we'd get the team talk off a Latin
teacher who looked after the second team and refereed our
home matches. Kick it up and chase it – great tactics, the epitome of the English game.

After swearing and aiming a kick against a kid with dark
curly hair from Stand Grammar, I was sent off by our team
coach after accusing him of pumping his gas at the self-service
stand. The fact that my nose was the victim of this other lad's
elbow and flowed profusely with blood didn't seem to matter.
Not only did he send me off, he then went and put me in
detention on the following Monday night with an essay title,
'A Good Sportsman Never Loses His Temper or Makes
Profane Remarks', or something of that kind.

Detention, now that was another great idea schools like
mine had. First you have a school bordering the roughest areas
in south Manchester and a rather inaccessible one at that. There
are pupils who travel in every day from as far away as Buxton
and New Mills, two bus rides and a train journey. So as a
punishment on a dark winter's night you put them in detention until 5pm and then say, 'Go on, get off home in the dark
now little 11-year-old, there's a fair chance you'll make it
unscathed.'

Competition is what the school prized most of all: compete
with each other, compete with other schools. This is fine if it's
contained and put into context, but this psychology ran
rampant through everything. It was like *Lord of the Flies* with
the lid just about kept on. Although there were only three
classes of 35 pupils in each year, each year's intake was divided
into four houses, all named after famous English saints. And
then, after the 75 per cent Irish majority in the school there
were Poles, Ukrainians, Italians. So, not only did we have inter-

class rivalry, social class rivalry, house rivalry, United–City rivalry, we also had ethnic purges.

Manchester Catholic schools always had a fair number of Polish kids. There was a sizeable Polish community in Manchester and about as far from the American stereotype of the dimwitted 'Polack' as you could get. These were the children and grandchildren of the air pilots who'd fled to England at the start of the Second World War to fight with the RAF. Although always affable enough, the majority of Polish kids were far too accomplished academically to be popular and we always thought they acted as if they were better than the rest of us. Most of their parents had money and they were extremely clannish, attending Polish Catholic church and going to their Polish schools and piano lessons on Saturday.

If you called at the house of a Polish kid, you'd rarely be allowed through the door. The mother would open it and look you up and down through the crack, shut it in your face and call her son, who would come straight out, never once saying come in and have a cup of tea. Still, they were honest, clever kids and never brought shame to their parents or mischief to the school – which was as good a reason as I can think of for not particularly liking them at the time. Although looking back now at some of the kids they had to share their schooling with, no wonder they chose to be quarantined from their fellow Catholics.

So, our friends of Eastern European extraction would routinely be accused of being Jew-haters and Nazi collaborators, teacher's pets and stuck-up toffee-nosed nonces. When one Ukrainian kid in our class once pleaded that his grandfather, far from being a Nazi collaborator had in fact died in a concentration camp, one wag commented that he'd probably fallen off the watchtower when he was drunk.

We were a bunch of begrudging, berating devils with honours degrees in sarcasm and training for PhDs in being totally obnoxious and there wasn't a more sarcastic, mouthy, green-eyed little bollix of a monster than me. I was a horrible little misanthropic shit. Playing football, whether for the school second team or the house team it was the same attitude: only pass to your mates in the team or someone you didn't dislike (certainly narrowed the options down).

I remember giving a goal away in a particularly fiercely contested match against Bury Grammar because I dribbled the ball around my own keeper in the penalty area rather than leave him to pick it up, because he'd taken the mickey out of my new outsize Parka in school all week. I was so busy keeping the ball out of his hands that I didn't see one of the Bury Grammar forwards lurch in and toe-poke the ball from between my legs into our goal. The result of this action was that no one on our team would pass to me, which was a pity as I was playing as a striker in that particular match. Still, my philosophy was we'd lost the match but I'd won the argument. I was sixteen years of age at the time.

My favourite match playing for the second team was against William Hulme Grammar one Saturday morning – but it was nothing to do with our win. Manchester United had made an early exit from the FA Cup, losing 1–0 at home to Ipswich Town (that bogey team again), so the next Cup Saturday United had arranged a friendly with Glasgow Rangers. As we played the last half-hour of our own game that Saturday morning we noticed dozens of these Scottish guys in tartans and blue and white scarves gathering around the pitch to cheer us on. 'Come on you blues.' We won 5–2 and sheepishly dodged past the Scottish hordes drinking Longlife and McEwan's from cans, and it had only just gone eleven o'clock. The Rangers fans loved us because we played in blue but their allegiances might have changed had they known we were a Catholic school.

Tragedy prowled on the horizon. United were terrible and so was the news. That unhappy year 1974 brought the saddest of tidings: George Best had gone for good. It was unbelievable. It was like a death in the family, and none of us could quite believe it, though we felt it was in some ways inevitable. Sure he'd gone before and always returned, only this time we knew he'd never be back. United without Best was unthinkable. There was a profound sadness because even though we were just kids, he'd always been there, our role model transporting all our hopes and dreams in every mazey dribble, giving us that sheen of glamour that other clubs lacked.

I'd seen Best win matches on his own at United, salvage victory from defeat with a couple of moments of brilliance – as when he returned after suspension, amid rumours he was going for good, and scored six against Northampton Town in the FA Cup. Best was Manchester United to many of us.

That was my problem with Manchester City. I'd gone along to see them quite regularly, and though they were good, they were never the footballing side United were. They had good players who worked hard for each other but they never captured the imagination the way United did. Colin Bell could run all afternoon and Francis Lee could score 25 goals a season but they weren't George Best or Bobby Charlton. Cocky Londoner Rodney Marsh could beat three or four players, but he never had the pace to leave them floundering in his wake on their backsides the way Best did, and he didn't do it as often either.

Marsh had been bought as a crowd-pleaser by City's ex-manager Malcolm Allison. His thinking was that City were consistently better than United, but United drew bigger crowds and the reason for that was George Best. Therefore if City bought an entertainer like Marsh, they'd start to attract the kind of crowds Allison felt their form and place in the league deserved. Alas it was naive to believe that Man. United fans only turned out to see Best and even more naive to imagine that Rodney Marsh could ever rival Best.

United had an aura, a history, a glory that other clubs could never approach, no matter how many great teams and players they produced or bought. United were special, a one-off and undoubtedly the greatest story ever in British sport. United were honest and all-inclusive, and football was truth; while school and as far as I could tell, life, was full of exclusion and cheating two-faced arse-licking bastards. And so what if our generation was queuing and spending Saturday afternoons on bleak terraces watching Paul Edwards instead of Duncan Edwards, it wouldn't always be the case. There was always the next game, the next season and, all too often at United, the constant rumour that lurking between the tuppenny-sheet programmes at reserve games was the next George Best.

12

A Test of Faith

Bless me Father for I have sinned, it has been six weeks since my last confession and these are my sins: I have been telling lies, I have been disobedient, I have been fighting, I have been stealing, I have been envious and I'm not sure if it's a sin, but I might not believe in God that much.

Hell had no fury like a man watching United collapse. My faith was waning as I saw United sweat and huff and puff, but there was no quality, no flow about the game. United were in disarray, totally demoralized. Alex Stepney took a couple of penalties and scored. A goalkeeper taking penalties, I ask you. Brian Greenhoff emerged from the reserves and youth team to become a United hero for his battling displays. Stewart Houston signed from Brentford, another Scot, surprise surprise. Sammy McIlroy came back into the side after his long injury, but never recaptured that devastating pace he'd had as a youngster. As the season dragged ever onwards, it felt as if Best hadn't played for United for years, and deep down I was glad he wouldn't be in a team that played football like this.

Hemmings was a flame-haired lad in our class, distinguished by being a Liverpool fan. Every school must have one I suppose, unfortunately for this carrot-topped misfit, he also had a very high-pitched voice like his hero Emlyn Hughes (and was a right moaner like him too). So we obligingly nicknamed him Castro, not after the Cuban dictator, but because his voice sounded to us like he'd had his bollocks chopped off.

'United are going down, they're rubbish, Liverpool are miles better, heh, heh. Bill Shankly says …'

'Bollocks to Bill Shankly you squeaky-voiced castrated Scouse-loving prat; Liverpool are the most over-rated, over-hyped cheating, time-wasting, diving and moaning team in the league. Emlyn Hughes is nowhere near as good as Martin Buchan, at least Buchan doesn't sound like he's had his knob chopped off when he's interviewed, and Macari's miles better than that curly permed ponce Keegan.' We believed it too: how dare Liverpool, just because they won more matches through their cheating and dishonest ways, think they were better than United who were just having a spot of bad luck.

City were having a fairly indifferent season too, but United were having a nightmare. Don't get me wrong, nobody was slaughtering us – we lost the first game of the season at home to Arsenal 3–0 and that was our heaviest defeat. Most of the games we lost were 1–0 and 2–1; we just didn't have the rub of the green and that's often more worrying.

It was a Wednesday night when United played City at Maine Road that season, and it was the first time I felt frightened for my life at a football match. I sat amongst City fans on the wooden ruler that was described as seating in the Platt Lane End, worrying about homework I hadn't done and about getting home before it got too late. The crowd were howling around me, with United fans in every part of the ground mixed in with City fans. It was war on the pitch with career-ending tackles flying in and then a massive punch-up between Mike Doyle, who must have been over six-foot tall and Lou Macari who was about five-foot six.

The referee had sent both players off but they refused to leave the field. The crowd were going mad and the violence on the pitch only intensified the atmosphere in the stands. The United fans goaded the City fans with chants of 'Wolves' and 'Derek Dougan', referring to City's Wembley demise in the League Cup Final ten days earlier, 2–1 to Wolverhampton Wanderers. Chants of 'You're going home by fuckin' ambulance' and 'City aggro / United aggro' rang around the damp night air. I wished I'd stayed at home. I'd lied and said there were lots of us going including my mate's older brothers; in fact I was there alone with a ticket I'd bought at school. All around there was violence and mayhem – ructions in the crowd, feet flying in and coins and bottles being thrown. Every time a surge went through the massed crowd a space would open up, the move away from the victim being kicked to the ground causing the crowd to crush sideways one minute, forwards the next.

The referee took both teams off the field and when they re-emerged neither Doyle nor Macari were present. I watched for a further five minutes and then headed through the cold wet night for the exit. I ran all the way through the back streets to Great Western Street to get the bus home, relieved when it turned up and comforted by the warmth of the smoky upstairs. I'd lied to go to this match and there was something about it that seemed alien. Violence in Richard Allen's books had a coolness about it but here in the cheap seats at Maine Road it exuded a terrifying darkness that sent a chill to the centre of my being. The noise of the boots and fists striking, the cold merciless fury of one group of strangers toward another, the weight of the bodies as they fell and struggled to get up again against the flailing feet and fists. I got home to find that the match had finished 0–0.

My mother heard about the trouble. No more night

matches for me. I looked at my unopened schoolbag with its homework lying undone and my football gear still wet and muddy from that afternoon's games lesson: United were in trouble, and so was I. In bed that night I prayed for George Best to come back, for the resurrection of Ian Storey Moore and for United to win and win well, and decided I'd hand in the wrong exercise books the following day and act daft, a gift I possessed in abundance.

The revival started at Chelsea, where Jim McCalliog, who United had just signed from Wolves (yet another Scot), made his debut and we won 3–1. Things were desperate, but none of us believed that Manchester United could go down into the second division. Governments would topple, royal houses fall, continents shift and Jesus rise again from the dead, but United were a permanent fixture in the first division just like the pyramids were a permanent fixture in Egypt. And just as the pyramids defined that country, so Manchester United defined first division football; it just wouldn't be right without United in the first division.

The thing is we all honestly believed United were better than any other side. We knew Willie Morgan was better than Steve Heighway, that Brian Kidd was better than Malcolm MacDonald, Lou Macari better than Kevin Keegan, it was just bad luck really. This team languishing at the bottom should really have been at the top. Well, I mean we'd drawn with Liverpool, Derby County and Leeds when we were playing crap and they were the top teams.

Chelsea weren't exactly the star-studded world beaters they'd been a couple of years previously, but beating them 3–1 at Stamford Bridge was good form. A draw with highly rated Burnley at Old Trafford in a six-goal thriller followed, with goals from McIlroy, a second from Alex Forsyth's superbly executed free-kick which blasted through Burnley's wall, and a third from Jim Holton. Our win against Norwich away 2–0 virtually condemned them to division two; and a particularly passionate 1–0 victory against Newcastle courtesy of a McCalliog goal at Old Trafford made it look like we'd be staying up in style. United were starting to play a bit as well as fight. The Scots in the team were all battlers and then we had the Irish faction with Daly and McIlroy; we were Mac United and Tommy Docherty's tartan army.

The Stretford End were in full voice, the terraces a moving mosaic of red, white and black scarves and the atmosphere crackling with electricity as United strode out to take on Everton on that Easter Bank Holiday Monday. The last four games read W-3, D-1: United were on a roll and everybody turned up for the games now as a sort of Easter duty, it was collective prayer. You would think it was a European final at every home game.

Everton had no answer to the relentless force that was United that day, with 50,000 willing them on to a 3–0 victory. Just four more decent results and United would escape the unthinkable.

I jumped for joy when McCalliog slotted his second goal of the game, throwing half a Wagon Wheel on to the pitch in tribute. 'We're going up the league,' the Stretford End chorused and as the blue Scousers chased shadows and Macari fairly ripped them apart. 'Six-foot two, eyes of blue, big Jim Holton's after you,' we sang, 'Greenhoff for England'; it was a celebration at Old Trafford that afternoon. So far United had beaten five of the teams who finished in the top eight that season. We couldn't go down, it had all been a misunderstanding. If we started the season now we'd be in the top three at least and on this form we'd be sure to win something next year. There was no doubt in our young minds. We believed it. We were that daft!

Southampton away was our next game; the heat was on but United were in good form. It was a crucial four-pointer because three teams went down this year for the first time and United were second from the bottom, with Southampton and Birmingham City just above us. We knew we'd win this one. The City fans could shut up mocking us and Castro could take his squeaky-voiced opinions and shove them up his Shankly. We drew 1–1. I felt gutted sitting in the kitchen, listening to the radio. Jim McCalliog had scored with a penalty, but all United's pressure had come to nothing.

A mere eight days after the drubbing at Old Trafford, Everton again, this time an evening match at Goodison Park. Surely this would be the one. We talked about nothing else, felt the nerves jangling all day, 'we'll beat them, we're on a roll'. On the Sunday after the Southampton match I'd gone to the back of church after Mass, put five pence in the box, lit a candle for United against Everton and followed it all up with some major prayer power aimed at St Jude, the patron saint of lost causes. The rest was all arithmetic, ifs, buts and maybes, and the discussion was like a convening of the pools panel; but basically we had to really win our remaining three games.

Another night in our cold kitchen, listening to live commentary from Goodison. We were unlucky and I have always hated Mick Lyons ever since he scored that goal, the goal that left my mind a jumble of mathematics and my stomach with a nauseating feeling like someone had tipped my flat Red earth upside down. Everton 1, United 0. I sat in disbelief, and then got a pen and paper out to work out the odds.

United had two games left and Norwich, Birmingham and Southampton only had one. Southampton were two points above United on 34 points, and Norwich three below on 29. Birmingham were on 35. Birmingham and Norwich played each other in their last game and Norwich had to win – unfortunately Birmingham were at home. Southampton were away to Everton. If United won both remaining fixtures and Southampton and Birmingham were to lose, United would stay up. And United's next game was against ... none other than Manchester City at Old Trafford.

The problem was how to get a ticket: to get one for the big games then, like United v. Leeds, Liverpool and City, you needed a set of tokens. These came in the back of first-team league match programmes and in a few reserve fixtures' teamsheets, which only cost two pence (it wasn't unusual to see up to 8,000 people at a reserve match just to get the special B-tokens). And then you'd stick them on a sheet, take them up to the ticket office, have a mark put through them, and get your ticket.

However, I'd stopped car minding. All the lads I'd done it with had moved on to shoplifting and other petty crime and I was fed up hanging around in the cold and wet. Instead I'd started going into town with my mates and hanging around Tib Street in the cold and wet. Either that or I was playing for the school second team, which meant I would only get home from distant away games at one o'clock, so there was just time to have some lunch and go straight to the match. This unfortunately meant I never had enough money every week to buy the match programme with its token, so I was short of the number required for a ticket and most of us were in the same boat.

Gerard Finucane was a solidly built, freckle-faced, ginger-haired 16-year-old. He helped out working on the turnstiles at Old Trafford for every home game and most of the reserve games. He stood sporting his Alun Evans-style bowl haircut outside the chippy, smoking a No. 6, holding court as ever on the goings on around United behind the scenes. He'd also tell us how he'd occasionally grab a few dozen spare tokens at the reserve games from the piles of unsold teamsheets. He prided himself on the fact he kept 15 full token sheets going at a time, mainly so he could get those scarce tickets for his Irish relatives when they'd occasionally come over to see a match. But he wasn't finished ...

'Anyway, we were dead busy, so Joe who was in charge asked me to count through the tickets and tidy up before we locked up and went up to see the match. There were quite a few late-comers that day straggling in and it was doing my head in. I kept saying, Can I go now Joe the match has been on for ages, I mean normally I'd be finished and up there watching by quarter-past three. In the end he says go on up, so I ran up the stairs and just as I got to where I could see the pitch McCalliog scored. I was screaming like a maniac jumping up and down grabbing people and they weren't moving – then suddenly this copper grabbed me and said, What do you think you're doing. It was only then I saw that I was the only one who was cheer-ing United's goal and then I noticed all these blokes in black and white scarves looking daggers at me: I was in the Newcastle end. Anyway this copper got us out of the way sharpish; if I hadn't been in such a hurry in the first place I would have noticed.'

We laughed at his story. Ged wasn't the type to make some-thing up to impress and he was absolutely fanatical about United, he'd have paid them to work there. When he first got the job he went round telling everyone like he'd won the pools and in a way he had, on all our behalfs.

Another scam Ged had going needed the help of his boss. When you handed in the token sheet with your money, the man at the ticket counter would mark it with a cross which went across the tokens to show the sheet had been used and you'd had your tickets. Ged's boss at the turnstiles, Joe, also worked on the ticket desk and every time Ged went up, he'd pretend to mark the sheets (in case anyone in the queue was watching) and give Ged his tickets. Then Ged would queue up again and get more, often as many as 20 or 30 tickets for the big games. Now Ged did have an extended family like all the Irish kids round our way, but not that extended: he'd sort us out a couple of tickets no problem, without asking for any reward – as a favour! Ged was a genuine local treasure.

Thanks to Ged we had our tickets for the United–City derby, but it was a bit pricey – the only tickets he could get us were 50p each in the United road end. So we were in the seats, but we were supposed to be accompanied by an adult. Ged said not to worry as they wouldn't really bother any of us there, especially not with an all-ticket match. It was worth it because this was the last home game of the season and the most impor-tant game United had been involved in since the FA Cup semi-final in 1970 when we were robbed by some shocking refereeing decisions in the third replay against Leeds.

At school all week the City fans tried to taunt us. City had spent two years in division two in 63/64 and 64/65; United hadn't been in division two since before the war. The City fans relished United going down, and although I used to quite admire City as a club, it always mystified me as to why their fans seemed unhealthily obsessed about United, regardless of which team was actually getting the better results or winning trophies. It was bitterness and jealousy.

In 1968 Manchester City won the League Championship for only the second time in their history, with United finish-ing two points behind them in second place, only to have that achievement overshadowed by United becoming the first English club to win the European Cup in the same year. When two years later City won the European Cup Winners Cup Final against the Polish side Gornik Zabzre, it wasn't even televised as it clashed with the replay of the FA Cup Final between Chelsea and Leeds United at Old Trafford. So in their most successful period City never got the praise and coverage they felt they deserved, whereas United whether winning or not were never out of the headlines.

I'd been to see City several times in recent years with David Lindsay and his friends from the flats in Brookes Bar, and although I'd enjoyed it as an afternoon out, it always seemed like they were a club without glamour, kind of fish-fingers to United's caviar. The atmosphere at City was somewhat depressing and the fans never really created the same kind of vibe as at Old Trafford. Even when the team were winning 3–0 at half time there'd always be someone moaning. It was and still is a ground full of people reminiscent of Harry Enfield's Old Gits.

There was never any wit from the terraces, just a passion for City and a depressing hatred for and burning obsession with United. City fans only seemed happy to me when they were moaning – so I would imagine their form in recent times has made the average City fan totally blissful. Even then with a decent side, City and Maine Road seemed like a team and a ground with one foot in the distant past. The pigeons on the pitch, the rosy-cheeked little boy mascot and the old lady with that annoying bell that she would ring to 'give the lads a lift'.

(Don't get me wrong, I don't usually mind eccentric things at football. I'll even forgive those pathetic inflatable bananas so loved by a few 'zany' fans some years back. It's all part of that depressing but forgivable type of 'wacky' mentality which thinks things like Gary Glitter or *Gladiators* are so crap they're good. We had it at United for a while with fans who loved – or pretended to love – Ralph Milne. But that bell belongs in the same deep and fiery pit of vengeance as the Sheffield

Wednesday band. I know various musical instruments at football matches aren't a crime, but don't you think they should be?)

When I used to watch City play at that time I thought the fans didn't appreciate what a good side they had and the fans weren't worthy of the team. Nowadays the team aren't worthy of the fans, but I suppose football clubs have a karma as well. On that fateful day, 27 April 1974, Manchester United met with their karma – his name was Denis Law.

Now, I could write a novella about Denis Law, but for the moment this'll do. Yes, George Best was our ultimate hero, but only because he was younger than Law and the type who dribbled around players. Law was a king amongst goalscorers. In front of goal his jumping and heading were the best I've witnessed for a player of his build. His sheer bravery, in those days when a lot of football was flying boots and elbows, fairly took your breath away. He'd stick his head in for a ball a foot off the ground amongst a ruck of defenders' boots kicking to clear, and the ball would flash into the goal. He had speed, tackling ability, skill and a first touch that would shame 90 per cent of today's internationals. But, towards the end of his time with United there were days when he seemed to lose touch with the game, unable to find his rhythm in a particular match. Having said that, he never gave up, and he would take any chance going.

I couldn't believe the tension inside me as I sat through that historic derby game. The teams were:

MANCHESTER UNITED – Stepney, Forsyth, Houston, Greenhoff, Holton, Buchan, Morgan, Macari, McIlroy, McCalliog, Daly; sub – Martin.
MANCHESTER CITY – Corrigan, Barrett, Donachie, Doyle, Booth, Oakes, Summerbee, Bell, Lee, Law, Tueart; sub – Henson.

In front of almost 60,000 fans, United looked good if a little edgy and as expected I suppose we pressed for most of the game. City had occasional threatening raids with Bell, Tueart and Lee linking up well. As a match it never really sparked, there was just too much at stake. United missed chances with clearances from Donachie and Barret foiling our attempts for a breakthrough. It had been United's problem all season: the lack of an out-and-out goalscorer. I honestly believe that had United scored a goal we'd have gone on to get three or four, but we seemed to be snatching at things and playing too hurriedly.

With about ten minutes left City had the ball in United's area, Stepney came out and the next thing, it was in United's net. The true horror unveiled itself as, in what seemed like slow motion, the City team ran towards the man whose razor instincts, for years worshipped on Old Trafford's terraces, turned away from the United goal; for once not celebrating and eyes downcast. 'Bloody hell, Denis Law … it's Denis Law.' Lee and Bell and other City players were converging in celebration but I could see Law: a shadow among the shades of Blue engulfing him, exposing his raw heart, a heart that we all knew was Red.

City were winning and United's players seemed completely deflated. The City fans were in seventh heaven. This was better, I suspected, for many of them than winning the League Championship, FA Cup and European Cup all rolled into one. We sat in our expensive seats and looked on glumly, tears invading our eyes as the City fans chanted 'You're going down'. There were shouts of abuse and several City fans who were sitting near us were being threatened by blokes as old as 50. This was a bad dream – I'd wake up and it would still be Friday night and everything would be fine. I realized how Denis Law must feel as he was immediately and mercifully substituted by City youngster Tony Henson.

United battled on for a few minutes, threatening an equalizer, but there were already one or two fans running around on the pitch near the Stretford End. Suddenly the United fans invaded the pitch en masse with around five minutes of the game to play, perhaps hoping to get the game abandoned and replayed. It wasn't so much hooliganism as a wish to express their love of United, who'd left it too late having battled so hard with little luck for at least half of the season. They'd be back next year, we knew that, and we promised ourselves we'd be back, we had to be, because we were United, rain or shine, second division or first.

On the streets of Old Trafford, even outside Mass the following morning, everyone seemed numb and shell-shocked. United were down. The fact City had beaten us didn't matter – had United beaten City 6–0 the result would have been academic, as Birmingham had beaten Norwich. No side can have felt as disappointed as United did: they were starting to play football, they weren't playing like relegation candidates, it wasn't right that they should go down. It was as if a huge black shroud had descended to cover the corpse of the United we'd grown up with and the usual detractors were queuing up to bury the body once and for all.

In school the following week there was tension. The City fans goaded us, bragging how they had a better team and how they'd sent United down. I said, 'Yeah City sent United down all right, Birmingham City.'

The season petered out for United with a 1–0 defeat away to Stoke. The FA Cup Final was coming up between Liverpool and Newcastle and the same weekend United bought a new striker for £200,000 from Hull City called Stuart Pearson. I have no doubt that had United bought Stuart Pearson a year earlier they wouldn't have gone down. Our defence and midfield were pretty good and deserving of at least a place in mid-table, but we couldn't put the ball in the net. The City fans still goaded us by flashing the *Manchester Evening News* headline of 'Stuart Who?' in our faces, and we did worry as to whether or not we'd just acquired a new Ted MacDougall.

As we watched Newcastle and Malcolm MacDonald demolished 3–0 by Liverpool in what must be one of the most one-sided Cup Finals of all time we were even more sure United shouldn't have gone down, because at least they'd have put up a fight. As for Liverpool and Leeds, well they'd better enjoy their success while they could because United would be back, they just had to be.

13

Changes

The truth about football fans is that they are allowed to be unbearable in victory and sour in defeat. For City fans this was their golden moment and to us Reds they were unbelievably annoying and goading. It was always the boys from Stockport, Gorton and that neck of the woods who claimed they supported City. They never tired of pouring all their young years of scorn on United and it was a supreme irritant.

For United fans the next season couldn't come quickly enough. Let the Reds escape the hellhole of mediocrity that was the second division and go straight up again, then we'd show City who the best team were. And as for Leeds United, they may well be champions, but they were only keeping the seat in Europe warm for United to get back and win the championship again. I was beginning to acquire some of our Tony's blind optimism.

Paul Hartnett was one of my best mates at grammar school and although he'd been at St Alphonsus with me for seven years I'd never really hung around with him then. He was loud and daft, a real-life Vic Reeves meets Robin Williams as Mork, with hair so blonde it was almost white. He was subject to an absolute fundamentalist fanaticism about Manchester United which continues both home and away to this very day. His parents like mine were Dubliners and he was a good, regular Mass-attending, occasional homework-doing working-class lad. And his biggest saving grace: he was one of the best thieves I've ever known.

Now don't get me wrong here, I'm not condoning criminal behaviour – I've never been into shoplifting or thievery myself. The majority of kids I've met who did that type of thing came from backgrounds with money or were always a bit spoilt by their mothers. But someone like Paul, who had the nerve to rob from big department stores, we admired; whereas the muggers and house burglars we saw as absolute vermin and poverty was never an excuse. House burglars invariably rob off poor people who've got nothing anyway, and to me and 99.9 per cent of working-class folk they are seen as lowlife scum – even in the prisons that's how they were looked upon at that time.

Back then when you were working class all you had was each other, and there was an unspoken code of honour with regard to what it was OK to steal and who from. And Paul, he was a master thief.

'Blimey Paul, this bedroom looks like John Menzies.' My admiration for his all-consuming kleptomania knew no bounds. Paul shrugged casually as I jealously eyed his bookshelves which were stacked with annuals and hundreds of brand-new paperback books. It wasn't as if Paul wasn't selective about his shoplifting. He was, as most of us at that time were, a huge fan of science fiction, fantasy and horror books, as well as Marvel comics, football annuals and magazines.

'Yeah that's why I haven't been doing that much homework. I'm on to the 'Swords Trilogy' by Michael Moorcock.'

To me his bedroom was Santa's grotto and the land of

plenty. Although Paul lived with his parents and sister in a terraced house, he had his own bedroom and his mother was naive to say the least (perhaps selectively blind) about how Paul had acquired such an extensive library. He had every single book available in both hardback (which he ordered especially and then thieved from Old Trafford library) and paperback written by Michael Moorcock; a full set of the Pan books of horror stories; Asimov books, Robert E. Heinlein, Brian Aldiss, Arthur C. Clarke, Ursula K. Le Guinn; and all stashed in alphabetical order, which told any casual observer that here was one avid science fiction reader whose spaceship had definitely come in.

'I nicked most of them from the precinct in Stretford and a few from the big John Menzies in town; well, Saturdays are boring now that there's no football on ... Here look at this.' He opened up a large suitcase crammed to the top with new glossy Marvel and DC American comics.

'Where'd you get those?'

'Well I got a paper-round, didn't I.'

A paper-round, everybody had a paper-round. The trouble was I didn't have a bike. Paul was lucky, his parents had splashed out thirty-odd quid buying him a brand new Chopper bike for passing his 11-plus. This meant a paper-round and a chance to steal all the latest American comics off the racks. No such bonus and productivity scheme existed in our house. I'd begged and pleaded for a bike, but to no avail: the cost was more than my dad earned in a week and if I had a bike then my younger brother and sister would demand one too. Although strictly speaking you had to be 13 to get a paper-round, one local newsagent would employ you when you were 12 as long as you had a bike and they had a vacancy.

I must have done the rounds of every newsagent looking for

a paper-round. There were no vacancies anywhere. Come the new football season it would go up to 35p to get into the Stretford End Paddock where all my mates went, and my pocket money was 20p a week. I needed that job.

Stephen White was going to Ireland for three weeks and had asked the owner of the newsagent if I could do his round for him while he was away visiting the relatives. He'd said yes.

'Did you tell him I haven't got a bike?'

'No I didn't, but if you go in early and tell him your bike's broken, he'll give you the easiest round, four streets all together: Leighton Road, Auburn road, Moreland Road and Reynolds road, all dead close to the shop.'

I staggered weighed down by my bag up the piss-soaked stairway to the fourteenth floor of Pickford Court – the only paper delivery there – then struggled with my overloaded bag towards the maisonettes on City Road. I couldn't believe anyone who lived this far, over a quarter of a mile away, would have their paper delivered from that paper-shop. I'd started my round at 6.45 in the morning, it was now gone eight o'clock and I was only just over halfway through. I still had to go home and get my schoolbag.

I tried to jog, imagining myself to be Alf Tupper out of the *Victor* comic-strip story 'Tough of the Track'. No Nike, Adidas or fancy pasta diets for Alf, who did umpteen jobs, lived off fish and chips and couldn't afford running shoes so drove some nails through an old pair of slippers or something like that, and won more gold medals than any of the posh kids or professional athletes twice his age. At least the weather was fairly fine.

I was bound to get in trouble at school for being late, and at our school, which didn't start until 9.30, that was a rarity amongst most pupils; but not in my case. I was more concerned with losing my paper-round and the grand sum of £1.15 that it paid. £1.15 for seven mornings a week and six evenings. My muscles ached, sweat drenched my school uniform and I used my tie to wipe it out of my eyes. I finished the round at five to nine: the paper-shop owner went ballistic.

'I've had people complaining already that they hadn't had their paper yet, what took you so long?'

'It's miles to walk and I haven't got a bike.'

The shop owner, a grey-haired decent old skin in his late fifties chuckled looking over his lowered spectacles.'

'You bloody daft ha'porth, why didn't you say?'

'Well I did tell your wife and she said we'll see.'

'Well you'll be late for school, so get off and I'll swap you with Gerard Sullivan for tomorrow.'

By the time I got home and picked up my bag for school I had 20 minutes to walk nearly two miles. I was on cloud nine as I strolled casually to school, mentally spending my £1.15 a week: I'd get a United yearbook, a new scarf, a couple of United badges, a Wrangler denim jacket, some patches to sew on it and I'd sneak off to some away games; hell, I'd even save up and buy a bike. I'd enjoy all the privileges of the working man.

The other paper lads, most of whom I had been at primary school with, took liberties I would never condone. While the newsagent was bundling the papers in order for our bags they'd be sweeping Milky Ways, Mars Bars, anything, into their bags. They'd take war comics and American Marvels off the rotating magazine racks. The more sexually aware amongst them rummaged for *Fiesta* or *True Detective* magazine, generally packing their paper bags with contraband.

On Saturday morning several houses would have comics delivered like *Victor* and the British editions of the Marvel comics like *The Avengers* and *Spiderman*. I'd take my time and the occasional bottle of milk off a doorstep and sit on a wall in the early sunshine drinking a pint of milk and reading the adventures of the Hulk and the Fantastic Four. This was the only perk of the job I'd allow myself. I didn't want to do the dirty on the newsagent who had employed me despite the fact I didn't have a bike and I was strictly speaking under age.

The school year finished and everyone was off, albeit not quite as early as Stephen White. It was a nervous summer as we discussed the merits of Lou Macari, what kind of season Sammy McIlroy would have, and how big a difference United's new £200,000 signing Stuart Pearson would make. Paul Hartnett was defiantly loud when he stated United would go straight up and Scotland, thanks to the number of United players in the squad, would undoubtedly win the World Cup. It mattered to some lads more than others.

Our mate Roddy Faherty for instance had weightier and more divine matters on his mind. He was the oldest son of six kids and was ruled by his mother with a rod of iron. She was a particularly devout Irish woman who believed strongly in hard work and going to Mass and had every room of their small terraced house decked with statues of the Infant of Prague, Our Lady in the grotto at Lourdes with a kneeling and praying St Bernadette, Sacred Hearts of Jesus, holy water containers, pictures of the Last Supper, all manner of saints and popes and crucifixions.

Roddy would often go to Mass every morning before going off to St Mary's secondary modern. I actually admired him for this. I'd always found church a comfort, if somewhat boring, and always wondered if it was possible to enjoy it and believe it at the same time. Mysteries abounded in the Catholic Church. Father, why does God kill little children with earthquakes and famine?' – 'Ah, it's a mystery.' Roddy was so busy with his mysteries he rarely had the time to play out with us. He was forever doing paper-rounds, milk-rounds, running errands and doing jobs for his mother and every old Irish biddy who lived in the neighbourhood. Despite his bulk and size, local kids would bully him. His mother wanted him to be a priest and campaigned furiously with the Bishop of Salford to have him admitted to a junior seminary to save him from the heathen excesses of St Mary's secondary modern.

I'd see Roddy in the library sometimes of a Saturday morning where we'd go to do our homework, like a lot of kids who had nowhere quiet at home to do it. We'd invariably get no work done, but spend the time swapping stories and talking about United and which girls we fancied. Roddy's only real pleasure was United, but all the money he made from his various jobs he'd invariably hand over to his mother, especially as his father had died recently. Also, she wouldn't allow him to go to football matches, with all the bad language, cigarette smoking and heathen hooligan capers.

So Roddy used to drop off enough money from his milk-round at Paul Hartnett's house, then tell his mother on the afternoon of the match that he was going to the library. He'd take his books to Paul's house around the corner, pick up his scarf, which he stored there and sneak off to see United with the rest of us, not putting his scarf on until he was several streets away. Man. United were Roddy's only escape and he probably needed and loved them more than any of us.

For United fans, that summer's World Cup was something of a consolation: most of them were on TV playing for Scotland in West Germany. The talk was of how United players were the backbone of what was undoubtedly the best Scotland team we'd ever seen. It was an extraordinary squad when you look at it now: Kenny Dalglish, Lou Macari, Martin Buchan, Joe Jordan, Billy Bremner, Jimmy Johnstone, Willie Morgan, Alex Forsyth, Stewart Houston, Jim Holton, David Hay, Eddie Gray, Denis Law, Peter Lorimer, David Harvey ...

England hadn't qualified for the World Cup, having fallen foul of Poland, but we weren't too disheartened: we all supported Scotland when they beat England at Hampden, 2–0 – well, there were no United players in the England side, and six in the Scotland squad. Come to that, besides Alex Stepney and Brian Greenhoff there were no English players in the United side.

In West Germany, Scotland had no luck. They beat Zaire 2–0, Denis Law making his last appearance ever in professional football. They then drew 0–0 with a very physical and lucky Brazil side (who'd also drawn 0–0 with Yugoslavia) and finally they played Yugoslavia, drawing 1–1 in a game which again the Scots would have won with the slightest bit of good fortune. In the end, Scotland didn't go through because they'd scored fewer goals against Zaire than the other two teams.

We all agreed that the best team in the tournament were Holland with Johann Cruyff, Johnny Rep, Neeskens and the rest playing a style the commentators described as total football. Unfortunately the Germans won the World Cup thanks to a dubious penalty and the biggest goalhanger of all time, Gerd Muller.

Nevertheless it was a comforting feeling for us United fans to know that six members of our team had played in the World Cup. We thought Scotland could have made the finals if it hadn't been for all those shit Leeds players like Bremner, Lorimer and Grey and Willie Donachie of City bottling it on the big occasion. Blimey, United nearly won the World Cup and would surely have no problems the following season in the English second division.

There was a sense of change pervading everything: it was like the Sixties were at last coming to an end and there was a certain nostalgic sadness permeating football. I can't remember a season of football with so much major upheaval as that of 74/75. Manchester United, Southampton and Norwich City down; Luton Town (with ex-United player Johnny Aston), Carlisle United and Middlesbrough (managed by Jack Charlton) up. The pitch invasions of the previous season, especially that at Old Trafford in the end-of-season derby, would be no more as the fences went up — the seeds of tragedy in our national game in years to come.

More changes and turmoil in the Charity Shield which kicked off in more ways than one. Bill Shankly sadly led out his beloved Liverpool for the last time before retiring, whereas Leeds were led out by Brian Clough. He'd replaced Don Revie who'd taken over as England manager after Alf Ramsey's dismissal. Liverpool v. Leeds is the sort of game where as neutrals we would want both teams to lose. Liverpool were beginning to look the business, especially with their second-half demolition of Newcastle in the FA Cup Final. Leeds were always a power in English football although rumours abounded about backhanders and corruption and we had all been witness at times to the cynicism of their football. Don't get me wrong, Leeds United had some great players, but should anyone other than a Leeds fan be asked to describe the style of their football, the word would be ... DIRTY.

Bill Shankly was a figure that even we as United fans secretly admired and loved. 'I'm not saying Liverpool are the greatest team in the world, but there's no one better,' was a typical Shankly soundbite. He was a football fan's football manager like Busby was, he never forgot his roots and knew that a football team meant a lot to the local community, especially the working man. His retirement was the end of an era, and I suppose it signalled to United fans that it was now OK to genuinely dislike Liverpool.

It was sad for Shankly but most entertaining for us as we

watched, on *Match of the Day*, Bremner and Keegan having a major punch-up and getting sent off during the 1–1 draw in the Charity Shield. This led to an unprecedented five-week suspension for both of them, which meant they'd miss more or less the first ten games of the season. Unfortunately United wouldn't be in a position to enjoy the benefits of this but we wished a curse on both their houses anyway.

United's season kicked off as we all expected with victory following victory. The opening day United played Leyton Orient at their Brisbane Road ground and swept them aside 2–0 with goals from Stewart Houston and Willie Morgan. United would be an irresistible force and an irrepressible attraction.

We used to meet up outside the chippy on Seymour Grove, impatient to get this season over with. Oxford bags and bad wedge shoes or Doc Martens and the most tasteless acrylic diamond-pattern jumpers one could imagine. The fashions and haircuts of the Seventies should be gathered from our memories, encased in a few hundred feet of concrete and then dumped in the deepest ocean trench, lest they emerge to infect innocent people in future generations. Or maybe we should just hand them out free to Newcastle and Leeds supporters.

We did very strange things back then, like spit on the ground every second word, walk with our legs sticking out sideways like trained chimps while we slumped our heads, and some kids even tied scarves around their wrists. I don't know whether we looked like the junior bootboys we hoped to or some out-of-sorts Neanderthal Bay City Rollers fans looking to give David Cassidy fans a good makeover. The thought of those Oxford bags and French pleat trousers with their forty-inch bottoms flapping around my ankles and having the nerve to brag about being the first to get some with turn-ups on horrifies me. For God's sake, we even bragged about designer tank-tops; and the less said about those horrible *Starsky and Hutch* style cardigans the better.

'Bloody hell lads, what have you come as,' was the kind of greeting we'd get in the ground from those old men who'd been going to United since the war and earlier. We'd settle in a good hour and a half before kick-off, behind a suitable crash barrier in the Paddock, only to have these pipe-smoking moaning old gits giving out behind us. Brian Greenhoff tries a speculative shot from 30 yards and these old blokes would start. 'Bloody hell Greenhoff what's that? If that had been Tommy Taylor he'd have broken the net from there.'

Every United player on the pitch would be compared unfavourably to a player from one of the golden eras. 'Blimey Buchan, Duncan Edwards could have intercepted that ball with his knob.' 'Harry Greg could have stopped a shot like that by throwing his chewing gum at it, wake up Stepney.' We were irritated by these constant references to the immortals of United's past, but knew it was a legacy of which we should be proud.

United being in the second division was a necessary cathartic experience for players and fans alike, an experience in which we'd grow together with some ebullience. United's travelling Red Army were the scourge of the second division bringing upwards of 15,000 visiting fans to every away game. This was how you proved your loyalty to the lads, by travelling to sleepy places like Hull, Bolton, and dare I say Birmingham, and robbing the shops and committing GBH on the opposing fans. Whatever the darker side of it, football hooliganism was in many ways comical.

It was Mike Brannan and Niall Kennedy who showed off their watchstraps outside the Seymour Grove chippy. The watchstraps were studded with drawing pins, with the sharp points jutting outwards.

'The thing you do is scrape it across their faces and then just stick the boot in, or if you're on the terraces you can sharpen ten-pence pieces and throw them like those kung fu stars, or throw frozen mars bars, they kill if they hit, like having a stone on your head.' Football's make-do guerrilla warfare sounded efficient and painful but a bit expensive. I mean it was 40p to stand in the Stretford End Paddock, never mind throwing ten-pence pieces at hapless Bristol Rovers fans or assailing them with Mars Bars that cost six pence each. Still the drawing pins through the watchstrap sounded good and it would give extra grip to United scarves which were now worn around the wrist in a fashion more reminiscent of The Glitter Band than *A Clockwork Orange*.

Chants from the terraces of 'Red Army', 'You're going home by fucking ambulance,' along with various eulogies about dying on the Kippax street with ten blue bastards at your feet and about walking home of an evening only to be accosted by a native of the city of Liverpool looking for a fight, were mixed up with that old favourite with a chorus about heads being kicked in.

Just like today the press loved it and loved United. We were in the second division but were the most reported team of the season, and 90 per cent of it was about our mindless hooligan following. Strange how things change and yet remain the same. Manchester United, their players, their fans – the biggest story in British sport.

Old Trafford in full voice an hour before the big games in the second division was a most intimidating place for opposition teams and fans alike. It would start like a jet engine taking off yards from you and build from the Stretford End until you could hear roaring from all four sides of the ground. In Duke

Street, where our old house was, was at least a mile away, you could hear that noise so clearly you could decipher the lyrics; and young children often stopped their games on the street to marvel at the sounds from that magic land which older brothers and fathers went to.

Our first home game in division two was Millwall. We'd heard all about the trouble in Manchester city centre already. Mainly London and southern-based United fans fighting with Millwall fans after travelling up on the same trains. About 40 Millwall fans had chased a 100 or so United fans down Gorse Hill and several lads we knew described how all these Millwall fans were in their mid-thirties, built like brick shithouses and wore big docker's boots with steel toecaps.

In the ground the Millwall fans were silenced as United blitzed their team 4–0, despite a world-class exhibition of goal-keeping from Bryan King, who went on to join Coventry City. United were rampant, with Gerry Daly, United's penalty king, notching up a hat trick and a goal on his home debut from Stuart Pearson.

United's next home game was an evening kick-off against Portsmouth who again brought trouble to Manchester. The victory on the pitch was United's, this time 2–1, a scoreline that flattered Pompey and their small number of rather fear-some travelling fans.

Outside the second division, football was, perversely enough, managing to go on without Manchester United. Manchester City were as ever in good form, winning games seemingly at will: they'd beaten Spurs at home and away, conquered the once mighty Leeds and given West Ham, now without Bobby Moore, a good 4–0 hammering on the open-ing day. Their only blips were a bruising 4–0 defeat at Arsenal and a scraped 2–2 draw with Coventry. After six games City had won four, drawn one and lost one. Their next visitors to

Maine road were Liverpool, hot favourites for the title that year, but if City were to beat them they would go top of the first division. We were keen not to miss it and check out United's opposition and maybe find some ammunition to goad the City fans at school with.

Me and the usual crowd went with David Lindsay, who couldn't resist winding us up about City being in the top three and United being in the second division. Maine road was packed that day, City having beaten (an albeit troubled) Leeds in their last home game. Liverpool were their next big test. They'd so far managed very well without Keegan thanks to his replacement Phil Boersma who'd been scoring goals for fun. The previous week Liverpool had beaten Tottenham Hotspur 5–2 at Anfield with Boersma grabbing a hat trick. This defeat sadly was the last straw for Spurs' gentleman manager Bill Nicholson, who retired after 39 years at White Hart Lane, another casualty of football's new age.

With the exception of their derby games against United, it was Manchester City's biggest home crowd for six years, as just over 45,000 fans settled into Maine Road that Saturday, with a large section of Liverpool fans making their presence felt. When walking up to the ground we were especially excited to see the huge outside broadcast trucks, vans and equipment of the BBC – the afternoon's match would be on *Match of the Day* that night. In those days there were only ever two games per week on *Match of the Day* and you didn't know until the programme which games those were. It gave added importance to the occasion and in contrast I wondered if United, who were playing away at West Brom. that day, would be on the Granada Sunday afternoon match highlights tomorrow.

We went as usual behind the goal at the Platt Lane end of the ground and looked at the pigeons as they settled on the pitch. Maine Road always seemed to have a certain unsymmetrical shabbiness about it to me, and those pigeons on the pitch, which have truly come home to roost nowadays, kind of summed it up. City had a cracking team at the time. Big Joe Corrigan had been dropped and replaced in goal by Keith MacRae, a £100,000 signing from Motherwell; at full-back they had Scottish international Willie Donachie and the much under-rated Geoff Hammond, a £40,000 snip from Ipswich Town. Mike Doyle and Tommy Booth were the centre-halfs, with Alan Oakes and new acquisition Asa Hartford joining Colin Bell in midfield. On the wings they had Mike Summerbee and Dennis Tueart and at centre-forward Rodney Marsh.

The Liverpool team, despite the absence of the still suspended Kevin Keegan, was fairly fearsome, including Clemence, Tommy Smith, Emlyn Hughes, Phil Thompson, Ian Callaghan, Phil Boersma, Steve Heighway and John Toshack.

From kick-off City took the game to Liverpool. Twice Bell crossed into the penalty area and twice Rodney Marsh blatantly brought the ball down with his hand before striking the ball past Clemence. Emlyn Hughes turned screaming at the referee who rightly disallowed them. It was third time lucky for Marsh when Bell again crossed fiercely from the right – Clemence missed but the hand of Rodney Marsh didn't and again he drove the ball into the net from four yards out. This time the referee allowed the goal, and we couldn't help but be amused at the whinging antics of Emlyn Hughes as he chased the referee all the way to the centre circle.

As the game developed Liverpool came into it more and in the second half had City on the back foot for most of the play. But then City broke effectively as ever through Bell on the right: his cross went over to Summerbee on the left edge of the Liverpool box, the ball was sent in and Dennis Tueart wrapped up the points for City in front of the scoreboard end. Man. City were top of the first division and Man. United top of the second, even though they'd only drawn 1–1 with a well-drilled West Brom. side.

The City fans would be unbearable, but Marsh had definitely handled the ball for the first goal and Liverpool were without Keegan, so there was enough ammunition to say they were lucky, which I did all the way home.

On the Sunday the Granada match did include highlights of United at West Brom. Don Howe had formed a well-organized team which was now without the outstanding Asa Hartford and relied on experienced players like Len Cantello and Willie Johnston. It was a tough test for the Reds who salvaged a point thanks to a Stuart Pearson goal. For some strange reason Mick Martin had been included in the side instead of Brian Greenhoff, who was on the subs bench. Martin was another of those workhorse type players United seemed so adept at picking up and which we fans never really understood. I mean, he isn't even John Fitzpatrick, never mind Stiles, so what on earth is he doing playing for us?

The irony was that Mick Martin was signed by West Brom. the following season to link up with Johnny Giles, who must have fancied him as his type of player. Thankfully for United, Docherty didn't that particular day and soon made amends. Greenhoff, within minutes of going on for the leather-lunged Martin, was involved in a nasty clash of heads with a West Brom. player and was stretchered off with concussion. A few minutes later a dazed Brian Greenhoff was pushed back on by a desperate Tommy Docherty. He took the ball, ran 20 yards, beating two opposing players and blasted a 30-yard shot which the keeper tipped on to the cross bar. Then, from the resulting corner Brian Greenhoff headed the ball from the edge of the box, past the keeper only to see it again hit the bar. The story that went round was that at full-time a still dazed Greenhoff turned to Tommy Docherty and asked, 'Who are we playing and what score is it?'

There were quite a few of us who supported United back then who'd watch United and City on alternate weeks. My excuse to all my fanatical City-hating mates for this strange behaviour was that I was scouting for United's return to the big time. But the truth was a lot of us desperately missed first division football and it was nice to go to Maine Road where there were always plenty of free spaces, you weren't buried up to your neck in fans and you could play spot the crowd. No wonder City had a crowd that averaged just over 33,000 that season.

A good pointer for anyone wondering about those days: United's home crowd for our opening game of the season against Millwall at Old Trafford was 45,000; meanwhile City's opening game against West Ham at Maine Road drew a gate of just 30,000. United were top of the second division and undefeated until they came up against what became our most hated bogey team that season, Norwich City.

United tasted defeat for the first time that season at Carrow Road where the fans rioted as Norwich took the game 2–0. What was particularly annoying was that Norwich City had Ted MacDougall playing for them and ... well we just hated him. We thought he was crap, he went to West Ham and now here he was at Norwich scoring goals for fun. Every article in newspapers and every bit of editorial in United programmes that season implored United fans not to act like hooligans, but there were so many people attending games and ... well we were United and we were youngsters and we were kind of proud that some fans had rioted at Norwich and climbed on the roof of the stand, throwing missiles and slate. Let's face it, when you are twelve it seems an exciting way of spending a Saturday afternoon.

The Norwich debacle did make us fans twitchy though: it wasn't so much the rioting but the fact we'd lost and we kept hoping that this wasn't going to be the start of a slump that would keep us in the second division any longer than the one season. We still carried around a hefty lump of pessimism after the shock of our relegation.

City fans at school were winding us up, gloating about their position, never out of the top three despite being hammered 3–0 at Middlesbrough. In school there was a simmering of discontent, arguments and fights. As you could almost have predicted, City were drawn against United in the next round of the League Cup at Old Trafford. This one game could make every United fan's season bearable and shut the City fans up for good. The problem was, United hadn't actually beaten City since the 1970–71 season when, after losing 3–0 at Old Trafford the team had then gone to Maine Road and run out winners in a 4–3 thriller.

City fans were quick to remind us of this and of our recent defeat at Norwich and stuttering draws against West Brom. and Nottingham Forest. We countered mercilessly with jibes about their home crowds of 30,000 despite the fact that they were top of the first division – albeit a first division where a mere three points separated first place from seventh.

Tickets were easy to come by and we were in our favourite Stretford End Paddock with a crowd of over 55,000 at Old Trafford on a blustery October night to witness this most important derby for United fans. Those City fans had to shut up and realize they were on borrowed time. I'd seen enough of City that season to be rightly worried: Bell was on fire, as was Tueart, and they looked good all round. Willie Donachie was out though, with veteran defender Glyn Pardoe included in the line-up; and Tommy Booth was also out with youngster Jeff Clarke deputizing at centre-half alongside Doyle. Otherwise it was the same formidable midfield and forward line of Bell, Tueart, Marsh, Hartford, Oakes and Summerbee United faced that night. Our main concern was Macari's absence from United's starting line-up.

As ever with Manchester derbies, the game was an edgy and ill-tempered affair. The crowd were noisy and every time City captain Mike Doyle went to take a throw-in he was showered with spit from the United fans, which, I'm not proud to admit, we found rather appropriate for this bitterest of Blues and self-confessed United hater. United looked the better side with Buchan, United's player of the season as far as we were concerned, keeping a close watch on Bell. At the back we were without Stewart Houston, and the young Arthur Albiston was clattered several times by Summerbee who was frustrated at the youngster's pace.

However it was the City youngster Jeff Clarke who decided the match by handling the ball in the City penalty area. Up stepped penalty king Gerry Daly, who not only never missed but had a knack of always sending the opposition goalkeeper the wrong way. In fact I never saw him hit the ball with any real power, just a sophisticated side-foot past a dopey keeper … and City were out of the League Cup.

'Told you you were shit, and we didn't even play Macari and Pearson at the same time to give you a chance.' Oh the joy of giving those Blues some stick after the months of constant torment they'd given us. 'Blimey if that lot are in the top three sides in division one, we'd have no problem winning the championship this season and if we're getting 46,000 fans on a bad week against the likes of Portsmouth on a Wednesday night, what sort of crowds would we pull if we were in City's position.' There's nothing like a good dose of scorn to cheer you up on an otherwise bleak Thursday morning in school. And back then, to all intents and purposes, Manchester City were indeed a big club.

14

In a Different League

United began to open up a gap on second-placed team Sunderland. This started with an away win at Blackpool which was our first outing as fledgling United hooligans (or so we thought). Blackpool and the seaside was too much of a draw for us to miss, although the supporters' coach was too expensive so we decided to go by train instead. We met at the bus stop in the gloom and drizzle at eight in the morning at Trafford Bar to get the bus to Victoria Station. Although we considered ourselves the hard lads from Old Trafford, now 12 going on 13, not one of us had actually told our mams where we were going. We'd all made up stories for our parents, who in light of all the hooligan activities concerning United fans wouldn't want us travelling to away matches.

As ever Roddy had told his mam he was going to do his milk round and then to the library, an excuse which wouldn't wash when he arrived home at seven-thirty. Me, well I'd just said I was going out like that Captain Oates bloke in *Scott of the Antarctic* and like that adventurer I was certain of a very cold and frosty reception upon my return. Paul Hartnett as ever amused us all by saying that when he got home that night he'd tell his mam that he'd gone to confession, and when she asked him why he'd been so long, he'd reply that he'd rather not explain the nature of his sins or Father Carter's subsequent penance.

Gary Johnson bragged that he hadn't even seen his parents since the evening before, and he'd lie and say he'd been at his gran's. In fact Gary was the one who had all the money and the shadier dealings, keeping lookout while the infamous O'Bannions and their gang of 14- and 15-year-old cronies robbed the gas meters of Old Trafford and burgled the houses of those who had nothing worth stealing in the first place. Gary knew that these lads were lowlives, but he enjoyed the buzz and excitement of a bit of crime, and the kudos it lent him. The only way to get more kudos was to be sent down to a reformatory or borstal, and it was a fact that some lads committed crimes with the full intention of getting caught and sent down to increase their standing in that strange, warped mini-society.

It never ceases to amaze me that these lads, many of them like Gary, very bright, were not prepared to knuckle down and learn at school, but relished the challenge of what they'd learn during a stint at reform school. In contrast, Paul Hartnett did crime purely for the material goods he could collect. Whatever the case we'd all have plenty of sins to share with God, the Virgin Mary and God Junior in the weeks to come.

We weren't exactly loaded with money, and although hungry decided that all the food at Victoria Station buffet was out of our budget and a bit crap anyway. It would cost us as much as 50p each for fish and chips in Blackpool, possibly more if we ate them in a cafe, then we'd need some money for the arcades and the Pleasure Beach. I was already panicking as, after paying for the train and the ticket, I had exactly 70p on me for my day trip to Blackpool. Even back then when you could get into a home game for as little as 30p as a junior, it still seemed expensive to us, especially where away matches and mid-week fixtures were concerned, and I'd stupidly been spending money going to see City as well.

Victoria Station was buzzing with young United fans and it wasn't even eight-thirty in the morning yet. Red, white and black scarves were on view everywhere, as were the bad haircuts, plastic bomber-jackets and tent-like Oxford bags. Everyone it seemed had the same idea. Kids the same age as us or a year or so older hung around, shouting across to each other, smoking cigarettes, sharing Watneys Party Sevens, bottles of cider and loud weak jokes. It was going off today, that was all we heard.

On the train we were packed in with hardly a normal passenger present, and more United fans got on at Bolton and again at Preston. Every stop more and more United fans were getting on. We heard that loads of older lads and hardcore hooligans had gone down the night before. A 15-year-old youth, with a denim jacket on bearing an assortment of Man. United, Wigan Casino and Keep The Faith sew-on badges, offered us some blues (a capsule form of amphetamine popular throughout my adolescence), six for a quid. We refused with expressions that said we did them all the time but were fed up of them now. Chants of 'I do like to be beside the seaside' rang through all the train carriages, the sound threatening and aggressive, and to our amazement no one checked our tickets. We were gutted – we could have saved all that money.

'Oh I do like to be beside the seaside, oh I do like to be beside the sea, oh I do like to walk along the prom prom prom, where the brass band's playing Fuck Off West Brom.'

Gary and Paul shared a cigarette they'd scrounged off some United lads from Moston and pretended that they went to all the away games. Gary was like a 13-year-old Walter Mitty as he engaged his new friends with aggro stories of his fantasy trip to Fulham a few weeks earlier. I wasn't even sure that Gary knew Fulham was in London, but these lads must have been impressed because they filled a plastic cup up with some warm pale ale out of a Party Seven tin and gave him another cigarette. Roddy meanwhile was wondering whether or not he'd made a mistake coming; he was very nervous of any violence, but unlike the rest of us he didn't bother hiding it.

Think of *Quadrophenia* and the seaside riot between mods and rockers, then replace them with what seemed like tens of thousands of United fans: that was Blackpool for three hours before the game kicked off. Nervous about the invisible enemy, we went with the mobs through the rain. There was nowhere to go as such, nothing to do but just run with the mob, change direction when they changed direction, and hope that some time that day you'd be watching Pancho Pearson outstrip the defenders and beat the keeper from 25 yards; and get home safely to tell your mates who hadn't gone how hard you were and how you'd help put to flight the combined terrace terrors of Blackpool, Burnley, Rangers, Preston and Blackburn on the pier and then gone home and bashed a motley collection of City and Luton fans at the station.

Of course that's not necessarily what happened when the plague of Red and white locusts descended on Blackpool in their thousands. We swarmed into Bloomfield road, took over the whole ground, sang United aggro for ages and watched Blackpool succumb to a rocket like shot from Forsyth's free kick and two pure pieces of cheek from Pearson and McCalliog as their team was as ravaged and ransacked by the boys in Red as their town had been before the match.

So did we find this threatened mob mayhem exciting and thrilling? Truth is we didn't spot one bit of bother. We saw loads of young Reds everywhere and hundreds of police, but no violence whatsoever. The sorts of young teenage kids who bragged about being involved in football violence (so-called) were mostly, for want of a better word, vermin and completely and utterly thick. I still bump into several lads I knew who went around with United causing trouble in the Seventies who moan about how they've been priced out of football, and although I feel sorry that something that means so much to them has been taken away, I can't help thinking good riddance.

Blackpool became Manchester for the day, and the only violence that we almost got involved with was with other young United fans who were bored by the fact that Blackpool had just been a show of force, as the Red Army partied in the wind and drizzle. Every team has its pondlife among the following, and United with their huge numbers of fans unfortunately had a lot back then who brought shame to the club along with their loyalty.

From them came the chants against Leeds of 'Zigger zigger zigger, Reaney is a nigger' and the chants against West Ham at Old Trafford for years aimed at their Barbadian player Clyde Best, 'We ain't got no niggers on our team'. How did Bobby Charlton or even Sir Matt view this when they knew players such as Paul Reaney and Clyde Best as individuals and fellow soccer professionals? How much success did this type of following cost United in the Seventies, how could players fight back from 1–0 down when they knew the stadium was erupting in hooligan behaviour, a different type of fight-back happening all around them.

The violence came from the neighbourhoods where poor kids grew up winning little victories within their warped macho codes. This was mixed with the fierce tribalism within areas in Manchester and the one ingredient that could be explosive and middle-class kids never seemed to need – passion. There was a huge recruiting pool for the Red Army, and not just in Manchester. There have always been large numbers of London-based United fans who travelled regularly to see United home and away. The draw for them wasn't just the football, but the sheer passion.

At Old Trafford every week we'd spot United supporters' branches from everywhere between Dublin and Peterborough, Hartlepool and Guernsey, Norway and Malaysia. For me and most of my mates every visit to Old Trafford, no matter at times how dismal the football, resembled a day out at Blackpool. Here we were, a bunch of lads who'd never left Manchester, except for the very odd occasion, spotting people at the match from all over Britain and the world, and they were 100 per cent Manchester United like us.

Nowadays much of Manchester United's support is denigrated for not being from Manchester and being part-time glory hunters. This may be true of the people who are on works outings at the corporate hospitality end. They all want to see United in the same way they want to go to the Opera or have a day's free drinking at he Test Match. United make a lot of money out of this kind of corporate entertaining and there's a definite drift of season tickets in that direction. Any businessman who owns three or four season tickets can use them to oil the wheels of his business by proffering clients tickets to important games.

Hence the huge numbers of people on corporate packages who were present for the recent European Cup semi-final at Old Trafford against Borussia Dortmund. Two Scottish businessmen occupying the seats behind me were asking each other whether they'd ever been to a live football match before, and then with the Reds trailing by a goal to nil with over 20 minutes of the game remaining, they got up and left.

There has to be some happy medium between the corporate and the regular fan if United want to keep any kind of atmosphere at Old Trafford, but the malaise isn't a sudden influx of huge support from outside the area. That was established long before I started going, and should come as no surprise in the Nineties when United are the hottest ticket in world sport. What's happened in the past ten years or so is that the club don't need or want a certain type of supporter; and conversely a lot of genuine supporters who can still afford the ticket prices to go and watch United don't need the team the way we did when we were young.

There were 47,000 people in Old Trafford for the evening game against first division high-fliers Burnley in the fourth round of the League Cup. With players like Welsh internationals Leighton James and Brian Flynn, centre-forward Ray Hankin and one-time England full-back Keith Newton, Burnley were near the top of the league, where only three points separated eight teams. They would be a good measure of how far the United team had improved and progressed.

For some strange reason Willie Morgan had been dropped to substitute for this game, the Doc mysteriously opting for McCalliog instead. We thought it odd that it was Morgan sitting this one out rather than Gerry Daly, who had been misfiring for much of the season. It was also unfortunate that Holton was out, replaced by part-time Yorkshire cricketer Arnie Sidebottom. United were 1–0 down and not far into the game when Brian Greenhoff picked up a knock and Willie Morgan came on against his old club with Macari switching from the wing to an inside position.

United stormed forward and Morgan slipped a lovely little ball through to Alex Forsyth who passed to Lou Macari whose first-time shot went past Stevenson in the Burnley goal. The crowd erupted, sensing a United side quickly coming to the boil. United peppered the Burnley goal with shots only to find themselves going in at half-time 2–1 down.

Within five minutes of the restart it was 2–2 as Willie Morgan celebrated a fantastic lob which floated over the mass of players in front of goal and into the net after a headed clearance from a corner. Now United were on fire and Burnley were chasing shadows. United camped outside the Burnley goalmouth and then, with three minutes to go, Lou Macari struck the ball, hit the post and then followed up to send in the rebound in and Old Trafford into a mass of noise and triumphant scarves raised to the floodlit night sky. Burnley fans seethed – they were big United haters and aggro merchants. We felt we could beat anyone at Old Trafford.

It was a dank, overcast, nippy November afternoon, but by two o'clock the Stretford End Paddock was a crush of people. There was no room near the wall despite our arrival at around 1.30. We'd managed to squeeze into a spot just in front of a crush barrier, but at times the sway of the crowd knocked us sideways or toppled us back on our heels, where we'd be forced to lean against the people behind the barrier, praying that we wouldn't fall over and be trampled underfoot by the surrounding multitude.

The stadium was shimmering with heat, the terraces around us emitting warm air and wispy clouds of vapour into the biting winter chill. The chorus from the Stretford End was at times more crushing in its emotion than the sea of people around us. But behind the songs, there was a genuine fear. Manchester United were faltering: we were still top of the division but Sunderland in second place were breathing down our necks and catching up. Today was the day – the second division top-of-the-table clash. Were we good enough to go up?

There were no certainties at Man. Utd: witness the team under O'Farrell in 1971/72. We'd been top of the table at this

same time: P-20, W-14, D-4, L-2. United looked like championship certainties, despite the suspect defending: Best and
Morgan were awesome on either wing, Charlton was playing
immaculately, Law looked back to his sharpest, Dunne was like
lightning, Gowling was scoring goals at will and Kidd was
looking like a real star. That was the best football kids our age
saw at Old Trafford. Despite all this their bubble burst on 11
December and they didn't win another league game until the
middle of March. There were no certainties at United.

What if United were starting on a slump? If that great team
of 1971 with all its superstar heavyweights could slip from
comfortable first to eighth, couldn't this lot, for all their
running and heart, do the same and miss out on promotion all
together? Could Macari, Pearson, Daly, Greenhoff and McIlroy
really keep it up? United had lost two out of the last three
games and to small-fry teams. Hull City beat United 2–0 in
what Tommy Docherty described as 'The most brutal game
I've seen for five years' and then humiliatingly Bristol City beat
us 1–0. United with the average age of the team around 23,
looked like boys against the Wearside veterans. We'd only really
played two decent sides all year, West Brom. and Norwich and
we hadn't beaten either of them. And Sunderland were more
than decent.

In midfield, and soon to be capped by Don Revie for
England was Tony Towers, a promising youngster from Man.
City who'd been part of the £275,000 transfer package that
had bought Tueart and Horswill for City. Towers was bloom-
ing now he was away from the shadows of Maine Road's big
star players. Also in midfield were Bobby Kerr and Ian
Porterfield, the scorer of Sunderland's goal in that memorable
1973 final and in goal Jim Montgomery, who had held Leeds
United at bay that day with a match-winning display. At the
back Sunderland were very solid, with England international

centre-back Dave Watson and former Scotland and Newcastle United captain and bruising stopper Bobby Moncur. The experienced Ron Guthrie and Dick Malone were at full-back. Up front they had the deadly pace of Scotland international Billy Hughes, the uncanny striking ability of Bryan (Pop) Robson and Vic Halom. This was going to be anything but easy.

The programme hailed the new player United had just swapped that week for George Graham. Graham had gone down to Portsmouth and United had grabbed ex-Southampton star and Welsh international Ron Davies. Would he be any good or another player past his sell-by date like Graham himself. We sang our hearts out to drown any doubts. For the faithful standing in the 62,000 crowd, what happened that afternoon would let us know more than anything so far whether or not United would be going up that year. And the BBC was there to capture it for *Match of the Day* too.

When Pearson scored the first, the crowd surged like a tidal wave. It was like the winning goal at Wembley had been scored as we joyfully jumped up and down and sang 'We shall not be moved'. On the pitch a battle royal was taking place, chances were made and spurned by both sides, with Stepney and Montgomerey making great saves.

From the kick-off the stadium was like a cauldron, and we knew this was going to be a classic. With the exceptions of Forsyth and Holton United were a very quick team then, and when things were going right, the sheer volume of noise and whiff of adrenaline coming from the terraces would spur them up to another tempo. The game was played at a furious pace and the quicker it got the more it suited United. Willie Morgan rampaged down the Sunderland flank and Moncur and Watson struggled early on with the pace of Pearson and Macari as they peeled off the back of them.

With Watson bearing down on him Macari slipped the ball through to Pearson, whose excellent first touch took it past Moncur. The skilful striker then rammed it low and accurate with his left foot from 25 yards, out of reach of the stranded Montgomery. Moncur spent half the game tapping at Pearson's ankles as Pearson backed in to him to receive the ball.

Sunderland grew in confidence and to our dismay took a 2–1 lead thanks to their nippy Scots forward Billy Hughes. We held our breath waiting for the comeback, relieved to see Buchan finally mastering Billy Hughes, taking him out of the game, and beginning to bring the ball forward into the Sunderland half. It was always a sign that United were on top when Buchan, to us Reds the best defender in the game, decided it was safe to attack.

Pearson drifted out left, pushed the ball up along the touch-line and drifted back in as he approached the box and sent in a cross. Willie Morgan slid in to claim the equalizer a split second before Montgomery could smother the ball. The crowd were going mad. 'Willie, Willie Morgan'. It was bedlam.

Then a tactical switch was forced on the Doc as Brian Greenhoff had to come off and ex-Southampton striker Ron Davies came on. More firepower up front, someone to challenge Dave Watson in the air. But with his first touch Davies sent a beautiful cross ball through to Alex Forsyth who was streaming through the centre. He slipped a ball through the Sunderland defenders to Daly who was coming in on the right-hand side of the box and we held our breath as McIlroy side-footed the Irishman's cross into the goal – 3–2 to United.

The crowd reacted as if our beloved team had won the European Cup. 'Hello! Hello! United are back, United are back.' 'So now you're gonna believe us, we're gonna win the league.' 'Just like a team that's going to win the championship [no mention of course of the shame we felt about the second division], we shall not be moved.' It was one of the greatest matches I've seen at Old Trafford in almost 30 years. United were back, we'd beaten the one team in the division we truly feared, and the loyal Reds would be around for all the good times to come.

The following week, still drunk from the headiness of the victory over Sunderland there was excitement and trouble of several different kinds. First, United came face to face in the fifth round of the League Cup with Jack Charlton's Middlesbrough. This was a side we considered cloggers, but they were effective enough with their long lobbed balls to Alan Foggon (later to have a mercifully brief stint at United) to find themselves top of the first division. It was the ninth time in five years that United had played Middlesbrough in cup ties, three of the previous eight going to replays.

Middlesbrough had Armstrong, Foggon, Graeme Souness, Willie Maddren, Hickton and ex-Leeds defender Terry Cooper. Listening that Wednesday night on the radio as the game finished 0–0 it was obvious United had been the better team, especially as the game moved into its later stages, although Alex Stepney was touted as man of the match. Now if United could beat them in the replay at old Trafford they would not only be top of the second division but also in the semi-final of the League Cup.

The week finished with another classic performance at Hillsborough but for a United legend there was tragedy. With the Reds leading 1–0 courtesy of a seventh minute goal from a Stewart Houston free-kick, United's Scottish international centre-half Jim Holton broke his leg in a tackle with Sheffield Wednesday's Eric McMordie. Only 15 minutes of the game had gone and United moved Brian Greenhoff to centre-half alongside Buchan and put substitute Ron Davies on. This time the magic didn't work as Wednesday grabbed a 3–1 lead by half-time.

There was trouble on the terraces again with United's huge away following battling throughout with the Wednesday fans.

In the second half, as Greenhoff settled better to his job at the back, United staged a Homeric revival. Within three minutes of kick-off, Lou Macari made it 3–2. Pearson levelled things, getting on the end of Forsyth's low, hard centre; and then tragedy as Wednesday scored again. United kept battling and with less than ten minutes left Macari drove the ball through a crowded penalty area for his second and United's fourth. 4–4: a wonderful game and a good result which stopped United suffering a third consecutive away defeat in the league.

But we still worried: life without Holton at the centre of defence. Who would partner Buchan in the centre of our defence? Surely not Arnie Sidebottom, a spindly misfit, a cricketer with Yorkshire who couldn't tackle, was good in the air, had a bit more pace than Holton but was slow to react. Or the even worse Steve James, who was experienced enough, good in the air and a good tackler too but didn't look effective even when playing for the reserves, as he lacked that do or die mentality and confidence needed when playing for United.

Our worst fears were confirmed when United huffed and puffed against Orient in a 0–0 draw at Old Trafford. Arnie Sidebottom played well enough despite some jeers from certain sections of the crowd who didn't see Arnie in the same class as Holton. There were also great performances from Daly (for a change that season) and Macari, but United always looked like losing a goal to a breakaway as they pushed forward more and more, especially when facing the pace of the young Laurie Cunningham (destined, as a West Brom. player to become the first black player to receive a full England cap). The terrier-like Tony Grealish also caused some problems in midfield.

The League Cup replay with Middlesbrough saw a crowd of just under 50,000 roar United on to one of their most glorious performances of the season. Nobody fancied playing Middlesbrough, the most competitive and hardest side in the league. They'd beaten all the big guns so far and were tipped by Bill Shankly to win the title (and indeed they were in title contention up to the last week of the season). This would be United's biggest test yet.

Middlesbrough were simply annihilated. United put three past them through McIlroy, Macari and Pearson. Middlesbrough looked like a broken team, bereft of ideas, as our heroes forced them into making mistake after mistake. On the terraces we suspected that were United in the first division we'd stand a good chance of winning it outright with opposition as clumsy and lacking in finesse as this. 'Blimey, Arnold Sidebottom played a blinder.'

All winter United stuttered and stumbled but stayed on top. A disastrous 1–0 defeat at Oldham. An injury to Pearson brought more bad results. The semi-final of the League Cup first leg at Old Trafford on a wet, windy night: 58,000 drenched fans spurred on United as they laid siege to Norwich, but Keelan in their goal played a blinder and Morgan and Macari missed a couple of sitters. The Stretford End were chanting with fanaticism 'We all fuckin' hate Norwich' in particular aiming our boos and pent-up frustration at ex-Red Ted MacDougall.

In a one-sided game United dominated, but without Pearson, like all the games he missed that season, we lacked a cutting edge. Norwich took the lead just on half-time through Tony Powell. Greenhoff was pushed into midfield, and Macari, who was playing out of his skin as ever, moved up front. Within six minutes of the second half kicking off, Jim McCalliog sent in a corner, Keelan in the Norwich goal punched it out, only for Brian Greenhoff to put the ball back in where Lou Macari, with his back to goal, scored with a cheeky overhead kick. Twenty minutes later the 5' 6" Lou Macari proved again what a footballing giant he was in a Red shirt. His back to the goal, he flicked the ball up a couple of times and then crashed in a low-angled drive from close range. Then, as Macari put Morgan through, Willie decided to go for a penalty with a soft dive rather than score and the referee wasn't having any despite howls of protests from the 58,000 zealots in the stands. A minute to go and Norwich equalize – 'fuckin' Ted MacDougall'. We are gutted, we *really* hate Norwich.

The following week, still missing Pearson, Norwich beat us in the second leg at Carrow Road 1–0, a goal by Colin Suggett against the run of play sending them through to the final, 3–2 on aggregate. They would go on to lose in an all-second division League Cup Final against Aston Villa, and both teams would follow United into the first division the following season, at Sunderland's expense. As for United, our dreams of Wembley were again shattered; it was the third time we'd lost in a League Cup semi-final, and I wondered if the day would ever come when I'd see the Reds lift a trophy.

The absolutely useless striker Tommy Baldwin came from Chelsea on loan to make his debut in a tense 0–0 draw with Sunderland at Roker Park. Reports hailed Stepney as the undoubted man of the match, and James and Buchan in the centre of defence gave outstanding performances in keeping a rampant Sunderland forward line out.

Pearson was still missing and Baldwin playing when Bristol City sent a cold silence over Old Trafford with a last-minute winner. They were the only team to beat United at Old Trafford that season and the only team to beat us in both fixtures. Bristol had hardly kicked the ball in United's half, the majority of the entertainment in the match coming from the Stretford End. Just before kick-off the tannoy announced that there had been a bomb threat phoned through and anyone wishing to leave could do so. The Stretford End immediately started singing, 'We shall not be moved' and then a chorus of 'We hate the IRA', which was swiftly followed by, 'We're gonna get our fuckin' heads blown off.'

It was a dull, scrappy game in which United without Pearson did everything but score. Baldwin showed some neat touches and missed a sitter which he contrived to hoof over the bar, and Steve James at centre-half stormed forward in Ronald Koeman fashion and sent a 30-yard drive against the Bristol crossbar, but we just couldn't get that ball in the onion bag. The game was finishing, and the Stretford End chanting the name of Stoke City striker Ian Moores for his hat trick in Stoke's 4–0 demolition of City at the Victoria Ground, when Bristol's ten-man defence finally discovered there was another half to the pitch. One attack, one goal. Not even the sound of a groan from near 48,000 people. Old Trafford was at its most silent.

For all their battling and possession, United had never really looked like scoring. It was a vision of the previous season when that lack of a sharp finisher had sent United down and we prayed that Stuart Pearson would be back as soon as possible.

Another defeat followed a week later as Oxford, in front of their biggest crowd in 30 years, cruelly rubbed United's nose into their New Year slump, 1–0. In the last nine games in both Cup and League, United had won two, drawn two and lost five. The Reds were losing ground and we were worried lads.

'I mean Daly goes off, and he's not been playing well. Tony Young, the "utility" player which means crap in any position, comes into midfield and we get beat by two of the shittest teams in the division.'

'Well haven't you heard? Ian Storey-Moore is coming back.'

'No way, where did you hear that?'

'My dad knows a bloke that goes drinking with Paddy Crerand and he told him. He's playing at Burton Albion and scoring loads of goals – his knee has healed up and if United pay the £170,000 they claimed in insurance, they can re-register Storey-Moore to play for them.'

Our eyes widened with disbelief. The lad who told us was one of my best mates and lived just doors down from Paddy Crerand … surely it was too good to be true. My mind misted over, dreaming of the sight of Storey-Moore on one wing and Morgan on the other, a perfect symmetry. Ian Storey-Moore: rationed to United fans on and off over less than 50 games home and away. Better than Giggs in my rose-coloured hindsight, with a bit of Beckham thrown in. On his day, he was better than Morgan. He was like a footballing treat you never quite got to devour. A quick taste of some of the most delicious football you'll ever witness: skill, power and pace, dancing on the toes of his white boots, a fierce shot from any distance. There were good Catholic kids in Old Trafford who prayed and lit candles for the resurrection of Ian Storey-Moore. There were times when from the terraces we'd confuse him with Best, and his career would finish in an even sadder way.

In the end salvation came not from Ian Storey-Moore, but from a crafty hardworking Scouse winger from Tranmere Rovers via Liverpool University. While the rumours concerning Ian Storey-Moore did the rounds, and were mentioned in the press by Tommy Docherty, United were lining up for what would turn out to be one of the transfer deals of the decade.

The opponents were relegation strugglers Cardiff City. We'd lost at Aston Villa the week before by 2–0 and it could have been more. Pearson was back now and on the bench was

United's £40,000 transfer from Tranmere Rovers, Steve Coppell. He played on the right wing, so would he get a game today? If so, we hoped he'd replace Gerry Daly, who wasn't on his game at the time. United lined up with Stepney, Forsyth, Houston, Greenhoff, James, Buchan, Morgan, McIlroy, Pearson, Macari, Daly.

In the first half United attacked the scoreboard end away from us. The final ball was lacking and they weren't playing with any real confidence, just a hurried desperation to play the killer ball and snatch that first goal. 44,000 people groaned and shouted, cajoled and urged on the Reds. We'd had enough bad luck these past seasons. We believed we'd go straight back up but the creeping doubts nagged: without a centre-half with the same ability as Jim Holton we were all too beatable, as Oldham, Bristol, Oxford, Norwich and Villa had proved in the last couple of months.

Half-time and it was 0–0. Fifteen minutes gone in the second half and it's still 0–0. Sixty minutes of frustrating football; of Gerry Daly still struggling with what had been his main asset, passing accuracy; of Willie Morgan getting round the final defender and sending the ball out for a goal kick with his cross. Then the substitution was made. Young Coppell, aged 20, for Willie Morgan. 'Why's he taking Willie off, that's daft, it should be Daly.' We were all mystified. But then it all fell into place.

Coppell didn't just cross the ball and beat his man every time, he kind of lobbed it on to a sixpence. The Cardiff defence were being stretched and United pushed forward with a vengeance. A Brian Greenhoff corner, a Stewart Houston header and the floodgates open. Cardiff are taken apart.

Good work from Coppell and Houston gives Pearson his fourteenth goal of the season; a lovely bit of skill from Sammy McIlroy and it's 3–0; and then an accurate lobbed cross from

Coppell and Macari heads it in, 4–0. Two goals made by Coppell, who played as if he'd been at United for years.

A new terrace hero was born, and apart from two more appearances that was the last we saw of our old hero Morgan, taken away from us so cruelly, yet replaced with a true wizard of the wing. Coppell wasn't as classy as Morgan at his best, but then he didn't try to play like he thought he was George Best the way Morgan did. Coppell was direct but pacey and skilful enough to beat his man and get in a great cross and he could shoot too. Morgan's final ball and shot had always been his weak points and Coppell's more disciplined, unselfish style and consistency suited United better.

Still the Red Army went across Britain. As for us, we didn't make a habit of away games, but that enticing away fixture at Bolton was too much. There were 37,000 people in Burnden Park, two thirds United, and plenty of gravelly ammunition lying around on one of the half-built, half-pulled-down terraces. In the bright sunshine missiles flew between the supporters. Ex-Liverpool winger, and my favourite all-time Liverpool player (yes, even I have one), Peter Thompson caused United all kinds of problems linking up with Terry Curran and Neil Whatmore; and ex-United hero Tony Dunne, who was playing a blinder at full-back and sometimes slotting in as a sweeper, kept the United forwards quiet.

Steve Coppell, wearing Morgan's famous No. 7 Jersey sent over a corner, Houston headed it, Siddall in the Bolton goal pushed it on to the bar and Pearson put in the rebound. It was a typical Pearson goal: his reactions were like lightening and over a short burst of ten yards his pace devastating with a strange short-stepped trot on his toes. Often first to a loose ball or rebound, he struck a particular sort of firm low shot that would dip in and bounce up in front of the opposing keeper like top Brazilian strikers did. So no longer 'Stuart Who?'

> The world has seven wonders
> But one thing you can bet
> You'll think you've seen the eighth one
> When our Stuart hits the net

More missiles filled the air, fighting broke out on the terraces, the police herded us to the bus stops and coach parks.

Next week it was Norwich at home – so far this season we'd played them three times, drawn once and lost twice. It was a big game, they were in the hunt for promotion, and this time we had Pearson *and* the new wunderkind, Steve Coppell.

56,202 people crammed into another cauldron-like atmosphere at Old Trafford. Chants of 'United reject' and 'If you hate Ted MacDougall clap your hands' rent the air. That old favourite, 'We all fuckin' hate Norwich', spiked with even more venom, was screamed from the terraces. United's ground was a wall of noise and animosity for Norwich City.

This is what we came for. We came from over-crowded housing estates where you could never show your true feelings or reveal anything, where emotions were often hidden underneath a veneer of respectability, trying to show that low income living didn't necessarily mean low-life. Yet on the terraces, you made a difference and you could boo back passes and take up the famous United chant of 'Attack, attack, attack, attack, attack!' The team had to play that way for us, swarm over the opposition, wear them down.

Tommy Docherty's side did that in pint-sized wave after wave. We didn't have a forward taller than five foot nine – a stiff breeze would have knocked half of them into the stands and would have blown Gerry Daly out of the stadium. But they were fighters, runners and winners. I've seen some great sides since at Old Trafford, but not even in the glory years of Cantona, Giggs, Kanchelskis and Hughes did United play with an attacking, devil-may-care, Celtic ferocity so in tune with the passions of the supporters.

Norwich surely wouldn't spoil our party? But of course Kevin Keelan plays another blinder in the Norwich goal. Pearson eventually scores another scrambled poacher's goal, but Keelan keeps making these incredible saves and McIlroy misses his usual quota of absolute sitters. With 20 minutes of the game remaining Norwich score and surprise, surprise, to rub salt in the wounds, it is ... Ted MacDougall! His fourth goal against United in four games that season.

After that United started winning and sealed their certain return to the first division with a 1–0 win at Southampton, on 5 April. Two weeks later a draw away at Notts County meant United were second division champions. The final match of the season at Old Trafford was versus Blackpool. Token sheets all round for this one, with United to pick up their first trophy since the European Cup ... but did it really count?

It was party time at Old Trafford: 61,000 paid homage that afternoon and roared the songs like 'Hello! Hello! United are back! United are back!' We dreamt of a new era to rival the Sixties and knew European Cups were not far off – we even relished the reserve games we'd have to go to to get those tickets for the big fixtures. United performed like champions, Blackpool were demolished 4–0 as per the script. And then the strange sensation of United receiving the second division champion's trophy.

It was a bit embarrassing. Yes, it was important that United went up as the number-one team, but celebrating that trophy was too distasteful for us Reds to handle. The players knew it too – Buchan looked disdainful. It was a tin cup. United were back, that was all that mattered.

15

United Are Back

Having kissed the second division goodbye forever we could relax and watch a dull FA Cup Final. Fulham's Dad's Army team, including press luvvies Bobby Moore and Alan Mullery, lost a one-sided game 2–0 to a bright and promising West Ham United. City fans retreated on sight, after their star-studded team cocked up what had been a promising season, winning seemingly at will at Maine Road, but falling apart and getting destroyed outside Manchester. They finally finished eighth with only four wins since March, much to the annoyance of their moaning fans.

City's bubble had burst and Derby County under the management of Dave Mackay won the championship, with some thanks to Francis Lee who had a brilliant season, capped for him by scoring a screaming winner in City's 2–1 home defeat against Derby. The best team I'd seen at Maine Road that season were Ipswich Town. City struggled the whole match and only scraped a draw thanks to a hat-full of missed sitters by Ipswich and a wonder goal by Colin Bell. He took the ball from the right side of the halfway line, went around three Ipswich defenders and the goalkeeper before coolly slotting the ball in the net. A superb breakaway goal, and a sign of how under pressure City were in the game.

Next season would be United v. City and United v. Ipswich Town, and it would mean new players and another five pence on the cost of a match. Liverpool were a spent force, Leeds were nothing special, neither were Everton, Ipswich always bottled it and Derby County were has-beens. Next season United would be champions and that is exactly what we told each other and all those jealous City fans, and that's what we believed.

So did United dip into the transfer market for a class defender like Mick Mills or Kevin Beattie of Ipswich, Roy MacFarland or Colin Todd? Did we buy a top-rated striker like Trevor Francis, Bob Latchford, Kenny Dalglish or even Ipswich's David Johnson? Did we swoop in for goalkeeping supremo Peter Shilton? No, we got a free transfer from Nottingham Forest – his name Tommy Jackson. Tommy was never a pretty sight, especially on a football field. He couldn't run, although I'd witnessed him almost break into a Teddy Sheringham-like limp on occasions, nor did he play a killer ball or score goals, but God bless him he must have done something right.

Frustratingly United's first two games of the season were away from home, at Wolves and Birmingham. United won both 2–0 with two goals each from Macari and McIlroy. All the signs were right.

It was still the school holidays when United played Sheffield United at Old Trafford for the first home game of our return to division one. The *Match of the Day* cameras waved us a cheery hello as we strode in the sunshine, badly dressed for the weather and any other season or decade come to mention it. Older lads with their 'birds', wearing the same daft jumpers, French kissing at half-time. Maybe sporting the bum-fluff of an offensive emerging moustache, a little silver necklace across their bare throat with their initial on it, a gift from the girl in the midi-skirt and plimsolls, hair in a bunch, who had also implanted the huge purple lovebites on his neck. Noise and colour: this was a great day to be alive, to be a United fan.

We knew Sheffield United weren't a bad side, with England midfield maverick Tony Currie the only real class in the set up. But this was United's day, and the faithful were turning up in their thousands to make sure Sheffield United's defeat would sound a warning to the rest of division one.

'Hello! Hello! United are back! United are back!'

Imagine an unexpected surprise that takes your breath away, and the profoundly inspiring nature of the sight is such that you breathe in and then forget to breathe out. United were unleashed that afternoon; pressing forward, harassing and firing hard, low, deadly crosses into the Sheffield United box; players in red and white with pace and heart, coupled with skill and sheer determination. Pearson got two goals, Macari, McIlroy and Gerry Daly one each. United were awesome, and the 5–1 scoreline flattered the Blades who'd been pummelled by a relentless onslaught.

They could have scored 20 and all captured for the *Match of the Day* cameras, spoilt only by Jimmy Hill who immediately dissected the secrets of United's speedy and at times suicidal offside trap for the benefit of our future opponents. Coventry adapted well to it at our next home game thanks mainly to the speed of Tommy Hutchison and Alan Green up front. The game finished 1–1 and we walked home cursing Jimmy Hill under our breaths.

We'd all gone 13 and in September we joined our local youth club. The local youth club was in fact just an under-16s disco in the school hall of our old primary school. Ten pence to get in and enjoy all the sounds of the Rubettes, Hot Chocolate, the

Drifters, Barry White and as much obscure Northern Soul as the resident DJs, Dave and George, could shove on their tuppence-ha'penny mobile disco turntables.

We'd got a record player off our Aunty May at home. It was one of those mono Dansette things; all we needed was some records. Kids then were buying stuff like Slade, T Rex, ELO, maybe Wizard. I quite liked Slade, but my favourites were the Beatles, the Jackson Five, the Temptations and Led Zeppelin and Pink Floyd because the covers of the albums looked cool and our Tony had them even though he didn't have a record player either. Tony was away at university by now, and he'd warned me not to play his few records on the dansette. I did obey him for a long time, until the temptation got too much and I had to listen.

I thought Yes were crap and I wasn't too sure about Led Zeppelin. They were heavy and all the lads at school, especially the older ones, liked 'heavy music', or so they said. Me ... well I liked soul music, we all did in Old Trafford, and reggae: Jimmy Cliff and all the Trojan label artists like The Pioneers and The Upsetters and the up-and-coming Bob Marley and the Wailers. I liked 'Machine Gun' by the Commodores and Al Green who was a big favourite among the girls round our way, more so than Donny Osmond and David Cassidy. But at school they all thought soul was shit, so I didn't let on that I liked it. Also the kid I hated most in our year liked soul music and had names like Ohio Players and The Chi-Lites written on his schoolbag. (There I was living a double life again.)

But we didn't go to the disco for music, or really for girls (we lived in hope, but we were unfortunately the younger end of the spectrum). No, we went to the youth club to show that we weren't scared to ... er ... go to the youth club.

My curfew was 11.30 on a Friday night. The disco went from 7.30 to 11.00. We'd meet up outside the Ayres Road or

Henrietta Street chippy at around 7.15, share a bottle of Strongbow cider, and make a cool entrance at about eight o'clock. We'd bundle in past Mr Donovan, the permanently boozed-up six-foot, four-inch Irish navvy who worked the door at St Alphonsus and made certain that even the roughest and toughest teen tearaways coughed up their ten pences. However, that's where Mr Donovan's job would finish. Any aggro inside would be over by the time he'd dragged his scary bulk up the stairs, and any real fights normally happened outside afterwards, by which time he was doubtlessly necking a few pints of Guinness at St Brendan's Irish club.

Then there was Father Carter, the Vatican's answer to Roger Moore. He had the voice, the accent (if a little Mancunian) and all the gestures and mannerisms, right down to the theatrically raised eyebrow. He also had that disturbing type of unfazeable demeanour – he would watch placidly as two 14-year-olds threatened to carve each other up with Stanley knives and philosophically dismiss it with a 'tut, tut, tut, boys will be boys', accompanied by that Mooresque disapproving eyebrow motion.

It's true that our youth club wasn't for the faint-hearted and I don't think anybody really enjoyed it that much. There were girls there, but only three or four that your peer group would agree were fanciable, and only one of them actually free. All the best-looking girls were going out with the O'Bannions, the Traceys or the Ryans, most of whom were older and harder than us. So assured were these 16- and 15-year-old lads of their faithful 14- and 15-year-old girlfriends, that they'd show up at the youth club to spy that no interlopers from Moss Side or Whalley Range were on their territory, and then invariably disappear off to the pub or Irish club to do the same thing there, without even bothering to let on to 'their birds'.

The O'Bannions were a big family of four brothers: Steven

who was 18, Sean 16, Martin 15 and Raymond who was our age. They'd all done some time in approved school although they weren't really hard-cases as such, just a bit psychotic and by nature bullies. Ray O'Bannion would always have a gang of ten or so urchin types with him when he came down the youth club, looking for victims to terrorize. We were dismissive of him as we knew if he jumped us with his gang, he'd be in receipt of payment in kind.

His older brothers had some very evil and hard mates, in particular Salvo Bentini, who had once stabbed a kid through the stomach with a knitting needle and Eddie Gilmichael who was a real street-fighter with a very bad temper and no sense of humour. Thankfully they didn't fight the O'Bannions' younger brother's battles for him, but then Raymond had a big enough crew to do that anyway.

Violence with its murky and at times highly sexual under-current brought Old Trafford's youth out in their full bloom into the night air. The great smell of Brüt and Hai Karate after-shaves mixed with Cossack hairspray for barnets lacquered into a variety of tasteless bouffants, centre-partings essential. The girls whiffed of Charlie perfume and Mum deodorant and danced in lines doing the stomp and shuffle, while us lads stood around the sides of the walls: feet crossed, arms folded or crossed over groins, rolled-up sleeves on our jumpers revealing the watchstraps studded with drawing pins, imagining that we looked like the front cover of a Richard Allen skinhead book, without the obligatory crops.

I knew most of the lads there, but I hadn't hung around with some of them since primary school almost three years earlier and while I'd been getting Latin shoved down my throat at grammar school they'd been toughening up at the local secondary moderns. I knew it would only be a matter of time before I was asked to prove that I hadn't, to put it in local parlance, turned into a pouff. Seven, eight, even nine years I'd known most of these lads and yet in a strange way my short time at grammar school had already put a huge distance between us. On this territory it was like I was an ex-pat pretending I was still a native and not sure whether I'd disowned my home country or it had disowned me. The only common ground we had was United and football.

Mike Brannan had been a mate of mine at primary school. He was never really rated as a fighter back then but now, aged 14, he was six-foot tall and weighed over 12 stone and was a regular attender along with his mate Niall Kennedy. Gary Johnson, although just 14, had dismissed the youth club and was now hanging around the Seymour Pub with the local hard-nuts and making excursions into town to clubs like Kloisters and Pips. Luckily for me Gary Johnson was a real mate and had a great sense of humour. He liked my company and was forever regaling people with the story of how we'd had a fight in junior four at primary school. It certainly helped my reputation, but it did mean that whoever had a pop at me would be very handy indeed, and while Gary's fighting had become a way of life, I was out of practice.

There was John Rafferty, the Finnegans, the Dunnes, all mates of mine, but they wouldn't bail me out of a one-on-one fight, nor would they be walking me home from school every night, so I again had to stand up and be counted. Fight or stay in were the rules in Old Trafford for the teenage lads − it's probably the same the world over.

Every Friday night I'd get home from school have a bath and an adolescent scowl at my younger brother and sister, and ignore my older sister as she teased me by enquiring as to whether I had a girlfriend yet. Then I'd get dressed in my horrendous best gear and toy with the idea of nicking my dad's Stanley knife from the cupboard under the sink. If I succumbed to temptation and fear I'd slip it through the lining of my Harrington jacket pocket like Paddington Bear packing an extra marmalade sandwich in case of an emergency, and then make my way out the door, promising to be in by 11.30.

Believe it or not, this was excitement. Out in the big bad world ready for anything. I've never had the same adrenaline pumping through my system as I did on those nights. The jokes outside the chippy always seemed hilariously funny, no matter how many times you'd heard them; the Cider bottles were passed around in the chill night air, a celebration of our youth. That's how it was, we never remembered the jokes, just the laughter – most of the stories were just the day-to-day episodic living that was our life as friends. The faces we pulled in the club had to be 'don't fuck with me' faces, practised in the mirror. Any smiling was only for your mates and then a kind of wry smile, a bitter grin that was a suppressed cruel laugh.

Trouble came on several occasions to our youth club. There was a black on white thing when the Reids came down with all their mates and it went off with Kevin McAuliffe, a hefty but pint-sized 17-year-old hard-case taking on the wide six-foot frame of Tony Reynolds. We spilled outside into the night air, the girls screaming, the lads eyeing each other up. Smack, Kevin laid Tony out with his full body weight behind a karate-style twisted punch to the underside of his chin. He moved in to finish Tony off, his mountainously high white platform shoes pulled back, about to kick him in the head. Tony scrambled on the floor and pulled out a ratchet-knife, arcing it in the air, slitting Kevin's hand open. The girls screamed.

Somebody shouted 'Fucking niggers' and more knives were flashed in what had been our primary school yard. Sean Brannan was stabbed in the arm by an unidentified member of Reid's posse, the sickening blow more a punch than a stab. Outnumbered Reid, Reynolds and mates scarpered. They didn't come back to the club, but Tony had a real hard-case brother who was the same age as Kevin McAuliffe. He caught up with Kevin a few weeks later, punched him to the ground, made him kneel down and beg for mercy. The story was passed around, but no one except Jimmy Millar, Eddie Gilmichael and Marco Bentini dared ask Kevin if this particular slice of Old Trafford folklore was true or not. Like several lads in our area, his temperament was like simmering fat in a chip pan, put the wrong thing in and it could bubble over and spit and scald. Silence was the best policy.

Ray O'Bannion terrorized the sort of kids who would or could rarely fight back, and he never seemed to have a square go with anyone himself. He was a nasty little piece of work, with a sadistic streak, who loved to cause bother. He was only the same height and build as myself, but had a sly mean look, somewhat reminiscent of a young Robin Asquith sucking a lemon. He spent his evenings at the youth club snogging his fetching, red-headed but dim girlfriend Cheryl and pairing members of his gang off with reluctant harmless lads, with no axe to grind, for a fight outside. The word would spread around the club.

Ray O'Bannion one night fixed it that Ballantine should fight Kubi outside. On that particular night the profoundly ugly Ballantine had picked on the smallest lad in the club. Kubi Ali was of Turkish descent, a Dickensian urchin, he was a lone operator, always on the go dodging and breaking into shops and ragging machines in the arcades around town. He went to the club just to dance to the Rubettes' 'Juke Box Jive' which he insisted they played twice a week, and he was an amazing dancer. We were all aware that Kubi was hard as nails, but Ballantine just saw someone very small who'd given him lip in front of all his mates.

O'Bannion's usual scam was that the protagonists would

have a square go outside, then seconds after the fight started the whole gang would just jump in. Kubi was so small and slight he looked no threat, but his speed and technique were out of this world. Within five seconds Ballantine's thick ugly head was being kicked all over the yard and O'Bannion's gang members were standing around looking at each other, worrying about the day, should they join in, that Kubi went looking for them individually, and they were right to think just that. Kubi when he felt threatened was a nutcase.

A few weeks earlier the gruesome Ballantine had supposedly been paired off with me by Ray O'Bannion. I'd seen them looking over at me and arguing a bit. It was obvious that Valentine hadn't been too keen. It was no secret that I was mates with Mike Brannan, Niall Kennedy and Gary J, none of whom unfortunately were there that night. I didn't think that the whole of O'Bannion's gang would pile in on me if I fought Ballantine – that would mean attrition between my friends and his, and his friends would be pretty thin on the ground once they knew who my mates were. But it was at the back of my mind and besides, if I lost or had a difficult fight with a no-mark like Ballantine, it would in my warped mind damage my tenuous reputation and that was a cause for some major concern.

O'Bannion, Ballantine and some of the others were sitting at a table looking over. I'd been snogging a girl who I'd met the week before who was half-Spanish and had just moved to Old Trafford from the other side of Stretford. That was the only reason I'd gone to the club, as none of my regular good mates were around. I sucked in a deep breath, asked the girl to hang on a minute and walked over to the table.

'Awright Ray, how's it going?'

'OK.'(Looking bemused, I hadn't spoken to him for about five years.)

'Who's is this?'

I grabbed a can of fizzy orange off the table in front of Valentine. As I lifted it up, Valentine grabbed my wrist.

'Ouch ... what the fuck ...'

His bony fingers impaled themselves on the drawing pins that protruded from the watchstrap around my wrists, at the same time I jerked my hand holding the drink away from him, scratching his palm and fingers in one deft move, then gave him some verbal.

'What are you fucking whinging about, it's only a bit of pop, I'm sure your mam'll buy you another one.'

Ray and the rest of his cronies were laughing. Valentine was Ray's right-hand boy, and they didn't really like the ugly syco-phantic sneaky little tosser anyway. Valentine was flustered. He knew I had the watchstraps on each wrist, he probably thought I had a knife as well. Seeing the consternation on his face I necked his pop, nearly gagging on the slimy warmth and the thought of his dirty crusty gob soiling the can, but making a point. He wouldn't start there and then. He wasn't going to do or say anything, but I had to make sure, be certain he was aware of who I knew and who my mates were, and that went for Ray and rest of them too.

'Oi, Ray do you know if Mike Kelly's out of nick yet?' Mike Kelly was a mate of Ray's older brother Martin and a very good mate of Gary J's. A few more names of mutual acquain-tances were mentioned and then I asked Ray where his red-headed girlfriend Cheryl was, a 14-year-old stunner, known to go all the way, and Ray was very jealous about her.

'She had to go to stay at her gran's in Salford tonight.'

'Nice-looking bird her Ray, I'll swap you for that Spanish bird I'm with when you're finished with her, I'll even get Valentine to buy her a can of coke.'

Ray laughed. He was scared too.

'See you around.'

I sauntered off, another great Friday night out in the wild west and I thought I was Clint Eastwood.

I was in training for my life at times. I'd been too mouthy at school, just as I had been at home, but now kids who'd been the same size as me were growing six inches taller, a stone heavier and coming back for revenge. I was wired all the time, every day I thought about violence: in school, walking home at night, always tensed up, always alert for it, it was the story of all our teenage years.

If you wanted to live happily in that world, you had to show you could be ruthless. Maybe on a certain level none of us liked each other that much. Part of being a teenager is bragging and lying to your mates, yet feeling all alone, like you are the only one who isn't allowed to go out every night or who hasn't got a girlfriend who goes all the way or who doesn't go to every United away game. We were a bag of inferiority complexes thrown together in a big adolescent playpen and had to fight for the toys and try to ignore the other babies' cries so we could play without disturbance. We had our pride and self-respect, and you couldn't give that up, not even for your best mate. If you couldn't say what you thought where and when you felt like it, then what was the point of living. All we had was our opinions on our view of the world – it was money in our pocket to us, it gave us status. Feelings and showing real emotions, well that was an unaffordable luxury.

Back then nobody really seemed to have any money and football was getting expensive, even though as juniors we got in for half price. In fact we blamed the players' high wages even then, echoing the sentiments of the national tabloid press as ever. 'Three hundred quid a week that ponce Keegan gets paid,' as astounded as the journalist who wrote the article at such a fortune being paid to someone for 'just kicking a ball around'. Funny how twenty-odd years later it's the same old story in the press, the same old criticism of greedy players and dull England team selections and managers and how 'it wasn't like that in the good old days'.

But it is true that prices (and transfer fees and wages) have escalated ever faster in recent years. If you take out normal inflation (ticket prices used to go up every year by a fairly regular amount) the price of football in the Nineties would have meant none of us would have ever been able to go when we were kids. Can you imagine even a not-too-badly-off working-class ten-year-old being able to afford £20, or even £10, to go to the football? Even back when it was less than 50p to get in, it was still a strain on our limited resources.

Money was tight as per usual at home, especially for me as I'd had to pack my paper-round in because of schoolwork. My dad came to the rescue by giving me 40p a week pocket money, enough to get into the match every two weeks and enough for the odd trip to the youth club but only money for one can of pop and a bag of chips. No more Strongbow and no more football boots with screw-in studs or new clothes or match-day programmes, that had gone up from eight pence to ten pence, or half-time Bovrils and Wagon Wheels.

Teenage angst is not easy to keep in control in an over-crowded council house – especially when we were moved out by the council down the rougher end again while our house was modernized. It would be temporary, three months we were told, while the council put in central heating, new windows and new plumbing and wiring. All our possessions were in tea chests, my mother's theory that it wasn't worth unpacking for just three months. The house we were given had been modernized but smaller. Just room for two beds in the rooms, our Tony having to sleep on the couch in the living room when he came back from college in the holidays; back to earth with a bump after hanging about with his posh mates at University.

After three weeks in our temporary home the damp seeped and black fungus started to grow through the new woodchip on the walls, making the whole house smell fusty and dank. It got on our clothes, gave us bad chests and we just couldn't get rid of it, even when the cold winter turned to summer. My mother was beside herself. We lived that way for almost a year, the council's idea of three months. We weren't even on the phone anymore.

I couldn't let anyone see how we lived. I was a self-conscious teenager and I'm embarrassed to say that I felt ashamed. Grammar school and what I thought of as posh kids had made me a snob about my own family and the way we lived, as if we were somehow failures and it was all our fault. The combination of being part of a family that dealt in necessity's, beyond the reach of advertising, and of being an adolescent in a consumerist world, meant that my spirit was cowed. All I had to be proud of was United and I'd be there for them, like they'd always been there for me.

16

Street Hassle

United were top of the league, followed by West Ham, QPR, Everton and Liverpool. We'd beaten Stoke City away, then Tottenham at home by a narrow 3–2 margin, booing Keith Osgood and their top scorer John Duncan throughout the game. We played Brentford in the League Cup, winning 2–1. Then we lost in the league to the Dave Sexton-managed Queens Park Rangers at Loftus Road 1–0.

This was no great surprise given the sheer quality of the QPR team at the time. A midfield of Gerry Francis, Don Masson and John Hollins; McLintock, Webb, Gillard and Clements in defence; and ex-United, Republic of Ireland international Don Givens alongside the maverick, ex-Manchester City, England international Stan Bowles up front. Alex Stepney saved a penalty from Stan Bowles, who then bragged it was the first penalty he'd ever missed. Jimmy Hill again on *Match of the Day* examined United's offside trap.

At home against a strong Ipswich side (albeit minus Kevin Beattie) United edged it 1–0; Coppell, Pearson, Macari and McIlroy in outstanding form, as was young Dave McCreery who replaced the injured Tommy Jackson. It was interesting to read the following letter in the programme for the

Ipswich match from a Joseph Camileri of Bexleyheath in London:

> Dear Editor,
>   When United were top of division one under Frank O'Farrell, not many may remember United's matches were often shown on TV. As we all know United slipped badly in the second half of the season and it is my opinion that one of the main reasons was that TV helps rival managers and coaches to spot the strengths and weaknesses of the team. The play backs and analysis in depth that we see on Match Of The Day and the Granada match gives away any special tactics. If United are to be successful once again I would like the club to restrict TV coverage at Old Trafford to once every three or four months.

I look at those old letters and press cuttings on United nowadays with great amusement. We weren't the champions, but we were the biggest draw in the English game even then. We were always in the headlines. If it wasn't a story about our uncontrollable hooligan fans, it was unfavourably comparing the current team with the great United sides of 1958 and 1968. It would be fair to say it was as a result of those two great sides and the management style and papal-like bearing of Sir Matt Busby that United were so popular throughout the country.

We played football in an attacking and entertaining way, and if we were going to win, it had to be played that way for it to count. As fans we understood this. We wanted to win the championship, but we wanted to do it with flair, style and panache. We didn't want to grind out results in the same workmanlike style of Liverpool or Arsenal, or cheat for victory like Leeds United. We wanted the glory first, the beautiful game.

Any longstanding United fans out there will remember how Dave Sexton was sacked after United won seven games on the trot. The point was, attendances at Old Trafford had dropped by ten or twelve thousand, because it had become like watching Arsenal under George Graham. Dull, effective, but not the sort of game you'd discuss excitedly with friends afterwards, or that would make you determined to get in for the next match. United always set the standard for English football whether we were winning games or not.

After a defeat at the Baseball Ground to the champions Derby County we faced Manchester City at Maine Road. City had a team of big-money signings lined up: Joe Royle, Asa Hartford, Dave Watson. They scored the first thanks to Royle pressuring young Northern Irish full-back Nicholl (who was in for Alex Forsyth) into beating Stepney with a bizarre own-goal.

Within minutes of the restart young Dave McCreery, making his debut in a local derby, equalized, and then Lou Macari headed a Sammy McIlroy corner past Joe Corrigan. Within minutes City had a corner, Mike Doyle picked it up on the edge of the United box, floated it in and Joe Royle met it to level up again. All the goals had come in a ten-minute period.

A 0–0 draw the following week against Leicester City at home was played in front of 47,878 fans, our lowest home gate of the season so far, and we all became obsessed and paranoid about the TV and press coverage. Liverpool, well they'd just say what a great side they were; Man. City they'd focus on Bell and Tueart; Ipswich they'd talk about the blend of youth and experience; but United, well they'd dissect every move in every game, assess each player's weaknesses and strengths, as if to say, Yes they are a good side, but not a patch on those other great sides, and we doubt they'll win the championship.

Victory against Aston Villa in the League Cup at Villa Park on the Wednesday night cheered us up and an away win 2–1 at Leeds sent us into pure ecstasy. We were in second place on goal difference behind QPR on 17 points when Arsenal, including our ex-hero Brian Kidd and ex-United keeper Jimmy Rimmer, came to Old Trafford. 54,000 witnessed United tear a rather indifferent Arsenal side apart. We were still joint top with QPR.

We all thought we'd win the league. We'd been first or second in the table for two months. It looked like all the years of supporting United could and would pay off at last. I'd felt our Tony had sold me a pup at times. The glorious Reds, League Championships, George Best, the European Cup, all that had disappeared since I'd been going to Old Trafford. Instead it had been relegation and disaster paraded behind a team that lost Best and Storey Moore, let Brain Kidd go and brought in no-marks like Tony Young, Paul Edwards, Mick Martin, George Graham, Jim McCalliog (who'd been transferred to Southampton at the end of the last season), Ron Davies and a plethora of forgettable players.

Meanwhile City had won the league, the FA Cup, the European Cup Winners' Cup and the League Cup; while the likes of Arsenal had won the double, Leeds, Everton, Liverpool and even a nothing team like Derby County had won the League Championship; and over-rated fairy teams such as West Ham, Sunderland and Chelsea had all won the FA Cup. When would United win something and become a name to be feared again, back where they belonged among the major honours of football? This season United would do it, surely. Otherwise, what's the point of putting up with school, scrounging the money for matches, having black fungus growing next to your bed, getting dumped by girls, and all of life's other tribulations?

We finally erased the Norwich City bogey with a 1–0 win at Old Trafford after losing against fellow title contenders West

Ham at Upton Park the week before. Liverpool were next, an exciting end-to-end game at Fortress Anfield where United attacked almost suicidally at times, losing honourably 3–1. Then disaster in the League Cup in midweek when Manchester City ran us ragged and triumphed with a mocking 4–0 defeat.

It was a somewhat hollow victory in the end for City who lost Colin Bell for a season and a half after a challenge by Martin Buchan, an injury which ultimately lead to his retirement and scuppered City's hopes of a serious title challenge that season. However City did go on to win the League Cup at Wembley that year against Newcastle United, thanks to goals by Dennis Tueart and Peter Barnes.

We blamed the dreadful beating on our startled-looking young keeper Paddy Roche and bemoaned the fact that Docherty hadn't bought decent cover for Stepney. Still we told ourselves that the League Cup was a Mickey Mouse trophy and we were challenging for the league and then Europe. Such dreams we had.

All those dreams came a sight nearer as United lined up against Aston Villa at Old Trafford, showing off our new £70,000 signing from Millwall, Gordon Hill. A left-footed, left winger with pace and a bag of tricks that had us mentioning him in the same breath as George Best and Ian Storey Moore. United were a dream to watch.

The minuscule Hill on one wing was mercurial, no wonder they nicknamed him Merlin; the tiny Coppell on the other was uncontainable; Macari, McIlroy and Pearson were a defender's worst nightmare. United poured forward in waves of pace, passion and skill. Villa walked off shell-shocked, hardly believing they'd kept the rampaging Reds to a two-goal margin of victory.

After that United blipped once in the next 15 games when they lost to Arsenal at Highbury; and, by the time they lost again, this time to Aston Villa at Villa Park, they were joint top of the table on 40 points with Liverpool and in the quarter-finals of the FA Cup. United were on for the double, playing perhaps the best attacking football, certainly the bravest, that the league had seen in ten years.

It was just too enticing a prospect for us when, a week and half later, the current United side, including our new hero Gordon Hill (but unfortunately minus Greenhoff, Macari and Pearson), played Man. United's European Cup-winning side (minus Johnny Aston but with the addition of Denis Law and Francis Burns) for Paddy Crerand's testimonial at Old Trafford.

On a cold Wednesday night 36,546 people queued up at the turnstiles, partly out of respect, but in our case to see George Best and how our new heroes compared with our old. The teams lining up that night were:

MANCHESTER UNITED 1975 – Paddy Roche, Alex Forsyth, Stewart Houston, Gerry Daly, Jimmy Nicholl, Martin Buchan, Steve Coppell, Dave McCreery, John Lowey, Gordon Hill.

MANCHESTER UNITED 1968 – Alex Stepney, Shay Brennan, Tony Dunne, Pat Crerand, David Sadler, Nobby Stiles, George Best, Brian Kidd, Bobby Charlton, Denis Law, Francis Burns.

It was a night of rare expectation as we settled down by the wall in the Stretford End, partly to save the five pence extra it cost for the Paddock to go towards the ten pence programme, and partly to experience the night in its full passion – after all we supported both teams. It was an even stranger match, with Stiles, Charlton, Kidd, Dunne, Best and Crerand playing some real exhibition stuff. The 1975 side had something to prove against a team which had become an albatross around all subsequent United sides' necks.

In a thrilling encounter with both Best and Kidd looking easily good enough to grace the current United side, the boys of 1975 ran in 7–2 winners with four goals from Dave McCreery and a screamer from Gordon Hill. We cheered every piece of skill, chanted 'Champions of Europe' until we were hoarse.

Then there was a magical moment at the end of the match when the Stretford End chorused at their old hero and epitome of United's fighting spirit, 'Nobby, Nobby, show us your teeth, Nobby, show us your teeth.' And beneath the floodlights Stiles jumped on to the advertising boards, flashing his gummy smile and reliving in his mind a hundred glorious moments. The 1975 boys had laid a ghost to rest, but to truly exorcise it they now had to win the game's top honours; and for a set of supporters as hungry and desperate as we were for trophies it couldn't happen soon enough.

With Hill and Macari looking magnificent, we came face to face with Wolverhampton Wanderers, who were languishing near the bottom of the first division, in the quarter-final of the FA Cup at home. Wolves would be swept aside, of this we had no doubt, all 60,000 of us.

Our mate Roddy was home for the weekend. The big 14-year-old had just started training as a Catholic priest at Upholland junior seminary near Wigan. We joked that Father Roddy, as we called him, had been putting in a good word for the Reds with the Almighty and we were happy to see him again, especially after the furore we had getting him enough tokens to get a ticket. God had sorted everything out, and there was only Derby County left in the whole competition who we were worried about.

The quarter-finals that day lined up as follows: Derby County v. Newcastle United, Sunderland v. Crystal Palace, Bradford City v. Southampton. With the exceptions of Derby and Newcastle, all the other teams were in division two or three. Crystal Palace were the big surprises, a third division side who had knocked out Leeds in an earlier round, and Derby had dismissed Liverpool. United's name was on the Cup all ready.

Wolves had deadly striker John Richards in the side along with Bobby Gould, Kenny Hibbit, Steve Daley and Willie Carr, and it was this midfield trio that caused United problems, stifling our build-ups and stopping us playing our usual game. United swarmed all over Wolves from the kick-off, but couldn't seem to score, last-minute blocks and tackles flying in. Phil Parkes in goal was playing out of his skin and then ... disaster: against the run of play, up pops John Richards and it's Wolves 1, United 0.

Then the crowd started up, shouting until we were hoarse, watching as McIlroy missed sitters and Pearson, Hill and Coppell struggled to find their shooting boots. At last the goal came. Gerry Daly, United's best player up front on the day, strikes a shot which deflects off Willie Carr, past Parkes and settles in the right-hand corner of the goal.

We urged and shouted, United won corner after corner, but the half chances went begging. Wolves had done their homework and rode their luck. It finished all even. The replay would be at Molineux, and we went home aggrieved but quietly relieved, because for ten minutes it looked like United were going out.

I hate listening to football on the radio, but that was the only way I could keep up with United and Wolves at Molineux that Tuesday. My mother kept popping into the kitchen to be updated on the score, as I sat with my homework books open, my good intents frozen as my ears filtered the commentary through the static of our old radio set. I felt sick: United were two goals down and time was ebbing away; and Macari had hobbled off, replaced by Jimmy Nicholl. I wanted to switch the radio off, go out, do anything. I'm glad I didn't.

Goals from Pearson and Greenhoff, who'd been moved up from centre-back to midfield and it was 2–2. Extra-time came and now there was only one team in it as McIlroy put United into the FA Cup semi-final for the twelfth time in their history. Forget homework, forget school, where's my token sheet?!

WOLVERHAMPTON WANDERERS 2, MANCHESTER UNITED 3

Manchester United reached the FA Cup semi-final at Molineux last night with a memorable performance that emphasised they have courage and determination with which to back the skill that already promises to make them as great a team as any of their illustrious predecessors.
DONALD SAUNDERS, *Daily Telegraph*

We were back in the big time. Had any team gone straight up from the second division before and then won the double the following season? United were still a young team: Hill was 22, Coppell 20, McIlroy 21, Daly 23, Greenhoff 23, Forsyth 24 and Houston, Pearson, Macari and Buchan veterans at 26. United oozed a will to win and pure class, both of which they'd need when they faced a star-studded side like Derby County in the FA Cup semi-final at Hillsborough.

United were still being hailed by the press on the one hand and yet excluded from the honours on the other. In the PFA selection of a league team, United didn't have one player selected in any position despite being second in the table, one point behind QPR with a game in hand and in the semi-final of the FA Cup. We couldn't believe the injustice of it. What on earth did players like Martin Buchan, Lou Macari, Steve Coppell and Gordon Hill have to do? Shag the Three Degrees and Princess Anne and then find a cure for cancer? The football world was jealous and small-minded when it came to United, the *cause célèbre* for outsiders and rebels.

I still feel sick about United's run-in to the end of that season with Macari, McIlroy and Pearson all missing important games. United lost three and won three, missing out on the title by four points to Liverpool and finishing in third place. It should never have happened. The United players were too distracted by the FA Cup, and our squad was weak in depth in comparison with Liverpool's. Two decent strikers, that's all we were short of squad-wise, and we would have won the double But United had too many games and the glimpse of glory that the FA Cup proffered was too tempting for a young, passionate side. So I'll remember the good times, but first some bad.

My mate Gary J was a bright lad, but his old man had always given him as much freedom as he liked, even down to taking him to the pub with him for a drink at the age of 14. Gary had been put away by this time. It was almost like a confirmation or bar mitzvah for the lads I grew up with to have been inside at least once by the time their sixteenth birthday arrived. Fines and magistrates didn't count, but respect flowed in proportion to how many three, four or six-month stints you'd done before you were old enough to leave school.

Gary was sent down for burgling shops, including breaking into the sweetshop on the corner of his street, where the woman who owned it had served him since he was a toddler.

Within weeks of being released, he was spotted late one Sunday afternoon in broad daylight on the roof of the same shop, trying to break in through the skylight.

Detention centre certainly made a man out of Gary. Inside he took up boxing, weight-training, got into fights and became more and more smart-mouthed, so that he could not only take the piss wickedly but also back it up physically. Within weeks of coming out of his second stretch, he had chinned a few people and bad-mouthed more. In an area where even to say you weren't scared of someone deemed to be higher in the pecking order was seen as an all-out challenge, Gary suddenly had lots of enemies.

Of course I was too busy with Latin, geometry, war games and wanking to be aware of Gary's recent escapades. Walking home from school one night, dreaming of United v. Derby in the FA Cup, I was accosted by my old *bête noire* Ballantine. He was standing with several older lads including Marco Bentini, Eddie Gilmichael and Ray O'Bannion's older and more evil brother Martin.

It was hard to have to switch on a macho image every time you walked the streets, especially alone – it always ended up as shaky as any Hollywood projection. I'd removed my school-tie as I always did on the long walk home and made myself look as unkempt as possible (not difficult), but whenever I trudged the streets of Old Trafford in my school uniform I always felt half-naked, vulnerable and soft.

Ballantine was an ugly wart on the face of humanity, but not that big. I had his measure, but I was unsure of his intentions and what would result.

'Oi, you're a mate of Gary Johnson's aren't ya?'

I felt slightly more at ease – I was recognized as someone, not a uniformed posh-school victim – but still suspicious.

'What about it?'

Ballantine approached me, and I allowed him to get uncomfortably close. His chest was stuck out and he leaned his face forward, a cocky, slightly menacing grin across his face. A face that you could punch and go on punching forever.

'Just that Eddie and Marco here were wondering if you'd seen him around or not recently.'

Then I made my big mistake. I could have sweetly and naively said no and innocently gone on my way, and that would have been the truth, but Ballantine's cocky manner really needled me.

'Oh aye,' I sneered questioningly, 'how come?'

Eddie Gilmichael swaggered over and grabbed me in a vice-like grip under the collar of my shirt, twisting it and hauling me up on my toes as I choked and heard several buttons pop off my shirt.

'Because he's been gobbing off about me and I want a word with him, anything wrong with that?'

I was crumbling, in fact I had crumbled, and in front of Ballantine too. I could feel the involuntary trembling in my knees, I fought against the shakiness in my half-choked voice.

'I've not seen him for ages, I, er, I just thought Ballantine was going to tell me he'd gone down again or something; I mean why would he ask me where he was, he knows where Gary lives ... I thought he was going to tell me something.'

Eddie relaxed his grip and pushed me away firmly and dismissively.

'Well when you do see him, tell him he's a gobshite, and if all his mates are as rock hard as you he'd better stay out of O.T. Now fuck off.'

I was off the hook partly, but hung around, hesitating. I couldn't just slink off, not in front of Ballantine and O'Bannion's older brother. As I was about to go on my way, Ballantine goaded me further.

'So don't hang around waiting to argue the toss, head out, go on, just fuck off.'

I was fuming inside. I edged away, fixing Ballantine with a look that was pure, lasered hatred.

'I'll pass the message on to Gary all right, and I'll mention you were asking for him too Ballantine!'

Eddie Gilmichael strode forward, tilted his head back and to the side, looking at me through slitted eyes.

'Pass this on then.'

My face felt like it had exploded as he headed the bridge of my nose like a football. I was gagging on blood as it choked in the back of my throat, my head swam and I was on all-fours trying to get off the pavement, knowing that at any moment they might start kicking me. The pain and humiliation were submerged by the numbing shock. I couldn't stand up and I was aware the real hurt and anguish would come later.

'Like he said, don't stand around here yakking and arguing the toss you little twat, when I say fuck off, do it.'

Shirt ripped, covered in blood and barely able to focus I staggered home. The shame engulfed me. I'd get a hammer or something and I'd kill him and that little slime ball Ballantine. As Mike Brannan had said later, when I told him of Ballantine's part in the in the incident. 'You don't waste your time on twats like that, if they give you lip, you just stick a knife in them.'

At home it was 20 Questions off my mam as expected. I told her I'd been in a fight, 'You should see the other guy', all the same old crap. I spent the evening very withdrawn, full of self-pity and seething with thoughts of bloody revenge. For the following weeks I never went anywhere without a sheath knife and my trusty watchstraps, even stealing a cricket box from the school sports store as added protection to wear down the youth club every Friday. Not that Gilmichael would be there, it was kids' stuff to him and he was pub age. It was Ballantine I wanted but he never showed.

I finally heard the story. Gary J and Eddie Gilmichael had been involved in an argument about who was next on the pool table in the Potters Bar at the Seymour pub. The argument had reached a conclusion when Gary wrapped the heavy end of his cue around Eddie's head and then kicked him around the floor until he wasn't going to get up. Not the Marquis of Queensberry rules, but then Eddie had a reputation as a boxer and street-fighter second only to Jimmy Millar in the area, and was built like a junior Charles Bronson, so Gary couldn't afford to mess around.

I was pleased at hearing the story, and made sure I spread it round. I made it sound funny, as if I had been there and the reason Eddie Gilmichael had done me over was because I was taking the piss out of him for it. I'd got beaten up by a hard-case, but I'd had the balls to laugh in his face first. I knew it was bullshit, but had people known I'd just been beaten up for being Gary's mate and a wimp, Old Trafford rules would have obliged me to do something about evening up the score with Mr Gilmichael, and to be honest, I was scared shitless of that.

It was a sordid world that Mr Gilmichael and the O'Bannions inhabited. There was a girl called Jeannette Barr; we all fancied her, she was so pretty, the only daughter of a single mother. We were too afraid of her striking beauty to ask her out – she seemed untouchable, the type of girl who made you feel that every pimple on your face was a huge, ugly boil shouting for attention. We'd compete to make ourselves amusing to her. Eddie Gilmichael had no such qualms.

Jeannette became his girlfriend, cowed and bullied. She lost her virginity to him aged 14 in an almost ritual rape witnessed by Kevin McAuliffe and Martin O'Bannion on an unmade bed in her own house while her mother was at work. Kevin

McAuliffe laughed when he told us how she lay there saying she didn't want to, but Eddie just went ahead, violent thrusting his foreplay. That was the underside to life in our area, bruisingly harsh with no sense of shame and proud of it.

I came out of the library one Saturday morning some four weeks after my nose job. I was daydreaming, it was United at home to Middlesbrough, a week before the FA Cup semi-final at Hillsborough. I had my red Mitre sports bag (bottom of the range) across my shoulders with my homework and books in; it also contained a broken Second World War bayonet my mother had used as a poker for our fire at home. Just as I turned on to Henrietta Street, I walked straight into Ballantine and two other cronies who hung around with Ray O'Bannion.

'Hey look, there's that little rocko.'

Ballantine got no further with his mockery: in a split second I was bouncing his head off one of the low garden walls, hanging on to his ears. I soon felt hands dragging me off as he slumped to the floor. I pushed the hands away. 'It's all right, I'm finished.' As Ballantine's two friends stepped away from me, I aimed a vicious kick as hard as I could at his prostrate bloodied head and then spat on him. There was no fear, no real exultation, only the satisfaction that I hadn't failed.

I turned to his mates who eyed me suspiciously, shrugged my shoulders at them, half-smiling and turned and gave Ballantine's whimpering figure another kick for good measure, splashing blood in every direction. 'Fucking animal,' one of the lads muttered. Then the exultation came: I'd made a point, I was safe to go where I pleased for the time being at least, ruthless enough to live in that warped world and pride had been restored. No visit to the library was ever quite as educational.

17

'Who the F*** is Bobby Stokes?'

Leppings Lane End, Hillsborough. It was packed, moving and swaying. An incident here years later has soured all my good memories, and I for one, despite people wanting to go back to standing on the terraces, will never do it again. On the pitch United v. Derby County: youth, fire, passion and skill meets experience, confidence, organisation and skill.

We'd lost at Ipswich 3–0 a few weeks earlier, and Derby County were a better side than them. God only knew what would happen. The semi-final draw had been cruel to both United and Derby, pitting the two first division teams against each other, while at Stamford Bridge second division Southampton played third division Crystal Palace. This was the real final; whoever won this game would undoubtedly win the FA Cup. The supporters of both teams felt that, and it was a game worthy of Wembley.

The teams came out to warm up. Derby County, solid and mean-looking, looked like giants next to United's midgets. Graham Moseley in goal, Rod Thomas and England international David Nish at full-back, and the dream international centre-back partnership of Roy MacFarland and Colin Todd;

the hard-tackling, running and shooting of Scottish internationals Archie Gemmill and Bruce Rioch in midfield; the sublime skill, pace and shooting of Welsh international Leighton James on the wing; and top strikers Roger Davies and Kevin Hector up front. The holding League Champions, they were again right up there with United, Liverpool and QPR, challenging for the title.

We were worried, and it was a worry exacerbated by the absence of Lou Macari, our player of the season. Instead of Macari we had the combative 18-year-old sheepdog lookalike David McCreery. It could all go so terribly wrong. Despite United being slight underdogs, no neutral wanted to see them win; it was the old story, the outsiders' team against the world, that's why we loved them.

The press and TV pundits were all tipping Derby County, giving the experience of the Derby players and the absence of the inspirational Macari as their reasons. United might make it go to a replay or if given the lucky breaks might snatch it, but not one had said, 'United will win'. The stands were two thirds red, white and black, with banners proclaiming Docherty's Red and White Army and the amusing 'Jesus Saves – Pearson scores the rebound' hoisted aloft.

MANCHESTER UNITED – Stepney, Forsyth, Houston, Daly, Greenhoff, Buchan, Coppell, McIlroy, Pearson, McCreery, Hill.
DERBY COUNTY – Moseley, Thomas, Nish, Rioch, McFarland, Todd, Powell, Gemmill, Hector, Davies, James.

From kick-off we breathed a sigh of relief as McCreery and Daly got straight in amongst Rioch and Gemmill, and the pacey jinking runs of Gordon Hill and Coppell signalled to Thomas and Nish that it was going to be a difficult afternoon for them. McFarland struggled with Pearson's acceleration and

Derby looked nervous and unsettled. Before they could even settle in they found themselves a goal down. In the twelfth minute Gordon Hill picked up the ball 20 yards out on the edge of the Derby box and unleashed a sizzling and swerving left-foot drive.

It was all over for Derby who were completely overrun. United made chance after chance, and although Nish managed to contain Coppell, on the other wing Hill destroyed Rod Thomas, making him look third-rate. It was Gordon Hill's finest hour for Manchester United, one of the all-time great performances in a Red shirt, surely even ranking alongside some of Best's moments. When Hill scorched in a long-range free-kick, like a 1970 Brazilian player, for United's second goal I even felt sorry for Derby and their fans. Final score: 2–0 and United were at Wembley. Derby couldn't have complained had it been six, it was that one-sided and breathtaking.

All that season, all the scrabbling around for tokens, going to shitty reserve games, trying to scrounge an extra ten pence to get a spare programme for a spare token, to do extra token sheets for absent friends – it had all been worth it. We were the famous Man. United and we were going to Wemb-er-lee. And I prayed that I'd be able to go too.

In my whole life I'd never really cried in public; not when beaten to the ground in a fight; not when as an infant I'd scraped my knee in the playground or street; nor when as a four-year-old I was caught stealing a bunch of grapes from outside the greengrocers and first felt my Dad's belt. On the deep terraced steps of Wembley the tears kept coming. It was 1 May 1976: it may have been sunny and bright, full of hope colour and noise, an experience to savour, but like a dark tragedy I've blotted every memory from my mind.

I'd spent every penny of my advanced birthday money and found myself yards from hoards of Wurzel-voiced, country-bumpkin, yokel Southampton fans celebrating as I vainly attempted to choke back tears that wouldn't stop. I hated Wembley, felt annoyed at Gordon Hill, aggrieved at Jim McCalliog kissing his winner's medal as he lapped the pitch wearing the colours of Southampton. It was the injustice and unfairness of it all. I'd been waiting half my lifetime to see United win something, and now I'd seen it foiled by the post, the crossbar, the Gods themselves.

There were those stalwarts who cheered United and continued in the face of devastating circumstances to applaud. We'd been the best team by far, we'd pushed them, penetrated their defences again and again, overrun them in midfield, squandered chance after chance and now all I felt was anger and hurt, and I was hungry and far from home.

Bobby Stokes ... I mean who the fuck is Bobby Stokes. Had it been Osgood, Channon, McCalliog, fair enough, at least they were somebodies. But Bobby Stokes was a mile offside when McCalliog slipped him through and what the hell was Stepney doing: he'd had nothing to save all afternoon, he must have been as blind as the referee or linesman. No matter where I am, what I hear or what I see, I'll refuse to believe otherwise and it's one thought I will take to the grave with me: Manchester United were cheated out of the FA Cup in 1976 by an offside goal and nobody except us Reds cared.

That's all you are getting in this book about that miserable day. I went home and tore the team photo announcing 'Doc's May Day Marvels' off the bedroom wall to display the damp black fungus which lurked behind. Eight years and we'd won nothing, seven years of our pocket money spent on watching the reds struggle and strain and all our hopes and dreams shattered. On the Sunday thousands turned out to greet the losing

United team as they paraded through town. Tommy Docherty said, 'If this many turn up to greet us when we lose, what would it have been like had we won.' I sat watching on the TV thinking, well there would have been at least one other person in that crowd ... me!

Martin Buchan, one of the all-time great United players and every inch the team captain, bravely stuck his neck out in the press. 'We'll be back next year, and we'll win.' I was heartened as this type of statement was out of character for Buchan, but I thought back to all those defeats: League Cup semi-finals, the FA Cup semi-final against Leeds in 1970, the European Cup semi-final against AC Milan in 1969 ... United hadn't won the FA Cup or been in an FA Cup final since 1963. Thirteen years it had taken us to get there, despite Best, Dunne, Law, Morgan, Stiles, Charlton and the likes. Deep down inside every one of us felt we were kidding ourselves.

Using the same token sheets we'd already bought our tickets for the last game of the season, Manchester United v. Manchester City. The following weekend the Home Internationals started and the two teams would provide 15 players for the various squads, with Greenhoff, Pearson, Coppell and Hill all called up to Don Revie's England squad. But first something far more exciting than international (yawn) football.

Again this was a grudge match for City. United had finished third in the league with no chance of overtaking either Liverpool who were champions or runners-up Queens Park Rangers. City had a chance of improving from eighth to seventh on goal average above Leicester if they won this one. It was the first time since the 1970–71 season that City had finished lower than United in the league and of course United wanted to avenge their 4–0 humiliation by City in the League Cup earlier in the season.

Just under 60,000 crowded into Old Trafford to savour the venomous atmosphere, added to by the fact that Tommy Docherty's son, Mick was playing in his first derby debut for Man. City. Both teams had injury problems: Bell had been out since the last meeting between the clubs, Scottish international full-back Willie Donachie and England centre-half Dave Watson were both out for City, while United were without Lou Macari and Brian Greenhoff.

MANCHESTER UNITED – Alex Stepney, Alex Forsyth, Stewart Houston, Gerry Daly, Arthur Albiston, Martin Buchan, Steve Coppell, Sammy McIlroy, Stuart Pearson, Tommy Jackson, Gordon Hill; sub – Dave McCreery.
MANCHESTER CITY – Joe Corrigan, Kenny Clements, Mick Docherty, Mike Doyle, Tommy Booth, Ged Keegan, Peter Barnes, Paul Power, Joe Royle, Asa Hartford, Dennis Tueart; sub – Alan Oakes.

We feared that United could be suffering a bad hangover after their Wembley disappointment a few days earlier, and given the injuries, we secretly dreaded a repeat of the previous November's humiliation. But Docherty's team was made of sterner stuff. Gordon Hill made up for his disappearing act at Wembley on his derby debut by scoring and United were just too strong for a City side who, after McIlroy had scored, were just trying to keep the score to a respectable 2–0.

In retrospect, the entertainment value to be had in those days for a mere 40p was simply overwhelming. The season was over and we faced a summer bereft of excitement, but hopeful that, with a couple of good buys, the following season we'd be champions.

We'd messed up the title by being in the FA Cup and not having a strong enough squad. Although the Cup was exciting, we longed to be back in the European Cup where we truly belonged, because we had been without any doubt England's most exciting and outstanding team that season. It was also sickening that City had actually won a trophy, even if it was the League Cup. After all Derby County had won the league the year before with 53 points, so we felt unlucky.

We had at least managed to finish in our best league position since 1967–68 season and we were above City, something we'd been telling City fans for years, although we invariably meant above them in the food chain rather than the league. At school the next day I went around collecting my ten and twenty-pence bets off the City fans foolhardy enough to have put their pocket money where their mouths had been.

As the 1976/77 season kicked off we were full of optimism, but with one reservation. United were in Europe, but those big summer signings had once more failed to materialize. While we dreamed of Claudio Gentile, Franz Beckenbauer, Johann Cruyff or Gunther Netzer, Tommy Docherty thought Alan Foggon from Middlesbrough was the missing piece in United's game plan for the top honours in football.

Alan Foggon was quite frankly absolutely useless. At Middlesbrough in his purple period he had pace and a decent shot; at United he just looked like a no-class lard-arse midfield clogger in a Red shirt, and that's the way the few United fans who recall his mercifully brief appearances will always remember him. Northern Irish defender Jimmy Nicholl in the meantime was brought in from the reserves to take over from Alex Forsyth at right-back. Nicholl had more pace than Forsyth and was a bit more effective at going forward, although he lacked the Scotsman's lethal shooting power. Otherwise it was the same team as the year before.

United's first game of the season was against Birmingham City and the Reds, still a young side, lined up as follows:

Stepney, Nicholl, Houston, Daly, Greenhoff, Buchan, Coppell, McIlroy, Pearson, Macari, Hill; sub – Foggon. Birmingham City, a team who – despite the talents of their striker Trevor Francis and ex-Everton midfielder Howard Kendall – would basically be battling relegation from the start of the season, were cannon fodder as far as we were concerned. Imagine our disappointment then at seeing United draw 2–2, despite Docherty's masterstroke of bringing on Alan Foggon for Gerry Daly late in the game.

Other teams had United sussed that season and we played like a decent middle-of-the-table side, a disappointment after all the heady promise shown the season before. The team failed to show any consistency. We drew away with Derby County 0–0 and then unbelievably lost 3–2 at home to Spurs (always a sign your form was average or worse).

We ventured into the UEFA Cup against Ajax of Holland, losing 1–0 in Amsterdam, before defeating them a fortnight later 2–0 in our first European game at Old Trafford in eight years. After that we trounced City at Maine Road (an important game as City were flying high) and had a good away win at Leeds, who were something of a spent force. Then disaster as we entered October and lost 4–0 at to West Brom. at The Hawthorns.

In the second round of the UEFA Cup United faced Juventus at Old Trafford. United rallied on that most celebratory of nights, inspired by the 60,000 crowd. Gordon Hill was rampant on the left wing against some of the most cynical and disgraceful tackling and refereeing we'd ever witnessed at Old Trafford. United should have had three penalties and several Juventus players should have been sent off. We screamed hatred from the terraces at the Italians and shouted ourselves hoarse as Gordon Hill scored a wonder goal, giving United a slender 1–0 lead against the Italian giants to take to Turin in two weeks time.

Juventus had already claimed Manchester City's scalp in the first round of the UEFA Cup when they'd lost 1–0 at Maine Road (thanks to a goal by ex-United hero Brian Kidd) and then beaten City 2–0 in Turin. It was important that United go to Turin and get a result. Unfortunately United's return game in Turin coincided with our worst form since we'd been relegated three years earlier and the Italians romped home 3–0 in front of a fanatical crowd.

United's confidence took a blow, a fact illustrated when they drew at home to Norwich and lost at home to Ipswich and away to Aston Villa. For almost three months, barring the home victory against Juventus and a 7–2 annihilation of Newcastle United in the League Cup, United didn't win a game. Finally Docherty, in search of some consistency, dipped into the transfer market for Brian Greenhoff's older brother Jimmy, a £120,000 snip from Stoke City, and at last we had an out-and-out striker of quality to play alongside Stuart Pearson.

I could write a book about Jimmy Greenhoff: no purchase has had such an instant impact on a United team except for Eric Cantona or perhaps Dwight Yorke, and I have no hesitation in putting Jimmy Greenhoff in that class. He had an eye for goal, worked for the team, had vision and great passing, just a good touch all around, and was undoubtedly one of the greatest uncapped players of his era.

Jimmy made his home debut for United at Old Trafford against a much-fancied Everton side bursting with big-money signings who had put three past United at Old Trafford three weeks earlier in a League Cup quarter-final. He pepped up United no end. Daly was dropped, McIlroy moved into midfield and at last United looked a better balanced side. Greenhoff (J), Pearson, Macari and Gordon Hill ran Everton ragged, bagging a goal a piece in a famous 4–0 rout.

In the next 20 games in both the league and FA Cup United

lost only twice. Passion and guts: that was what Docherty's United team showed. Nobody shirked a tackle or hid on the pitch, there were no strollers in that team, with perhaps the exception of Gordon Hill, who made up in sheer impudence and skill what he sometimes lacked in competitiveness. Docherty's Babes were turning into men, and United were only one or two players short of being a championship side.

It was the Cup again that inspired United that year, as they scrapped with Liverpool, Ipswich and Manchester City for the league top spot. United's Cup run began on a dull January day against Walsall – a game in which the lower league opposition fought tigerishly – a solitary goal by Gordon Hill beginning United's march to Cup glory. The next round saw Queens Park Rangers dispatched by the same scoreline, this time thanks to Macari. Round five and United were drawn away to the hated Southampton who'd deprived us of glory the year before.

In a fierce contest at the Dell, honours were even. At Old Trafford ten days later, under the floodlights, another close game saw United run out 2–1 winners, thanks to two goals by the superb Jimmy Greenhoff. As we watched the game unfold, we couldn't help but wonder if this was a good omen, if we would really be returning to Wembley for what was rightly ours. The Gods seemed to favour us with a home tie against a more than useful Aston Villa who were just two places and three points below United in the league and boasted Andy Gray, the first division's top scorer at the time.

All my mates were so sure that United would win the FA Cup and I echoed their words … but inside I was a doubting Thomas. We'd beaten Villa 2–0 at Old Trafford a couple of months earlier and we had to fancy our chances against them, but who could predict anything in the FA Cup? Who could have predicted McIlroy's header hitting the bar or Southampton playing as they did and winning the final on that blackest of days last May? Yet in front of 58,000 at Old Trafford Southampton had played ten times better than they had at Wembley and lost ... funny old game.

18

Living for the Moment

She lived near the library and I'd met her at the parish dance. All the lads I'd gone to school with fancied her, but it was me she talked to all evening. She laughed at my daft jokes and turned other lads down when they asked her to dance or offered to buy her a snowball at the bar. It was a dance with a licensed bar, but then it was an Irish Catholic church's fundraising dance for St Alphonsus parish, and the Irish were fairly liberal about underage drinking. In fact most fathers in our community would have worried if their sons hadn't had their first pint by the age of 15, and teenage drinkers were accepted as long as they were accompanied by an adult – kind of a night out on the beer with a PG certificate.

I'd had two pints of snakebite and my head was with the fairies as I fawned over my new admirer. I'd snogged a couple of girls before, even had a three-week romance with a girl I'd walk home from the youth club, dodging down entries for a snog and a fumble. Then one day she just ignored me, and whatever slight she must have felt I'd caused her wasn't as bad as the slight she'd paid me. But this girl, well she was perfect.

Dark sandy-coloured thick hair that reached down to her waist, greeny-blue eyes, the body of a woman hugged by a dress, she towered three inches above me in her heels. I was just pleased she acknowledged my existence, never mind spoke to me and showed amusement and interest in my conversation while forsaking all others. So after several hours of conversing with this girl and her friends and discovering several of my old primary school friends were her cousins, did I offer to walk her home, ask for a date, or did I play it cool and let her do all the running? Well, none of those things really.

I didn't walk her home as I didn't fancy having to walk back at midnight from Old Trafford Community Centre on my own without an escort of friends for at least two thirds of the journey. I daren't ask her for a date, because she would no doubt refuse and laugh in my face for having the cheek to think that a girl like her would ever be interested in a little scruff like me, with his school shirt and trousers on, and a bad fawn-coloured jacket that was too big and being paid for on the weekly out of the GUS catalogue at home. And besides, if she said yes, I didn't have enough money to entertain both her and Manchester United and where could I take her?

St Alphonsus youth club on a Friday with its law of the jungle atmosphere? Then having to walk her home on my own through some of the most dangerous streets in Old Trafford, crawling with enemies and muggers. I could take her to the pictures, but it was expensive and what if she wanted to go to see an X-rated film. They'd never believe I was 18 and although I was nearly 15 I still got pulled up when I'd gone to see an AA certificate because the woman at the ticket kiosk didn't believe I was 14. All I could see was my ultimate humiliation in a relationship like this. My mother wouldn't let me out at night, I couldn't invite her round to our house as there was nowhere for us to be on our own there – no room, no space, too many nosey brothers and sisters who'd tell stories about me and make me look stupid, especially as I'd pretended to her to be something I wasn't, i.e., fairly well-off family, confident, witty and a bit of an intellectual man about town.

I said nothing, didn't even let on to my mates that I fancied her like mad as they teased me about her all the way home. I saw her sitting a few rows in front of me at evening Mass that Sunday. Evening Mass was the adolescents' Mass. All the Catholic teenagers went to the 6.30 Mass: it was like a halfway house before we stopped going altogether and turned into Catholics of the lapsed variety. All the lads I knew went there to ogle at girls they fancied and the girls would always look their going-out best, with their best dresses on, make-up, heels, stockings and gallons of perfume.

We'd sit, kneel, stand throughout the service, staring at the objects of our desires, hoping to catch their eye with a cheeky wink as they returned to their pews after receiving holy communion, our eyes nearly popping out as they bent on one knee and genuflected, before kneeling in quiet meditation to absorb the body and blood of Christ our Saviour. Irish Catholic girls, such beautiful faces and womanly ways. They knew we were looking and, eyes downcast, they'd occasionally smile as we winked at them, never totally acknowledging our interest. If they glanced across and we caught them gazing in our direction, they'd swiftly avert their eyes to one of the stations of the cross that went around the church.

Such impure thoughts and right in the house of God too; how hard-faced could you get. And I was the worst offender, brazen in my sin and wantonness. I looked at Jesus on the cross above the altar and wondered if asking for forgiveness would be like murdering my parents then asking the judge for mercy on account of being an orphan. Such poetry in my soul then, such ideas and none of this 'One day I'll be a millionaire and everyone will think I'm great' type stuff.

On a personal level I aspired to having a job that didn't

mean working on a Saturday; clothes that I didn't wear for school all the time and a jacket bought from a shop, not a catalogue; the freedom to stay out late at night; a front room where I could take a girlfriend in private for a snog and enough money to take her to the pictures on a Saturday night, and dancing at St Brendan's Irish club on a Sunday, and to discos in town on Fridays without being asked my age; and still be able to afford to go the match on Saturday. Maybe I'd even be able to go to away games without having to scrimp and save and lie to my mam or worry in case I got found out.

In terms of attainability, these modest personal aspirations were as far away as if I'd dreamed of curing world hunger, being a millionaire or George Best or a film star. And no matter how different and special I'd occasionally think I was inside compared to other people, I knew that as a teenage boy I was a dead loss – no longer quite the lad I'd been, grammar school had seen to that. Yet I didn't really fit in with the type of person that my education wanted me to be because I was scared that if I did I'd be a traitor to all the things I'd grown up with and I'd be a kind of no one.

These thoughts tortured my head for weeks. Like a good Catholic boy I went to Mass – 6.30 Mass on Sunday evening, the one she went to, disappointed if she wasn't there. Then it was an unusually busy Friday night at the youth club. We'd decided by now we were men, so we'd slip away from the club at around 10.30 and head to the Seymour for last orders; just enough money for one pint of Wilson's bitter in a pub that was like a fourth and fifth-form school convention.

In the Seymour the atmosphere made everything else, all the worries and insecurities and dissatisfactions, seem irrelevant. Outside the Potters Bar, Gary Johnson and Eddie Gilmichael sold quarters of Moroccan hash for £6.25, £3.50 an eighth or

a wrap for £1. They were sworn enemies turned allies in business, part of a little firm. They were always smiling, always
popular with girls buying us drinks and inviting us to illegal
blues and student parties in Chorlton. They seemed to be
having a ball. This was what people like me should do: try to
live for the day, get some money, snog girls, laugh and drink
beer. Everything else just seemed like a glum and miserable
way to spend your life: work, marriage, future, prospects, paying
rent and bills. Not me God, never me, I'm not going to get
trapped by that, anything except routine. I want a life of flying
by the seat of my pants, no big ambitions, I'm too impatient,
just a raw appetite for living now, like George Best had an
appetite for the ball and wouldn't pass it during a game.

But then I'd think of all my parents' sacrifices to bring us up
decent, despite the unfairness they'd suffered in their lives. And
then I'd think of the sometimes unfair punishments dished out
by them, the burden of my mother's ambitions for us to take
her past and turn it into something – but where, when and
how? It was just like Manchester United: Docherty had built a
team that was entertaining, promising greatness, and yet, like
every United manager, it would suffer the memory of those
great Busby teams of '58 and '68 corroding its future.

Even at that young age I understood to an extent that all
those years of gallivanting about with my mates, wanting the
same things as them, that would have to go – I'd have to let go.
I clung on, dogged by those unrealizable childhood dreams of
being George Best. I now had no role models and I secretly
despised all those things about myself that I knew were working class and that I thought would hold me back in other ways
of life. But equally I despised the pretend me that tried to fit
in at school, the me that was almost a betrayal.

Even so I couldn't give up the Manchester United part of
that dream. I'd cling on to United like a dog to a bone and yet

there was no earthly or logical reason why my life couldn't have been happier without them. Strange that several years later at Old Trafford I nearly gave up on United. Here was a team that played football, went forward fearlessly, almost recklessly at times. They played like champions, yet they never seemed to win the league.

I think it was a Wednesday evening against Everton, either way it was Easter time, cold wet and miserable with it. I looked on as the previous year's champions, with nothing to play for, packed their defence, looking for the 0–0 draw they eventually got. I felt a strangely intense anger about it, a howling resentment at the injustice, almost as if there was a conspiracy to prevent United ever winning a championship, like an unofficial glass ceiling that keeps the working classes and blacks and Asians out of the top jobs. The spite of it almost drove me away forever. But even then, I didn't despair completely. United were what linked my past with my present and my future for better and worse.

Women, music, drink, breaking the rules and an appetite too strongly rooted in the present was too seductive a mixture. I sold my LPs at school for a pound each, sold my old United and City programmes from previous seasons for five pence and ten pence each, my *Shoot* annuals, my younger brother's Marvel comics, sold anything I could to get enough money to take the object of my desires out.

It was in the library on a Saturday morning the week before the Villa game. I passed Siobhan's house on the way, wondering what she'd be up to, if she was in, whether she ever spotted me carrying my homework past the net curtains. In the library I settled down, school textbooks out on the huge table in the corner, restless in the quiet. She suddenly materialized and sat down opposite me and I was in sheer panic, blushing beetroot.

She'd caught me looking scruffy and dowdy, doing home-work in the library like a swot, what kind of man was I? She'd never let me take her out now, even if I dared utter the words to ask her.

'Hi.' She uttered the word so shamelessly and in such a nonchalant, friendly manner. I gulped and squeaked a 'hello' – I could feel my face glowing and immediately looked down at my text book, unworthy to gaze at such a pretty face. The page may as well have been blank. This was the girl I'd been daydreaming about for weeks and now here she was. I'd gone through this scenario time after time in my imagination, and now in reality it was even more unreal. It was as if I was back at the old Imperial faced with an actress in a film I couldn't join in with.

'Are you going to the match today?'

'Er, er, yeah, course I am.' I was aggressive, oh God I was too aggressive. Thankfully she didn't notice.

'I'd love to go to a match, who are they playing?

'Leeds.'

'Can I come with you?'

'Er, yeah, I mean no, it's all-ticket.'

'Do you ever go to St Brendan's?'

'Er I've been [lie], but not really.'

'Oh you should come tonight, we always go on Saturday.'

'Who with?'

'Oh some of my cousins and my mam and dad.'

St Brendan's was a big Irish club on City Road on the borders of Old Trafford and Hulme. It was known to be a very traditional type club with Irish show bands playing a mixture of Irish ballads, ceilidh and country and western. It sounded like a nightmare to me, I was into reggae, soul music and the Beatles. But the more vexing problem was that I knew my mother would never let me go.

'Er, yeah, but I can't go tonight, what about next week?'

'Oh that's a shame. OK, next week, but don't let me down.'

'Well how can I arrange to meet you?'

She smiled and handed me her phone number that she had already written in fountain pen on a neatly folded piece of paper like a calling card. I was open-mouthed: all the struggles and worries and then she as good as asks me out, at least I think she had … she must have, or maybe she just sees me as a friend. This was too complicated.

I didn't tell my mates anything about the incident in the library, they'd just spend the whole match taking the piss and if she did indeed just want to be friends they'd mock me even more mercilessly. Leeds were woeful, United nearly as bad, making hard work of their goalscoring chances despite the capacity 61,000 crowd roaring them on to victory. My head was away with the fairies again and struggling with the week's problems to come, when an arm went round my neck and a roar exploded across Old Trafford as the ball spun from Steve Coppell's foot to rebound off Trevor Cherry for the only goal of the match.

United were in championship form, playing poorly at times but getting results. We whispered about possible league and Cup doubles, but quietly in case fate was eavesdropping and ready to act the despoiler.

United dumped Aston Villa unceremoniously out of an open FA Cup quarter-final. Villa were supposedly tired out after their League Cup Final replay at Hillsborough in midweek, but we couldn't care less. United were the better team and won 2–1, deservedly so. We wondered who we'd draw in the semi-final, hoping it wouldn't be Liverpool and praying that we'd be able to go.

Financing football was becoming more and more of a struggle. The semi-final was to be against Leeds United, who were well past their peak of earlier years, and like last year's semi-final it was at Hillsborough in Sheffield. We knew it would cost around a pound for the ticket and between £1.50 and £1.75 for the return coach fare, which meant we'd need four or five pound each to make a day of it. And then there was Wembley: at least £2.00 for the ticket and nearly a tenner for the coach or train down there. These amounts could have been scraped together by some lads, but I would have to become a hermit for the next eight weeks or so to achieve this. My finances were of course now complicated by having the extravagance of a girlfriend.

She was definitely the pick of a fairly good bunch, but she was an Irish girl. Her parents were both from County Mayo, staunch Catholics with their own ideas on courtship even at that age. Old Trafford's Irish community was a B-film scripted moral throwback to an Edna O'Brien Ireland of the 1950s with a touch of John Ford's *The Quiet Man* thrown in for good measure. It was a romantic ideal and even puppy love relationships were seen as a possible pre-cursor to the sacrament of marriage.

The script read that you started courting a girl at the age of 14 or 15, with her family's approval of course. Engaged at 16, when ideally you would both be working. Save up for a deposit on a house which her family may well help out with if they could afford it. Marriage at 19 or 20 and then it was three kids by the time you were 25. Respectability and decency with a capital R and D, everything above board. Manchester's Irish clubs played out these mini-soaps in thousands of people's lives and I've no doubt other Irish clubs across Britain were stages to similar scenarios. My first date with the girl of my dreams at St Brendan's Irish club was a real eye-opener.

We'd been hankering for straight-legged black corduroys as flared jeans and trousers fought a dogged rearguard action against the encroaching drainpipe trousers which heralded the emergence of punk rock. Punk was a big thing at our school, as the 16-year-old drummer with the Buzzcocks, John Maher, had been a pupil there until Christmas, and he'd also gone to primary school with me. We all thought it was the coolest thing in the world that he'd left the sixth form after a mere eight weeks to go on tour supporting The Clash (even though his punk ethics didn't stop him being a regular at 9.30 a.m. Mass every Sunday at St Alphonsus church). I'd recently invested £8.99, a discount price, in a pair of Castaways black cord jeans and wore them mismatched with my wide-lapelled nightmare fawn-coloured jacket to pick up Siobhan from her home at 7.30 p.m. to go to St Brendan's.

I'd lied to my mother telling her I was going to a house party at a friend's on Ayres Road and I'd be home around 11.30. She wasn't too pleased at this decadent suggestion but allowed me the liberty. There was no way in the world my mother would knowingly allow me on any licensed premises. Siobhan looked a dream, even if she was a little over dressed for girl her age. Her charm bracelets hung with solid gold, she had gold necklaces and four rings on each hand, including a solid white gold Claddagh ring and huge gold pendant earrings. She was her father's eldest daughter and had a younger sister of ten, who was shunted into the front room of her house to act as impromptu chaperone as I finished my cup of milky tea. Before taking her big sister on what I now realized was very much a date to St Brendan's, I was informed, as if in warning, that her father would be along later.

Her hand felt warm, her perfume heavy and sweet. Two hours she'd spent drying her hair which was full and thick, falling to just above her waist. I felt like a king, proudly walking her to St Brendan's while I worried as to whether they'd just turn me away at the door for looking too young. I had £3.20 in my pocket, so as long as I didn't get dragged into any big rounds I'd have enough to pay the 50p each admission and buy the drinks all night. My hand gripped hers tightly as we approached the two huge red-faced men on the door.

'Good evening Siobhan, you're looking lovely, is Eamon coming along later, how's your mother?'

They knew her. I scrambled in my pocket taking out a pound note, reluctantly handing it over. She then asked me if I had five pence for her to put her coat in. The club was only a quarter full, as it had only just gone half-past seven. It was a largish place with a stage for the band, a dancefloor, tables around the perimeter and a huge bar. Framed charts on the wall displayed the coats of arms of the famous names of Ireland, O'Byrne, O'Rourke, O'Brien, O'Connor, Fitzpatrick, O'Neill and so on, and a huge map of Ireland displayed those famous names and their colourful crests in the various Irish territories and Tuatha which were their strongholds.

I was fascinated by the coats of arms, searching vainly for Christian, and was dismayed to find it wasn't included, not even with a prefixing 'O' or 'Mac'. I suddenly felt like I didn't belong, as if I couldn't even be Irish properly. I was reassured by the coats of arms of the O'Cullens, which was my mother's maiden name, and O'Byrne, which was my paternal grand-mother's maiden name. But I felt aggrieved that if I wasn't Irish enough to have a coat of arms or a territory on this chart, then where did I belong?

Siobhan dragged me upstairs to a different bar with a large seating area which overlooked the dancefloor below. There were very few people in and we sat awaiting the arrival of her cousins and assorted friends who would join us during the course of the evening. By nine o'clock the place was almost full to bursting and getting fuller as the night went on. I was happily surprised to find myself sitting with several lads I'd been to primary school with, some of whom were Siobhan's cousins.

We talked football of course and United's chances of the double, and they talked of money-making schemes and helping out doing building work for their fathers and uncles at the weekend and why hadn't I been down to St Brendan's before. They offered to buy me drinks until I had four pints of bitter lined up in front of me and I still hadn't finished my first. Somehow I felt they were more grown-up than me, even though they were the same age, perhaps because they went out drinking with their girlfriends every Saturday and Sunday night. They assured me that Sunday night was even better and more full of life than it was tonight. With the alcohol affecting my brain I gazed at the black velvet jackets and beige bags that smothered their stocky frames and wondered if it could be true that if you couldn't see your shirt collar with your peripheral vision it wasn't fashionable enough. And all the time the music blared from The Ranchers showband below: 'The Wild Side Of Life', 'I Recall A Gypsy Woman', 'The Blanket On The Ground', and it was as if I experienced the whole thing by proxy.

I was guided down the steps to the dancefloor to join the assorted O'Briens, Kellys, Donegans, Brogans and partners for a slow dance to a romantic sounding air with far from romantic lyrics.

> It was down in the town of O'Bantry
> Where most of the fighting was done
> It was there where a young Irish soldier
> Lay shot by a Black and Tan gun.

As he raised himself up on his elbow,
The blood from his wounds it ran red
He turned to his comrades beside him
And these are the words that he said

Won't you bury me out on the hill side
So I can see where the battle was won
So they buried him out on the mountain
Beneath a cross that lay facing the sun.

It wasn't Marvin Gaye singing 'Lets Get It On ', but it certainly hit the spot with me and by the time the dance had finished I was more than ready to cry 'Up the Republic'.

At midnight they played the Irish national anthem, 'The Soldiers Song', and we all stood. Drinking-up time, collecting coats. By the time I got home it was nearly one o'clock in the morning and my mother had been round to the false party I'd told her about to find a house asleep and herself shamed and an inch away from phoning the police. The wrath of my parents descended: I was grounded and there was no way I would be going to the FA Cup semi-final against Leeds.

Had it been worth it? Worth selling my treasured copy of *Songs in the Key of Life* by Stevie Wonder for £2.50, *Dr Buzzard's Original Savannah Band* LP for a mere £1.00 (an album which was until recently impossible to find again for less than £30), *Desire* by Bob Dylan for a quid, *Breezin'* by George Benson, *Jail Break* by Thin Lizzy. I wasn't quite so attached to these records as I had been, besides we didn't have a stereo at home and punk rock was coming to the fore and reggae was seen to be cool. Still, sacrificing two thirds of my record collection for one night in a dodgy Irish club, to say nothing of United in an FA Cup semi-final, proved romance wasn't dead. But as Jim Capaldi sang around that time, 'Love Hurts'.

The night had taught me that, no matter how Irish my

parents were, we didn't belong to that wild western Irish tribe with their country and western music, building trade money or reels like The Siege of Ennis and songs about martyred IRA men and ambushing Black and Tans. It was a life that could be open to me, but it was all too strange, something to escape from rather than embrace. But where would I be escaping to?

A working-class kid with an education meant being a schoolteacher or a civil servant. Other jobs were possible, but to compete with those well-spoken middle-class kids was an uphill struggle. Like Accrington Stanley playing the Brazilian 1970 world champions. Even at that age we all understood this was the case. You could fight and rail against it, but it would be like running a 52-mile marathon rather than a 26-mile marathon. Everything seemed difficult, and choices were so limited.

As we go through life we make more and more decisions which mean we leave other selves behind, as if we carry on somewhere in another dimension, living that sort of life, with that woman, doing that job. It's a bit like the round, square and oblong windows on the old children's programme *Playschool*. Through one window I'd have been living off jam butties play-ing with a Johnny Seven; in another I'd be the star forward for Manchester Boys' under-15s football team with a forthcoming apprenticeship at United and singing rebel songs in the Irish clubs of Manchester; and in another I'd be a local Jack the Lad, in and out of approved schools and borstal, selling dope outside the Seymour pub, robbing shops and having fights, impressing the girls and my peers.

All different lives to the one I had, and I was too young to genuinely articulate any dissatisfaction which had taken root, to see what haunting lives peered back at me, beckoning and saying, 'If you had come here you would have been happier'. Because whatever choices I'd make, one constant would run through them all: inside I felt a lump, a malignancy like a belly-ache of bitterness made up of a reservoir of slights, both real and imagined, of my own uncertainties about who I was, where I belonged and just all the crap things that felt as if they were building into a giant straw that would one day break the camel's back.

I was a teenager on that adolescent rollercoaster of ups and downs and yet I could look back at the streets and kids I'd known, how I'd been and how I was and all that was there was a wasteground of paradoxes and contradictions with no shape or real focus. When the irritations of life got too much, I'd lash out verbally and, more masochistically, mentally at the things around me: the middle-class kids at school and the way the teachers drilled and bullied us until we denied the worth of our own parents; the plastic Paddies in Old Trafford with their pre-ordained destinies and almost fascistic zeal for living a certain way; the Catholic Church; the Government, any authority figure. Rebel without a cause turned rebel with every cause.

It was like somewhere there was a tap dripping messages of self-loathing into my being, and occasionally it would over-flow, infecting me and those closest to me. And the only balm to this deep anguish which would be with me and others who silently felt the same way, in which ever life we chose, was Manchester United Football Club – they told us who we were, where we belonged. I was Mancunian first and Irish second. The Mancunian was more important: it had given my parents a place to work and the chance to live decent lives. No dewey-eyed sentiment in a young Republic of Ireland with all its inherited English snobberies could have given them that, but Manchester, the great immigrant city of Europe could. And Manchester United, with all its fearless passion for attacking football and glamour, splashing out money worth a couple of pools wins on players, was our Celtic pride: an antidote to the various indignities life visited upon the members of our class, the immigrants' team, the holy of holies for outsiders.

19

The Price of Commitment

I lent my token sheet for the semi-final ticket to a lad at school for the princely sum of 50p. The tokens had been stuck on with flour and water and I was missing the ones given out for United v. Huddersfield reserves and United v. Sheffield Wednesday reserves. I was a teenager in love with a girl I wasn't allowed out at night to see and with a football team who were about to play in an FA Cup semi-final that I also wasn't allowed to see. How many injustices could an honest, decent young boy take?

Roddy hadn't been to many games that year as he was tucked away boarding in the junior seminary near Wigan. The seminary had its main intake from the dioceses of Salford and Liverpool, with a few lads from the North-east, mainly Newcastle and Durham. Although strict, the discipline wasn't overbearing. In bed by ten o'clock, no transistor radios allowed, no television after seven o'clock. This was easy for Roddy – the toughest part was that he had no money, tokens and, or freedom to get to the semi-final. But he did have faith that somehow God would help him get to the final at Wembley and he inadvertently helped me to get there too.

While Roddy was most certainly a devout Catholic, in a sense we all were: in so far as religion was the way we'd been taught of getting the world to make some sense and our lives sometimes resembled waiting rooms for a place we never quite reached.

You would think a junior seminary for would-be Catholic priests aged 14 to 18 would be a haven from the wickedness of the world. Not this particular seminary. It was run by a gang of Geordie lads who extracted money with menaces from the other kids, and when, in the case of Roddy, they found he had no money, decided that they'd physically and verbally humiliate him every chance they had. Roddy was a big broad lad, yet he'd never laid a finger on anyone in his life, never having allowed the anvil of an Old Trafford childhood to shape his nature. He now found himself bullied, without any friends to bail him out or a home to run into with a front door to shut out his troubles.

His persecutors lived right next to him 24 hours a day and so the inevitable happened. One day he just flipped, receiving a beating off all five lads but finally standing up for himself. And then, like the hero of some old Western, he went after them one at a time and kept it up until they felt like they were the ones being persecuted. He came out of his shell, releasing a lifetime of put-downs and humiliations into the most caustic of solutions, and finally adopted some of the Old Trafford boy's exterior, letting the hardness and badness act as a casing for all the good in his soul.

Roddy was broke, his mother was bringing up his four sisters and brother on her own after his father had died the year before. So he bet the other inmates at the seminary 50p each that he would run naked around the full perimeter of the college grounds just before morning Mass, when the yards were full of the senior priests who taught the boys and ran the college.

So there he was, a blue-white naked figure streaking around the grounds with an audience of every boy who'd sponsored him and several open-mouthed priests, including the rector of the college. Roddy was dragged in front of the inquisition. Why had he chosen to defile the sanctity of these grounds, including the consecrated parts, and make a spectacle of himself and a laughing stock of his teachers and vocation?

'I'm sorry Father, I've got no money and I did it as a bet, 50p off each lad.'

To Roddy's surprise his rector and the other priests just laughed and told him to let them know if any lads didn't pay up their agreed 50ps.

Now Roddy missed that easy semi-final victory against Leeds United at Hillsborough and was beside himself as the prospect loomed of missing the FA Cup Final. His redemption came via a competition on Manchester's commercial station Piccadilly Radio. It was a couple of weeks before that Wembley event, United v. Liverpool, with Liverpool heading for an historic treble having won the league. They now had to face United in the FA Cup Final and Borussia Moenchengladbach in the European Cup final in Rome.

They looked unstoppable, with England striker David Johnson, Kevin Keegan, Jimmy Case and high-scoring super-sub David Fairclough in fine form, it was as if other teams collapsed and rolled over just because they were Liverpool. It rankled with United fans that Liverpool had made it to the final of the European Cup and were so lauded by the media and feared by opposing teams.

What we really wanted was no English team to win the European Cup until United got back in. Alas, the dire state of European football in the late Seventies early Eighties and the weaknesses of what were once great continental sides, meant that English teams would win it no less than six times. United's

4–1 victory against Benfica in 1968 meant we were the first and, until 1977, the only English team to have won Europe's top honour; and, in our minds at least that spring, we were still the true English champions of Europe.

In the oppressive seminary there were two other Irish Catholic boys from Old Trafford. Liam Heffernan was one of them. Liam was a nice lad, but someone must have been having a major laugh to imagine him ever becoming a priest. His brother Michael was known in Old Trafford for being a drinker and a fighter and to be truthful Liam was no different, except of course he was training for a life of serving the Holy Roman Church. Rules at the seminary were strict for such a free spirit.

Liam was the one with the illegal radio. From 11 p.m. until 2 a.m. every weekday night there was a brilliant phone-in show on Piccadilly Radio. One night they had a phone-in competition to win one of three pairs of tickets to the FA Cup Final at Wembley that Saturday. The question was 'Who is the only Manchester United player to ever play on the losing side in a European Cup Final? This was a tricky one, nobody had the answer … except Roddy: Johnny Giles, who had indeed played for Manchester United and then later played in the Leeds side that had lost to Bayern Munich in the final a few years earlier.

Liam suggested that they should break into one of the priests offices and use the phone. So at one o'clock in the morning, armed with a screwdriver, Roddy and Liam crept along the hallowed corridors of this ancient Lancashire seminary with a vocation greater than themselves in a quest for the holy of holies, a pair of tickets to see United at Wembley. The door opened, they slipped inside, phoned the radio station and duly won. But that was only half the battle. They had to not only face the rector but also ask for a Saturday off, when they would normally be serving on the altar at various weddings and Masses in the local parish, along with their usual weekend chores.

'I know you are all honest boys, and I know that you all know who broke into Father Quincey's room last night. Nothing was stolen, but the door is broken and has to be paid for, and I promise that whoever owns up here and now will not be punished other than paying for a new lock. I'll be in my office this afternoon, so the boy or boys responsible can come along in private and no one need know other than me and the boy or boys concerned, but until I find out who did this all TV privileges are cancelled and all weekend leaves are suspended for the next month.'

Roddy and Liam were in a fix: they either confessed and hoped the Reverend Father would understand, or they would be in even more bother when they slipped off on the Saturday, when all leaves had been suspended. Besides which everyone knew who had done it and as most of the young trainees were either Liverpool or United fans there was a certain amount of envy going around about them having the tickets. And, of course, not owning up meant none of the other boys would even be able to see the game on TV.

Roddy decided to own up. He had a feeling ever since his streaking incident was forgiven that the rector had a soft spot for him and if the worse came to the worst they'd probably get five, maybe even ten or twenty quid for the tickets. It was a sob story Roddy gave the rector who was at first furious about the radio and the breaking and entering.

'Father we're both from Old Trafford and we're both United fans and it was just too much temptation. We'll pay for the lock and the phone call and we promise nothing like this will ever happen again.'

The grovelling before one of the Almighty's representatives

on earth worked. In exchange for their humility and promising to catch up on all their chores and pay off the damage, Liam and Roddy were granted permission to go to Wembley.

Meanwhile, I was still short the two tokens. I went round to the Scotts, Mulvaneys and Ryans on Seymour Grove, my old partners in the match-day car-minding business. I offered to give them 50p for the two-pence programme sheets for each of those games. They made it their business to find out which reserve matches were token games and would go down to the ground buying 20 or 30 programme sheets each and then flog them for upwards of 20p each. Some people after all had enough money and enough sense not to be bother watching Alan Foggon, Alex Forsyth, Peter Coyne, Colin Waldron and various no-hope youngsters on a miserable Monday night in September or October.

The programmes were produced by Jimmy Mulvaney; the small square just below the left-hand corners where the tokens were supposed to be had been ripped away.

'What do you think I am, some bleeding stamp collector checking up on the number of reserve games Paddy Roche has played this season or something. I want the tokens, I'm not bothered about how the teams lined up.'

'What for twenty-five pence each! You'd be lucky to get those tokens for a quid each, everyone wants them for Wembley tickets.'

I looked at Jimmy Mulvaney in amazement: what the hell did he think I wanted them for? It was hopeless, nobody had any tokens, they'd all gone. I was in abject despair. A Wembley Cup Final ticket was £2.50 but rumours that people were selling the B-tokens for up to £5 each frightened me. Then there was the travel as well.

Roddy's story gave me an idea. Piccadilly Radio was the answer. I rang in and wrote a pleading, begging letter to tell the biggest white lie of my life to date. I'd lost my schoolbag, someone had stolen it on the bus home from school (I actually walked home from school) with my token sheet in it, so I couldn't go to Wembley; could anybody help me? The sob story did the rounds, the radio station milked it. Through the post at no charge I received a ticket for the West Stand Upper. Wembley for the second year running! The United captain Martin Buchan's prophecy the year before had been spot on. United were back, and so was I.

Love – it was getting in the way. How could I give up something so pure and beautiful, something that kept me awake at night in bed dreaming and longing? A smile, a wave, and yet fulfilment seemed so far away, so unreal. The warmth and the poetry filled a need in me, and yet I couldn't have everything I wanted, not when it was so expensive. So I decided to keep my money, go to Wembley and ditch Siobhan.

It was ruthless but me and Manchester United were too much of a good thing together. We made a lovely couple and even the most cynical teenager needs something far greater than himself to love.

Now even at such a young and selfish age (is there any other for a male?) I was aware that it is hard to explain to a girl that life is all about difficult choices, and with only a limited budget, it had to be her or Manchester United. You see I still cared about the girl, found her eminently attractive, fantasized about her, but ever since I'd missed that semi-final against Leeds, I kind of held it against her. To be honest, had she looked like Raquel Welch and been as rampant as Linda Lovelace, her presence would still have reminded me of how I'd missed out on seeing Leeds dumped out of the semi-final with goals from Jimmy Greenhoff and a fantastic volley from Steve Coppell.

I explained to her that I had too much homework and not enough money and I didn't want a steady girlfriend. I was accused of being a part-timer, of being disloyal and not caring. Not by Siobhan for packing her in, no it was worse than that ... the abuse came from my mates for not being there at Hillsborough. But what can you do?

The story of my magical ticket did the rounds. Some lads said 'jammy bastard'; I preferred to think of myself as enterprising. Like a priest I had given up the company of women for a greater love. My life was littered with sacrifices made on behalf of United.

United v. Liverpool: the true champions versus the unglamorous machine-like pretenders to our legend. There could be no treble and certainly no domestic double; it wouldn't be right. We discussed at length what a disaster for football it would be if Liverpool were to win both the FA Cup and European Cup to add to their league trophy. No team had ever done it, and only one team ever would, but for now ...

Ever since qualifying for the final United's form had been up and down. We lost heavily away at Middlesbrough then scraped a 1–0 win at home to QPR. Then it was Liverpool in a midweek game, and we lost 1–0. The truth was, for much of the game we'd been the better side, and Tommy Docherty, playing mind games, said he had seen that night how we could play to beat Liverpool in the final. We crossed our fingers and hoped he was right.

Strange looking back now, but I didn't know anyone who really wanted a ticket for that final who didn't get one. Nowadays people scrabble around for a ticket for United v. Leicester in a meaningless Coca-Cola Cup tie, announcing it to their mates as if they've just got the best seat to watch

United play in the European Cup Final or found the winning lottery ticket. Can anyone remember at United when the real fans came first in the raffle for Wembley tickets?

We'd all decided to travel by train, partly because it's quicker and more fun, but also because we just wanted to do what we hadn't done the year before and break the hoodoo or jinx. Roddy turned up with Liam, about ten minutes before the special football train was about to depart. Already at the station were Gary, Paul, Gerard and some of the older lads from round our way. Roddy and Liam were laughing, showing off their free tickets for the posh seats they'd won. They'd got the train from Wigan to Piccadilly Station and acted as if they had escaped from borstal for the day. We soon discovered why.

As I explained earlier, most of the lads at the junior seminary they attended were from the dioceses of Salford and Liverpool and so these trainee men of the cloth supported in the main either Manchester United or Liverpool. As a rule there was no TV after 10 p.m., but they had been granted a special dispensation the night before to watch the Granada TV special, *Who'll Win the Cup?*, with expert analysis and the opinions from both sets of fans. By the time the trainees of the Catholic priesthood had settled into their seats to enjoy this televized treat, the bickering had already started.

Voices that every day responded to the Mass, studied theology and tried to love their neighbour as themselves, started rankling at each other: 'You Scouse/Manc bastard'. Soon the bad tempers turned to violence as the lads started shoving and pushing each other, then fists started flying. Then Liam Heffernan, about to be assaulted by an older trainee from Liverpool, swung his canvas-backed metal chair at the approaching figure of his enemy only to miss and send it crashing through the television screen. The huge enamelled dispenser for boiling water for making tea and coffee was ripped off the wall, the steaming water scalding some boys. The whole TV room, including the door, windows and metal chairs lay scattered and broken as if the wrath of God had descended on the Philistines. I personally can't remember how provocative that Granada TV show was, but it certainly caused a mêlée amongst this normally pacific and holy congregation of trainee priests.

Excommunication wasn't on the cards, but all the trainees were grounded the next day, and as the television was the only one in the seminary (outside of a couple of portables in some of the priests' rooms), it meant nobody got to see the match the following day and the TV wasn't replaced for six months. As for Roddy and Liam, they crept out at six in the morning, clutching their Wembley tickets and carrying their little sports bags to hang around the local train station waiting for the first train to Manchester like nervous escapees in a Second World War POW film.

Luxury, that's what travelling by train was to me. I always felt sick travelling by coach, bus, or car. One of the main reasons I never made much of an effort to follow United away from home was an urgent need to vomit after spending half an hour in any form of motorized transport. This would hardly have made me one of the top boy hardcases of United's travelling army, pleading with a coach driver to pull over on the hard shoulder while I puked my ring up for the tenth time. But then the train was too expensive to take all the time (although I can't remember seeing any United fans ever being asked to show their tickets on the train).

The journey was pure excitement, and part of me wanted to stay on that train forever. The year before when we'd travelled down to London by coach for the ill-fated Southampton final it seemed to take an eternity, especially the traffic coming off the motorway at that end of the M1. I was sat on two seats on my own, disowned by my peers, holding a Tesco's carrier-bag containing a pint of vomit that had collected in it since our last stop just outside Birmingham. But this year, it was all going to be different.

I was the teenage bore on the train with one story (of how I'd wangled my ticket). I think I told the whole train, including the driver, the woman and bloke in the buffet car, people who were just getting off at Stockport and people who got on at Stockport and off at Macclesfield. I even told some Liverpool fans, said it was an omen, my luck was in, and so would United's be and Liverpool would also get stuffed in the European Cup Final by Borussia Moenchengladbach and a good thing it would be for football too.

The day wasn't without its worries. Stewart Houston, our Scottish international full-back, was out with a broken leg, and we wondered whether the 19-year-old Arthur Albiston who had come into the team as his replacement would be experienced enough to cope with Kevin Keegan. We looked for omens, discussing at length the game United had played against Liverpool at Anfield, and how Docherty planned to play. For that particular game we'd had Stewart Houston, but had been missing both Brian Greenhoff and the rock on which our side was built, Martin Buchan. Today we had them back but, as well as Albiston, Gordon Hill was a worry: would he freeze again on the big stage as he had done the year before against Southampton?

Our doubts plagued us and we whispered them to each other conspiratorially in case any of the older fans scoffed at us for our negativity, signs of disloyalty and lack of faith. I mean we could have said, 'Well there's no way a team can lose an FA Cup Final two years running.' But then we looked at United's dubious FA Cup record. We had lost the 1957 Cup Final 2–1 to Aston Villa and then one year later, in the aftermath of the

Munich air disaster, we were beaten by Nat Lofthouse's two goals for Bolton Wanderers (one of which was, of course, a blatant foul on our keeper Harry Gregg). Other than that United had only won the FA Cup three times: in 1909 with George Wall in the side they'd beaten Bristol City at Crystal Palace by one goal to nil; then they didn't win it again until 1948 when the first of Matt Busby's great sides beat Blackpool 4–2; and in 1963 when they'd beaten Leicester City 3–1. And we had never played a team so on form as that Liverpool side heading for the treble in 1977.

20

Prayers Answered

Walking up Wembley Way it felt very different to the previous year. There was a much greater tension of rivalry. It was after all Manchester v. Liverpool, opposite ends of the East Lancs road, Mancunians against Scousers, two tribes at war. Red and white was everywhere, the banners dragging in the stiff breeze that fought with the bright sunshine drenching the throng. We listened as older blokes moaned about London prices. 'Forty pence for a pint of lager! I said at least Dick Turpin wore a bleedin' mask.' Everything was more expensive, fish and chips, burgers, pies, hot dogs, but the biggest rip-off on the day was the match programme. It was a shock to us to say the least.

Now we are talking 1977 here: a pint of bitter cost between 25p and 28p in Manchester, and a United programme cost 12p. We expected to pay extra for an FA Cup programme. The year before the Cup Final programme had cost 20p, twice the price then of a United programme, so we expected the programme this year to cost 25p or at most 30p. But no ... 50p! Fifty sodding pence for a programme that had nothing special about it. We moaned at the programme seller, who just shrugged, as we reluctantly parted with our 50ps. It was the Queen's Jubilee and this was the Official Silver Jubilee Programme. At least the year before both the Queen and Prince Philip had actually been at the match; this year it was the Duke and Duchess of Kent, whoever they were and whatever they did or didn't do for a living.

We muttered curses under our breath and laughed at how we'd witnessed several ticket touts being turned over outside the ground in full view of the police by both United and Liverpool fans. 'How many tickets have you got there mate? Can you get all twelve of us in? Right get him lads!' We fantasized about the smug programme vendors receiving similar treatment and prayed that there would be no more unpleasant surprises today.

We split up to go through the turnstiles, just before one o'clock. The ground, just as it had been the year before, was a sea of red, but noisier, almost deafening. The long wait in the sunshine was interspersed by the grimmest entertainment ever, with parachute display teams and the obligatory massed bands of the Royal Marines. I wondered if they were really considering conscripting football hooligans into the army or something; they were trying to brainwash us with Colonel Bogey into joining up and marching off to Aldershot or wherever it is the army go nowadays.

Then just when the pre-match entertainment seemed to be getting really dull, on came a display of police dogs. No doubt the dogs would stick around for the match, should the Liverpool and United supporters get a bit lairy. They jumped over little fences and through hoops and tackled a pretend armed assailant. We joked that it was like *Blue Peter* and next Tommy Docherty would come out and show us how he made Alan Foggon out of sticky-back plastic and used toilet rolls. The dogs got all the applause that the Marine band and aerial display team didn't, but we were eager for the game to start.

The North-west had taken it's rivalries to Wembley for the day and with sweaty palms clutching my 50p programme I roared with the crowd, ignoring 'Abide With Me' and the national anthem and cheering on the team as they came out into the bright sunshine.

> MANCHESTER UNITED – Alex Stepney, Jimmy Nicholl, Arthur Albiston, Sammy McIlroy, Brian Greenhoff, Martin Buchan, Steve Coppell, Jimmy Greenhoff, Stuart Pearson, Lou Macari, Gordon Hill; sub – David McCreery.
> LIVERPOOL – Ray Clemence, Phil Neal, Joey Jones, Tommy Smith, Ray Kennedy, Emlyn Hughes, Kevin Keegan, Jimmy Case, Steve Heighway, David Johnson, Terry McDermott; sub – Ian Callaghan.

United were playing in their usual red shirts, Liverpool in white shirts and black shorts. The noise from that Wembley crowd greeting the players was unbelievable. In my mind I said all the prayers I'd learned as a child. For all those years I'd gone to see United, dreamed about them regaining the glories of the Sixties, and here was the crunch. Last year's final had been a terrible humiliation, losing to a second division team; but how much worse if United lost now, giving an historic double to Liverpool and a chance for them to scoop an unprecedented treble – what team could ever hope to match that?

The tension and strain was on every United face around the ground. Would Hill play better than last year, could the inexperienced Albiston contain Keegan? In that day's papers some of the so-called experts said that had Houston been playing they may have fancied United, but that Liverpool were too strong and were without doubt the best team in Europe, if not the world, and it all added up to another disappointing year for United's young side. It seemed an awesome thought that in 90

minutes we'd know the answers to all these questions. What if
we were humiliated and lost 4–0, what if we played really badly
and spent the whole game defending? Nightmare scenario
after nightmare scenario went through my head as the Duke
and Duchess of Kent shook hands with the players from both
sides, the last friendly act to take place on the pitch for almost
two hours.

United were known for their freestyle attacking football;
they might concede four goals, but were as likely to score five.
Liverpool were a well-oiled machine, strong and fiercely
competitive in all departments and above all overwhelmingly
efficient. As a Cup Final it wasn't a classic for the neutral. It was
all fearsome lunges in midfield, with Liverpool in control for
long periods of the game, United defending well and Lou
Macari battling for everything in midfield. We waited for the
tide of the game to turn in our favour. Arthur Albiston settled
in quickly, winning important tackles against Keegan, Case and
Heighway and the United fans outsang our Liverpudlian rivals.

Liverpool looked to be getting stronger as the game went
on, while United seemed to lose possession of the ball too
easily. Pearson and Greenhoff struggled at times to hold it up
at the front long enough for Coppell, Macari and McIlroy to
join the attack from midfield. Meanwhile Gordon Hill was a
shadow over on the left touchline and may as well have been
the ball boy for all his involvement. We were happy when half-
time came, 0–0, and believed that United had surely weathered
the storm and would come out playing 100-mile-an-hour,
penetrating, attacking football in the second half.

United tried to be more enterprising but seemed locked
down by Liverpool. They were endeavouring to go forward,
Arthur Albiston running with the ball the full length of the
pitch, rousing the voices of the United supporters in the
crowd. It was a tight game, but it was hard to see where a

United goal would come from. Then the ball was hoofed into the middle near the centre circle; Kevin Keegan's misdirected header was intercepted by Sammy McIlroy who headed the ball forward for United; a flicked-back header from Jimmy Greenhoff found Stuart Pearson with half a yard on Joey Jones, and with his pace that's all he needed; he then struck a low shot with his right foot that surely must have been covered by Liverpool's England international keeper Ray Clemence … but no, it was in the net! 1–0 to United and Wembley erupted … this was it, surely this was it.

Less than three minutes later Keegan found Jimmy Case outside the United penalty area and from the edge of our box he struck one of the best shots ever in a Cup Final, which bulged the back of the net. It was 1–1 and our shoulders slumped – it just didn't look like United could come back, they'd hardly created a decent chance the whole match, whereas Liverpool were dominating the game more and more.

Two minutes later and United got the ball forward. Macari challenged Tommy Smith and struck a speculative shot from the edge of the Liverpool box – it ricocheted off Jimmy Greenhoff's chest, wrongfooting Ray Clemence and nestled in the back of the Liverpool net: 2–1 to United. The next 30 minutes were hell as Liverpool stormed forward again and again, United clinging on at times by their fingernails until we cheered every pass back to the keeper and every time a defender put the ball, even for a couple of seconds, in the Liverpool half.

The final whistle and it was all our Christmases at once. United were back. Liverpool were dominating domestic football and would soon go on to dominate European football too, but they couldn't dominate Manchester United and for now that was enough for us.

We'd seen the bad times in both life and football. On the

one hand, poverty, Victorian parental discipline, overcrowded housing, a school system that treated us with disdain, and the school of hard knocks on the streets. On the other we'd seen our hero hounded away from us by the press and the pressures of stardom, seen our great team destroyed and suffered the humiliation of relegation into the second division. And now was the start of a new era, of a new all-attacking United under Tommy Docherty, whose name we roared from the terraces. Years of pain and now triumph and a horizon decked with bigger and better victories to come.

'Hello! Hello! United are back! United are back!' In my head I whispered a prayer of thanks for victory and for Manchester United, an interchangeable 11-man religious icon that granted absolution from the seemingly predestined narrowness of all our lives.

Epilogue

Tommy Docherty's United triumphed in possibly the least stylish way imaginable. But those 11 players had prevented United's reputation being eclipsed by a Liverpool side threatening a the ultimate treble. And more importantly there was a trophy gleaming in the cabinet back at Old Trafford and over the next 20 years visits to Wembley and winning trophies would become the habit it always threatened to be.

Behind those trophies was a work ethic, a religious ethic, honesty and endeavour mixed with God-given talent and determination, of a game played the Matt Busby way, inspiring kids who had nothing else. Manchester United: big business ... oh yes indeed, but the people behind the now successful United are descendants of that humble man of the people, who had respect for the fans, and a glorious vision of how football should be played and of a footballing team who would play it that way: Sir Matt Busby.

Tommy Docherty had restored United's pride, restored our faith and given us supporters the team we had dreamed of. No other team in my memory played with such a youthful zest or devil-may-care attitude that had us screaming and shouting from the terraces until we thought our lungs would give out. That was the beauty of it you see; it's what football gave us that the cinema, the Scouts, the fairground, school and work could never allow us. We could vent our feelings. If we thought Peter

Osgood was a wanker we could yell it until we were blue in the face; if we thought one of the United players wasn't pulling his weight, we could scream at him too; and we could dole out as much stick as we liked to the referee and the chairman and any number of managers, to say nothing of opposing fans. We counted out on the terraces, our opinions were included there for all to hear, whether at the ground or picked up by the TV microphones. That was Docherty's United, a dream team come true for us Old Trafford lads.

Dave Sexton, though a good manager, tried to turn us into a Don Howe-inspired Arsenal. Fans that were still drunk on the headiness of Docherty's sides suddenly felt the hangover of Sexton, and United weren't the big draw they'd been previously, despite challenging for honours.

Ron Atkinson brought back the entertainment as an antidote to Sexton's hangover years, although I doubt many United teams suffered more hangovers than Atkinson's. The age of heroes began again: Bryan Robson, Norman Whiteside, Remi Moses, Mark Hughes. United were back.

I look on with amusement as I watch Ferguson's sides develop. They have the big names of Atkinson and at their best much of the work rate, passion and fire of the Doc. No wonder every other football fan is jealous.

But this book wasn't about United or the glory years, it was about a feeling they gave us when we were callow youths, in a world where we felt excluded by everything that was glamorous and exciting, except Manchester United. They gave us an appreciation that went beyond mere trophies or something to do on a Saturday afternoon. Passion and living in the moment, that was why football was made for and by the working classes rather than the middle classes.

Everything about the middle classes has a practicality: plans for the future, investment in education, investment in the stock market, investment in football, climbing up the slippery career ladder, new cars, nice houses, wealth which can be quantified. For us it was something to argue about vociferously, to care about, to live and breathe, to fight about and embrace. One in a list of passions like dancing to soul music or falling in love, pissing your money up the wall and scrimping through the week and doing the same thing over again... living. We were rich in experiences and there would be great ones to come.

Before Alex Ferguson arrived, how many true United fans could bear to watch old TV footage of Best, Law and Charlton without a lump coming to their throat and succumbing to a quiet, desperate depression? That feeling that perhaps we'll never have it so good again. We are all nostalgic for the smells of our childhood, but Fergie, for all his infuriating team selections and tactics, has cast a light over the dark years and brought United as close to the fans as any large business venture can be in the late 1990s.

The memories are all there for me. The eight lads from Ayres Road who travelled down to the Milk Cup final in 1983 in a clapped-out greengrocer's van used by one lad's father for his deliveries and collecting his stock. The way it overheated, squirting viscous, snotty-green anti-freeze on to the boot and windscreen as it finally gave up with a bone-dry radiator just outside Watford Gap. Then the lads taking it in turns to urinate into an empty 7-Up bottle to fill the radiator, before giving up and getting a lift to Rugby off a coach full of ... rugby players. Then taking shelter in a pub and getting caught up in a huge wedding party and drunkenly hitching back to Manchester, arriving at midnight, still clutching their unused Wembley tickets and oblivious of the fact Liverpool had won the game.

The terraces behind the goal at Villa Park in the semi-final of the FA Cup in 1983, separated by a fence from the Arsenal fans. The contorted faces of those North London boys as they went a goal up and held their hands up, moving fingers and thumbs like a beak as if to signal that someone was talking too much, while chanting, 'Gowing aht, gowing aht, gowing aht' in their glottal-stopping cockney accents; and then, after some genius by Robson and Whiteside, finding themselves 2–1 down and en masse we Reds aping their beak-like hand movements and accents and throwing the same 'Gowing aht' chant back in their faces.

Liverpool's last-minute equalizer in the semi-final at Maine Road in 1985, God punishing us for daring to celebrate and count our chickens before the clock had run down. Singing 'Always look on the Whiteside of life' after Storming Norman had lead United's ten men in that glorious topsy-turvy FA Cup Final victory over Everton.

George Best decking the Argentinean Estudiantes defender who'd kicked him all the way through the World Club Championship and the Stretford End singing 'Estudiantes, pull down your panties'. Danny Wallace's winner in a 3–2 thriller in the fifth round of the Cup at St James Park against Newcastle in 1989, when the excitement was so great, it looked like the two sets of fans from opposite ends of the ground would end up meeting on the halfway line as they spilled on to the sides of the pitch in a frenzy of excitement. The eerie thwack of the ball as Hughes volleyed in the legendary FA Cup semi-final winner against Oldham at Wembley, when United's most glorious season seemed about to disappear down that gaping also-rans drain. And of course there was Eric Cantona ... it's all pure gold.

Nowadays we are always looking back. It's probably our age. I look at my friends. Roddy, once a poor kid raised on council grants and free school meals. Now a millionaire with his own business. He gets stick for it. On a recent weekend stag trip, we were wandering the labyrinth of our working-class youth, and we said that Roddy wasn't working class. Enraged by this slur, Roddy reminded us of how tough his upbringing was.

'Yeah, but Roddy, you can't be working class any more! You own the means of production!'

I look at Paul, still loud and brash, following United across the world. No longer the light-fingered kid we once knew. Mind you, he is married to a policewoman.

Gary now lives in Amsterdam, involved in the risky import–export business. Weird thing is he flies regularly from Amsterdam to Manchester for the games. Yet he always flies back via Brussels and then drives a hire car from there to Amsterdam. Perhaps he loves the Flemish countryside as much as he loves the Reds.

Jimmy Martin never made it as a professional footballer. A trial for Man. United was a fiasco as he was merely watched playing a game of one touch, unable to show his magnificent dribbling and shooting skills. Disheartened, he had trials with Bolton and a stint in the youth team at Bury. Having to bus it to trials on his own, without his dad there to push the scouts and coaches, he was a bystander as the life he'd always dreamt of slipped away.

Manchester United isn't the same any more. The cost of matches now means that kids from poor families can't afford to go, unless their dads are really prepared to scrimp and save for tickets, or a season ticket (assuming they can get hold of them). It's unbelievable that a scarf is a quarter the price of a ticket and not the other way round. There are other things to distract kids now as well.

But they are still there, ten-year-olds trying to jib in behind us at the turnstiles to witness their heritage, which football's crazy economy is denying them legally. They still mind cars like we did too, even wearing luminescent jackets and putting up signs written in felt pen in front of empty office forecourts that say 'Car Park £3'. Yes, football is all about money now, and every young scally is aware that that's the way life is in the Nineties. The little kids in Old Trafford might have all the things we didn't have – the latest replica shirts, both home and away, the boots as sponsored by Giggs and Beckham, the posters and paraphernalia of Manchester United Plc. But they can't turn up on a Saturday with two bob in their pocket and see Law, Best and Charlton, the way their dads could.

In many ways it's the fate of the immigrant, particularly the Irish. Our forefathers were the miners and sappers of capitalism, sent in to build the foundations on which the wealth of the industrial powers was erected and then when they were finished just discarded, never to share fully in the rewards of the wealth they had helped to create. Likewise the working-class football fans, who supported and screamed for their teams through the lean times until, in the case of Manchester United, they became so big and powerful, they no longer needed them.

All the time, nagging at the back of the mind, is the feeling that the working-class fans in football are like the Sioux Indians living in the Black Hills of Dakota: once the big businessmen found gold there they were driven off and had their land taken from them. Yes, there are still a few of us Indians around on the reservation, but we wonder whether Old Trafford and Manchester United, like the Black Hills, are still as sacred and meaningful as they used to be. For us they were the one thing we valued that didn't make us feel excluded.

Finally to Alex Ferguson himself. There were doubters when he cleared Old Trafford of our heroes like Whiteside, McGrath and Strachan. Yet we as Old Trafford boys had faith in him. We'd heard you see, we had inside knowledge. Ferguson attracted some boo-boys, but not, I'm proud to say, us. We had faith because the husband of our old dinner-lady from primary school, the now late Harold Moore, had told us.

Harold was in his seventies and was passionate about the club and doing good work for St Alphonsus parish church. For years he worked in the offices at Old Trafford while Ron Atkinson was manager, yet not once had big Ron said so much as hello, goodbye or kiss my arse to him. Ferguson, within days of starting at Old Trafford, had, like the great Sir Matt Busby before him, made a point to go and meet and speak to every worker, cleaning lady, gate-man and tea-boy at the club, and actually genuinely wanted to know them, asking about their families and their lives, making them feel part of the club and feel important, as every human being is.

That's why Alex Ferguson is a great manager. At heart he's a lover of football and people, who wishes to make Old Trafford a huge family. So what if there's this big corporate monster known as Manchester United nowadays and some fans whinge that they can't turn up en masse on a Saturday and stand on the terraces for two bob. Is United not still a family because it's the team, the coaching staff and the supporters that make it? Or is it now something more sinister: a money-making, branded theme park to be visited twice a year by middle-income families, like an outing to Alton Towers?

To us older fans, still hanging on to an ideal that we grew up with, it's still what goes on out on the pitch that inspires, the way the game is played, win, lose or draw, that ultimately counts. As long as Ferguson and the big-money boys remember that, Manchester United will always belong in some part to the people, or at least the ones who can still get tickets and afford to go. Look at the crowds at Premiership games, look at the chants at every ground around the country: 'Stand up if you hate Man. U.' There are few clubs left in the world which provoke as much passion as Manchester United.

Four friends stood in a crowded stadium in Rotterdam. The outward gruffness, laddishness and broad accents identified the friends' backgrounds: the council estates of north-western England. Whatever their finances, all three were rich beyond mere wealth.

The blonde lad was loud and shouted himself hoarse as he had home and away, both in Britain and abroad, for the last twenty-odd years. He shared joint with a smaller guy who wore shades and a misshapen bush-hat as if in some crazy disguise. Another, a hard-faced but humorous man was being scathing against the Spaniards, stating that for all the crime he'd committed, had he robbed the Brinks Matt bullion, the last place he'd skip off to with the money would be a land peopled by cockneys and dagos. It had been a holiday, two days of Manchester in Amsterdam, with a jaunt over to Rotterdam, and there was a feeling of happiness all around and a big party night to come.

A Welshman, strong enough to shoulder the burden of a stadium full of hopes and dreams, sent a ball goalwards from an impossible angle – the noise rose into the night sky and bodies jumped and threw themselves in an orgy of several different types of ecstasy and waves of frenzied joy. In the middle of this avalanche of human happiness, was a short man. He didn't cheer when the goal went in and as his friends pulled him round, he just wanted to stare at the pitch. Suddenly from under a bush-hat tears flowed, sheltered by a pair of Ray-Bans. This he would cherish, remember and store with other moments special to him and shared with friends.

It could have been a memory stirred, of a time when all the good things in life these friends wanted were in the drop of an

Irishman's shoulder, the speed of a Scotsman's reflexes and the power of an Englishman's boot. Signs to them growing up that there was a better life, a better future and if not, there was always this Saturday. Because they bore a legacy, an inspiration, an inner world of heroes in legends that would be passed from generation to generation like the Celtic myths they'd heard as children.

They were born and raised in Old Trafford, believed in living life like the game played by the team they loved – positive, determined, unstinting, unselfish, honest and always inspiring. They were more than just working-class kids made good; thanks to Manchester United, they knew where they came from and always would. They were forever grounded, part of a big wide world beyond the narrow streets they'd grown up in. Yes there was a deep fear of leaving everything behind, a fear of a middle-class world in which they suspected they'd never belong no matter how much money they may have made. Fear was the unknown. Fear was not belonging. Most of all fear was to discover and sign-post their limits as human beings. Manchester United nullified the symptoms of those anxieties, made them realize they weren't alone because they had each other even though some of them hated themselves. Most of all United gave them a belief and a limitless horizon to share with their team and bathe in all its reflected glories.

They had chosen their world now and would never desert it, would live in it with all their hearts, promising that while they lived in it they'd add to it, and survive in the middle of it, because they had been and would always be, Reds in the hood.